CRUDE POWER

CRUDE POWER

Politics and the Oil Market

ØYSTEIN NORENG

I.B.Tauris *Publishers*
LONDON • NEW YORK

Published in 2002 by I.B.Tauris & Co. Ltd
6 Salem Road, London W2 4BU
175 Fifth Avenue, New York, NY 10010
www.ibtauris.com

In the United States of America and Canada distributed by Palgrave Macmillan, a division of
St Martin's Press, 175 Fifth Avenue, New York, NY 10010

Library of International Relations Volume 21

ISBN 1-86064-818-5

A full CIP record for this book is available from the British Library
A full CIP record for this book is available from the Library of Congress

Library of Congress catalog card: available

Typeset in Garamond by A. & D. Worthington, Newmarket
Printed and bound in Great Britain by MPG Books Ltd, Bodmin

CONTENTS

FIGURES

PREFACE

The present book is the final report to the Petropol Programme of the Norwegian Research Council from the project Oil Prices, Market Power and Politics. The intention has been to prepare a comprehensive book on the interaction of economic and political forces in the world oil market. Generous funding and patience from the Petropol programme during the years 1997–2000 has provided the author with extensive resources and time to carry out the project.

The author is grateful for advice and critical comments from many colleagues and friends and would like to thank in particular Bjørn Brochmann, formerly with Norsk Hydro, Irene King, formerly with J.P. Morgan, Daniel Heradstveit of the Norwegian Institute for International Affairs, Svein Andersen of the Norwegian School of Management, Helge Hveem of the University of Oslo, Paul Horsnell of Chase J.P. Morgan, formerly with the Oxford Institute for Energy Studies, Angel de la Vega of the Colegio de México, Valery Kryukov of the University of Novosibirsk, and Pierre Terzian of Petrostrategies, Paris. In addition, the author is forever indebted to two old friends and mentors, Jean Carrié and Jean-Marie Bourdaire, both formerly with CFP-Total, the latter presently with the Cambridge Energy Research Associates, CERA.

Without the competent and enthusiastic help of research assistants the book would not have materialized. The author would like to thank Tonje Irene Horn, Leif Wollebæk, Erik Rindvoll and Per Anker-Nilssen for meticulous and patient efforts in collecting and processing data and finding sources, as well as in dealing with the author's moods.

The author has the sole responsibility for the present book, including errors, mistakes and misjudgement.

Øystein Noreng
Oslo, 5 October 2001

CHAPTER ONE

THE NECESSITY OF OIL

The ambition of the book

The aim of this book is to analyse the world's persistent dependence on Middle Eastern oil and why oil prices cannot stabilize at any level. The ambition is to investigate the economic and political pressures, and the shifting relations between the major oil exporters of the region as well as outside powers that cause oil market instability and oil prices to move. Crude power in this context means the ability to unilaterally raise or lower oil supplies so that prices move up or down, subsequently influencing the world economy. From this perspective, the world oil market is as much shaped by political forces as by economic factors.

Middle Eastern politics directly affects the United States and the rest of the world, at times in most unexpected ways. The 11 September 2001 terrorist attacks on New York and Washington are a brutal reminder of the importance of Middle Eastern politics to the rest of the world, not only because of oil.

One view is that the attacks were carried out by fanatics motivated by a violent religious sensibility, and were unrelated to the economic, social and political problems of the Middle East, such as poverty or Israel's occupation of Palestine.[1] From this perspective, fighting terrorism means eliminating individuals and small groups, and oil is not an issue, neither as a cause of terrorism nor as a potential fatality.

Another view is that a terrorist network has thrived on the political and economic bitterness felt in much of the Arab world and the Middle East.[2] From this perspective, terrorists are motivated by oppression and by the corruption and authoritarianism of certain Arab governments, supported by the United States and other Western powers. Fighting terrorism means not only eliminating individuals and small groups, but also comprehensive economic, social and political reforms.

From this perspective, oil is a key factor, as it has provided huge revenues for the rulers but neither political reform nor sufficient prosperity for the people. Since 1970, oil revenues have profoundly changed the Middle Eastern societies, but there has been little political change to cope with the ambitions of the more numerous and better-educated younger generations.

1

The outcome is a society with rising social and economic inequalities and generational conflicts. The bitterness is also caused by Arab defeats at the hands of Israel, the plight of the Palestinians and the enduring sanctions against Iraq.

The extent and the intensity of the resentment against the rulers in place and their Western allies and protectors are difficult to grasp because of the limited freedom of assembly and expression in most, if not all, Arab countries. The West is a victim of its own trap in the Middle East. By supporting corrupt and dictatorial regimes for immediate economic and strategic advantages, the West has prevented necessary change to stabilize the countries concerned through representative government.[3] Western oil interests and economic stability are shaky when dependent on moribund political systems and paralysed societies. The United States has provided military, political and at times economic support in return for access to oil. At times the United States, again often supported by allies, has also actively destabilized Middle Eastern governments with a popular mandate, as happened in Iran in 1953.[4]

Rising Western dependence on Middle Eastern oil since the 1960s has not been matched by an effort to stabilize the region politically. Although the United States is increasingly dependent on oil imports and on the Middle East supplying the world market with volumes sufficient to stabilize prices, there has, so far, been little interest in or insight into Middle Eastern affairs. The wisdom of giving unquestioning support to corrupt and authoritarian regimes because they export oil is not obvious. The error has been to equate secure oil supplies with regimes that were more dependent on Western backing than on a popular mandate.[5] Such a policy can back-fire, as it did for the United States in Iran. From this perspective, the September 2001 terrorist attacks may appear as the forerunner of more trouble insofar as they express a widespread, so far hidden, discontent. Insofar as United States relations with Israel are constant or even improve, relations with the Arab world deteriorate as the conflict between Israel and the Palestinians escalates. As long as the United States appears to be siding unilaterally with Israel and is incapable of halting the violence and imposing a political solution, it is exposed to a terrorist risk as well as an economic risk from the Middle East. The terrorist risk has been manifest since 11 September 2001, even if more terrorist acts are likely to further weaken sympathy for the Arab cause and consequently prove politically counter-productive. The economic risk is linked to oil and money.

The rising violence between Israel and the Palestinians, triggered by Ariel Sharon's September 2000 visit to the Temple Mount, the site of the al-Aqsa mosque and the Dome of the Rock, marked the end and failure of the Oslo peace process.[6] The danger is that the attempted peace process will be followed by a countdown to a more comprehensive conflict, which ultimately could set large parts of the Arab or even Muslim world against Western interests.[7] In that case, oil supplies and oil prices would be at risk. From this perspective, the September 2001 attacks on New York and Washington may embody an escalation to a new stage of conflict, with the open and uneasy question of what will come next. The terrorist attacks caused a serious setback for the Arab cause in the United States and led to greater sympathy for Israel, but such considerations seem to be absent from the terrorists' minds.

The US dilemma is conflict between the need for Arab oil to stabilize the market and sympathy for Israel. Therefore, Israeli policies toward the Palestinians and the escalating conflict represent a liability for the United States. For Israel, the US dependence on Saudi oil represents a security risk in the sense that in an escalating conflict over Palestine, the United States might give a higher priority to Saudi Arabia and eventually withhold economic assistance to induce Israel to withdraw from the occupied territories, as former president George Bush Sr threatened to do. One way out for Israel could be to make a proactive move, creating new political realities.[8] Israel could incorporate the occupied territories and eventually also expel parts of the Palestinian population. Such an extreme move would possibly provoke Saudi Arabia to use the oil weapon, or the Saudi regime to be toppled, but in both cases US dependence on Saudi oil would be reduced, which would appear advantageous to Israel. Even if the United States should suffer from sharply higher oil prices, there would be little risk of Israel losing its major ally. The alternative for Israel could be to accept a Palestinian state on viable terms, which seems even less likely after the end of the peace process.

In this situation, the United States would be looking for new oil suppliers, with Russia as the most obvious choice.[9] In terms of oil reserves and costs Russia cannot replace Saudi Arabia, but by playing the two countries off against each other, the United States could hope to induce a struggle over market shares in the world oil market, leading to lower prices.[10]

Israeli military superiority is uncontested and guaranteed by the United States, which is losing political influence in the Arab Middle East, affecting Middle East politics, the regional balance of power and the pattern of oil supplies. The cost of US and Israeli military domination could be the loss of moderate pro-Western regimes in the Arab world.[11] Repercussions for the oil market and the world economy could be serious.

Since the Afghanistan War of 2001, Saudi Arabia is at times seen as an untrustworthy ally of the United States because of its restrictions on American military operations.[12] Therefore, some important voices in the United States favour a military retreat from Saudi Arabia, in spite of the US economic interests at stake. The alienation seems to be reciprocal.

The dilemma for the moderate Arab regimes is that maintaining close military and economic relations with the United States conflicts with the need to placate domestic public opinion and to take a stronger stance in favour of the Palestinians. Political survival has priority over US interests. Facing anti-American sentiment in the Middle East, especially among the younger generation, some Saudi rulers appear uncomfortable with the US military presence, allegedly arguing that the kingdom and the regime would be safer without it.[13] In military terms, a withdrawal would deprive the United States of air bases that have projected US power in the Middle East since the 1990–91 Gulf War. It is also doubtful whether it would be politically feasible for the United States to maintain bases in other Gulf States after pulling out of Saudi Arabia. Consequences for oil supplies and prices could be substantial.

In political terms, a military pullout would weaken links between the United States and Saudi Arabia, which would have to reorientate itself more closely toward its Middle Eastern neighbours. The immediate beneficiary would be Iran, whose relations with Saudi Arabia have improved steadily since 1997. The next beneficiary could be Iraq, provided that the regime appears less hostile. If Iraq should renounce its claims on Kuwait and disarm, it would eventually establish a new political order in the Middle East, based on improved relations between Iraq, Iran and Saudi Arabia. The current militarization of the Iraqi regime is an obstacle to good neighbourly relations and consequently to Iraqi influence in the Gulf.

In the case of better neighbourly relations, the economic effects could be a reduction in Saudi arms purchases and consequent reduction in the need to sell oil, improving conditions for OPEC co-operation to defend high oil prices. For the oil market, the most salient effect would be to discontinue the link between US oil imports and Saudi oil output that has stabilized prices during long periods since the early 1970s. Alternatively, weaker Saudi links with the United States could help Iraq assert a regional hegemony, also with profound repercussions for the oil market.

Apparently, US–Saudi relations are approaching a historical turning point with potentially ominous results for the oil market. The prospects of a stronger Iraq, eventually on better terms with Iran and Saudi Arabia and emerging as a regional leader, are as frightening to Israel as to the United States, where some voices favour attacking the country to topple the Saddam Hussein regime.[14] The motive would be not only to eliminate a military threat, but also to open Iraq for US oil investors.

From this perspective, US policy toward the Middle East seems to be approaching a historical crossroads, the choices being either to continue the military engagement commenced during the 1990–91 Gulf War and eventually bring down the Iraqi regime by force, or pulling out of the Middle East. In the first case, the United States would be seen as the only superpower to defend oil interests by military means, conducting resource warfare, as during the Gulf War.[15] The cost of the reduced economic risk would be a heightened terrorist one. In the second case, the United States would be seen as stepping down from the role of global superpower, exchanging a heightened economic risk for a reduced terrorist one. The economic risk would comprise the potential loss of capital inflows into the United States by the recycling of Middle East oil revenues and eventually the ability to pay for oil imports by printing dollars.[16] In either case, repercussions for the oil market could be profound.

The world remains vitally dependent on Middle Eastern oil. Almost 30 years after the first oil price shock of 1973–74, oil remains of critical importance to consumers and producers alike. OPEC, the Organization of Petroleum Exporting Countries, is still alive and doing well in spite of repeated announcements of its demise and occasional allegations of the irrelevance of oil. Despite concerns about greenhouse gas emissions from burning fossil fuels, the world economy remains highly dependent on oil, which provides 40 per cent of the world's primary energy. Oil powers travel and transport, heats houses and is the feedstuff for plastics, chemicals and fertilizers. Despite the extensive search for oil elsewhere over the past 30 years, more than half of the world's oil reserves are located in Middle East OPEC member countries.

In the unsteady economic situation after the September 2001 terrorist attacks on the United States, oil is again of critical importance to the world economy. Should oil prices stay moderate, around $18–20 a barrel or less, they would facilitate an economic recovery backed by co-ordinated monetary policies of the major central banks. Should oil prices shoot up, for example as a result of political unrest and subsequent supply cutbacks in the Middle East and North Africa, they would compromise efforts to enhance economic activity, and could be a factor in pushing the world economy into a prolonged recession.[17]

The interests of the major powers in relation to Middle Eastern oil are as acute as ever. The 1990–91 Gulf conflict was over oil, not democracy in Kuwait. Because oil prices influence trade balances, inflation rates and levels of economic activity, they matter to governments throughout the world. Repeatedly, oil market turbulence has contributed to Western presidents not being re-elected, as happened in the United States to Gerald Ford in 1976, to Jimmy Carter in 1980 and to George Bush Sr in 1992, as well as in France to Valéry Giscard d'Estaing in 1981. Economic distress in Germany as a result of high oil prices may have contributed to Chancellor Helmut Schmidt's downfall in 1982. Against this backdrop, control of oil gives political leverage. Middle Eastern oil therefore remains of vital economic and political importance both to the United States and to the other major powers. To safeguard oil interests, the United States needs friends and allies, not foes, and cannot, as the only surviving superpower, defend important interests unilaterally. Russia seems to be a winner.[18] Iran may forgo a historical opportunity to become more closely integrated economically and politically with the outside world because of the conflict between reformers and conservatives. From this perspective, the continuation of the US sanctions against Iran, embodied in the Iran–Libya Sanctions Act, ILSA, renewed in the summer of 2001, appears thoughtless and contrary to US economic and political interests. In the redefinition of the United States' friendship needs, Israel may lose, especially as the Sharon government has managed to embarrass the United States and appear as an active force of instability in the Middle East.[19]

Alternatively, Israel may emerge the winner, appearing as the only stable democracy and friend of the West in the Middle East, as a result of US uneasiness over the stability of the Saudi regime.[20] In an extreme situation, after a military pullout from Saudi Arabia, the United States might eventually consider using Israel as a bridgehead to portray military power and to defend oil interests in the Middle East. Such a choice would imply a conscious confrontation with the Arab world, unlikely to stabilize oil supplies and prices, raising both the economic and the terrorist risk.

Because oil resources are concentrated in the Middle East, OPEC has control of the market when key members agree. In 2000, the Persian Gulf countries, Iran, Iraq, Kuwait, Qatar, Saudi Arabia and the United Arab Emirates, produced nearly 28 per cent of the world's oil, while holding 65 per cent of the world's oil reserves. From this perspective, the West's dependence on Middle Eastern oil is likely to increase and OPEC's power over the oil market is likely to strengthen. Because the cheapest and most plentiful oil is in the Middle East, OPEC has the power to set oil prices. Non-OPEC oil supplies are more precarious, largely dependent on prices set in the Middle East. This underlines the importance of caution when dealing with Middle Eastern oil fields, regimes and societies, not only in the fight against terrorism.

The concentration of oil supplies in the Middle East means that oil prices are necessarily unstable, unless there should be robust agreement on oil prices or major oil exporters should choose not to price oil far above their marginal cost of extraction. Neither seems likely. Stakes are economic as well as political. High population growth means that practically all Middle Eastern oil exporters face rising revenue needs, which is a strong argument in favour of high oil prices. The Middle Eastern oil exporters also face the risk, however, of high oil prices contributing to an economic recession that reduces oil demand and sends oil prices down. This dilemma is unlikely to be settled in the foreseeable future.

Political concerns also count. Those Middle Eastern oil exporters that depend on US military protection, essentially Kuwait, Saudi Arabia and the

United Arab Emirates, have so far not wanted high oil prices that could harm the United States and allies.[21] Oil market stability ultimately depends on Saudi Arabia investing in sufficient capacity and using it to make supplies meet demand. Politically, this requires a finely tuned Saudi balancing act, weighing concerns for the consumers and especially the United States, against those for its own as well as its neighbours' oil revenues. From this perspective, Saudi Arabia's political stability and foreign policy concerns are pivotal for the oil market. Political conflicts in the Middle East were the cause of the embargo imposed in 1973 by Arab oil exporters on Israel, the Netherlands and the United States, as well as the oil price rises in the wake of the 1979–80 Iranian revolution and the 1990–91 Gulf War. Persistent political instability in the Middle East means an unrelenting risk of another oil price shock. Against this backdrop, a US military pullout from Saudi Arabia could have a signal effect on the region and make concerns for US interests weigh less in oil policy making in the Gulf States. Such a change of policy does not require any radical political break in the Gulf States, but could be implemented by moderate regimes desiring to take political distance from the United States in order to stay in power.

More than ten years after the Gulf War, Iraq remains a risk both to neighbouring Middle Eastern oil exporters and to the world's oil importers, but it is not the only one. Iran is politically unsteady with an economy precariously dependent on high oil prices. Saudi Arabia's enduring distress, the result of a quickly growing population and consequent income requirements rising faster than oil revenues, has been temporarily masked by high oil prices since 1999. Domestic constraints make Saudi Arabia's balancing act in the oil market more difficult, and unemployment is a growing source of dissatisfaction among Saudi youth. Saudi reservations about the use of military facilities in the US anti-terrorist campaign in the autumn of 2001 may be a sign of more profound apprehension.[22] In that case, securing Middle Eastern oil supplies should be a top political priority, but not using historical methods.

Oil prices, market power and politics

Energy markets, especially the oil market, provide surprises and high risks. Even after decades of turbulence and analysis, our understanding is meagre. There is no general explanatory theory of oil or energy relating to social science, in spite of many partial studies and much available data.[23] The world market crude oil price seems unsustainable at any level. Volatile oil prices with sudden moves up or down represent a high risk for all parties involved and the world economy.[24] In 2000 and 2001, high oil prices bothered consumers and again put oil and energy in general on the political agenda.[25] Fears over oil supplies and prices have spurred concerns over inflation rates, trade balances and government complacency. When con-

sumers call for government action on oil and other energy supplies, oil
matters and is politicized.

No single theoretical discipline of the social sciences has been successful
in analysing the energy markets with results of a predictive value. Insight
into oil and other energy issues is fragmented. Basic philosophical questions
over energy are unsettled. There is no coherent general theory of energy
that can be used to analyse the impact of increasing energy supplies on the
political economy of different societies, such as that of the relationship
between capital and labour.[26]

Engineers, physicists and historians often consider energy to be the
primary factor input in industrial and economic development, but economists tend to ignore energy as an input factor, often considering it as but
one of many intermediary inputs.[27] The classical economists, notably Adam
Smith and David Ricardo, overlooked technology and energy among the
factors of production, selecting only capital, labour and land.[28] In classical
economic analysis, only these three factors were considered sources of
value creation.[29] In hindsight, it is remarkable that energy and technology
were overlooked at the unfolding of the Industrial Revolution, when coal
and the steam engine significantly enhanced the efficiency and value of
capital, labour and land.[30] From an energy perspective, the Industrial
Revolution was essentially the replacement of the muscle power of men
and animals with fossil power, with a subsequent huge increase in commer-
cially available energy.[31] Since the start of the Industrial Revolution,
economic growth has been largely synonymous with increasing energy use,
generally at declining real prices. In the nineteenth century, increasing coal
supplies at declining real prices fuelled the Industrial Revolution. In the
twentieth century, rising supplies of electricity and oil, also at declining real
prices, facilitated the subsequent stages of industrial development. In the
twenty-first century, electricity and natural gas supplies seem increasingly
critical to economic performance, but oil remains important.

There is no coherent theory to link oil demand, trading and supplies,
and explain and predict oil price formation. Attempts at economic modelling of the international oil market have generally been unsuccessful,
yielding few reliable predictive results.[32] The essential economic variables
are insufficiently known or unstable. Reserve estimates are constantly being
revised upwards as a result of exploration and technological progress. Cost
estimates are being scaled down as a result of the development of technology and organization. Demand patterns change because of competition,
economic growth, social change and shifting consumer preferences.
Trading patterns and the mechanisms of price formation also change over
time.

The world oil market has repeatedly performed in ways that appear to
violate basic laws of economics. Oil prices seem to move independently of

supply and demand, and vice versa.[33] Since 1970, total oil supplies to the world market have not been price elastic, meaning that oil price changes do not seem to affect global supply volumes.[34] The leading Middle Eastern oil exporters have shifting interests and objectives that at times coincide, at times conflict, so that any formal modelling of the supply side of the world oil market is hazardous. Economic analysis often takes institutional, political and social premises for granted.[35] Political, legal and social analyses, however, often overlook the fundamental economic aspects of practical problems. For the oil market, neither provides an explanation of a predictive value. The functioning of the oil market and the oil industry is difficult to explain only in the traditional economic terms of marginal cost, supply and demand. Concepts of economic rent, imperfect competition and especially oligopoly have to be included in the analysis.[36]

As in other markets, the balance of supply and demand ultimately sets oil prices, but the oil market is striking by reason of its imperfect competition and a structure dominated by supplier concentration and power. The oil market has a large number of sellers and buyers, but suppliers are fewer in number and some have market power in the sense that they can influence prices by adjusting volumes. In economic terms, the oil market is an oligopoly, dominated by few sellers, and intrinsically unstable, making oil supplies more volatile than demand. The abrupt oil price changes since 1970 have been triggered more by sudden changes in volumes supplied than by demand fluctuations. In the oil market, the major oil suppliers are governments that often consider longer time horizons and more diverse concerns than do companies, because countries have more complex interests than firms.[37] Oil supplies and prices are in the last instance set by a small number of Middle Eastern governments working through OPEC, which makes the oil market a unique meeting place of economic forces and politics. Because the major suppliers are located in the Middle East, regional politics have an impact.

Oil demand is a composite of actual consumption, stock building or drawdown, subject to seasonal and cyclical variations as well as speculative movements. It is essentially conditioned by economic forces, such as the growth of incomes, consumption, trade and production, the cost of substitutes and energy taxes, as consumer governments intervene with diverse motives and measures.

Within this framework, economic rent, excess profit above the normal return on capital, offers a clue to oil market performance. Oil-exporting countries, companies that extract, transport, refine and sell oil, as well as oil-importing countries that tax oil products, are rent seekers in the sense that they pursue transfers of wealth through privileged positions and imperfect competition.[38] The huge difference between the value to the consumer from using oil products and the technical cost of crude oil supplies leaves ample space for bargaining and struggle over income between producer governments, consumer governments and the companies. Economic rent, keeping market prices well above the cost of most supplies, to a large extent cushions supply patterns from price changes. For consumers, the most expensive petrol or fuel oil is usually the barrel that is not available in the market. The struggle over economic rent can somewhat explain sudden price moves triggered by political events and unexpected shifts in bargaining power, quite different from marginal adjustment in competitive markets. Landowners, usually governments, restrict access to resources and levy taxes, while consumer governments also impose duties and taxes. There are important economies of scale in most oil industry operations. Economic rent, excess profit, is essentially a function of the size of an oil field, because development and operational cost per barrel tend to diminish with rising volumes.[39] The economies of scale provide strong incentives for joint ventures and tacit co-operation.

These factors distinguish the oil market from many other commodity markets, making it more sensitive to political interference, leading to the importance of the Middle East in oil matters. Oil price formation is highly sensitive to real or perceived changes in the balance of supply and demand. Oil price stability would require a fine-tuning of oil supplies, so that they adjust to demand, controlling inventories. A multitude of suppliers, none of which would have much influence on price formation, but with different costs, would adjust to changing prices. One or a few large suppliers operating together, agreeing on price levels and market shares, acting as a residual supplier and a price maker, could also provide stability. This was to some extent the case for decades until the 1960s as a cartel of integrated multinational companies dominated the world oil market.[40] Since 1970, the concentration of low-cost oil supplies on a small number of countries in the Middle East has been a major source of instability, because each major oil exporter has sufficient market power to influence prices, at least temporarily, and they often disagree on price levels and market shares.

Faced with shifting oil demand, the low-cost oil suppliers have the discretion to adjust volumes or prices or both. This is the core of OPEC politics. When OPEC does agree on an oil price and a corresponding supply level, it is a compromise bridging different economic interests and political concerns, at times responding to past market development rather than anticipating future trends. Fine-tuning of supplies in relation to changing demand is difficult by means of political compromise. In late 1997 OPEC ignored the East Asian economic crisis and increased oil supplies when demand was falling, sending oil prices down.[41] The price collapse was exacerbated by suddenly rising oil supplies from Iraq in early 1998. In March 1999, prominent observers remarked that oil prices were likely to stabilize around $5 a barrel and stay there for a long time.[42] Within a week,

OPEC, supported by Mexico, Norway and Oman, reached an agreement that reduced oil supplies and sent prices soaring, at times above $30 over the next two years. Oil demand was rising as the East Asian economies resumed strong growth and Iraq no longer had the capacity to increase oil exports. It is equally risky to predict that oil prices will remain high.

When OPEC does not agree on prices and volumes, the key member countries give conflicting signals to the oil market, often competing for market shares, undermining what stability might exist. OPEC and oil market stability are hostages of Middle Eastern politics, as has been made clear many times since 1970. Iraq with the world's second largest oil reserves is currently the joker, absent from OPEC deals since 1990, and remains pivotal to Middle East and oil market stability.

Doubts and uncertainties concerning oil supplies from the Middle East are likely to persist. Iran, Iraq, Kuwait and Saudi Arabia have oil market power in the sense that each one is usually able to increase or at least decrease output, influencing prices and pursuing separate interests, acting in collusion or challenging each other. Venezuela is the only oil exporter outside the Middle East to have a similar oil market power. In economic terms this distribution of market power means that each one can act as a price maker for oil, at least for some time, and force the others to be price takers, to the eventual detriment of their revenues and economic interests. In political terms this means that the countries mentioned have the potential to harm each other's stability, as the regimes with few exceptions are precariously dependent on oil revenues. High population growth aggravates this dependence. From this perspective, the relations between the leading Gulf oil exporters are more complex and potentially more hostile than are relations between companies taking part in a cartel. The leading Gulf oil exporters also represent political and military threats to their neighbours, in addition to economic rivalry, as Iraq has shown in 1980 in relation to Iran and in 1990 in relation to Kuwait.

The only prolonged periods of relative oil price stability since 1973 have been the years 1974–78, 1981–85 and 1991–97. During 1974–78 and again in 1981–85, Saudi Arabia acted as a residual supplier and price maker with market power through the combination of excess revenues and excess capacity. Saudi Arabia set residual volumes and decided the price, and the others had to follow.[43] In the late 1970s, the political condition was a certain minimum of trust or at least the absence of overt conflicts between Iran, Iraq, Kuwait and Saudi Arabia. The balance was upset by the Iranian revolution in 1979. During 1981–85, Iran was marginalized by revolution and war with Iraq. During 1991–97, OPEC collectively ruled the oil market through target prices and quotas, but with the conspicuous absence of Iraq and with Saudi market power as the disciplining factor. Iraq's sudden oil export expansion in early 1998 was an important factor, but not the only one, upsetting the balance.

With rising dependence on Middle Eastern oil, the political balance between Iran, Iraq, Kuwait and Saudi Arabia will remain the key to oil market stability. At first, revolutionary Iran was seen as the troublemaker and political threat; subsequently the culprit has been Iraq, with the Saddam Hussein regime appearing as a military menace to three neighbours. The absence of political normalization between Iraq and Kuwait or Saudi Arabia precludes oil policy co-operation. As long as Iran or Iraq appears to threaten Kuwait and Saudi Arabia, but without dominating them, they compromise oil market stability as the two latter countries need foreign protection, essentially from the United States, which thus gains greater weight in the balance shaping their oil policies.[44] Oil market stability today will require either the replacement of the Iraqi regime, or alternatively Iraq succeeding in dominating the Gulf. The continued moderation of the Iranian regime is also essential.

Oil prices affect the inflation rates, trade balances and macro-economic policies of all countries, as well as government re-election chances. Public forgetfulness and political complacency are remarkable when energy supplies are abundant and prices low. When supplies tighten and prices rise, the public makes politicians responsible, as in the United States in 2001. Suddenly, energy supplies and price security become government matters, too important to be left to market forces and private initiative alone. Political rhetoric aims to calm public apprehension, but real measures have effects not always in tune with intentions. The freshly elected conservative George W. Bush administration in the United States has promoted a national energy policy to secure supplies and moderate prices.[45] This is nothing new. Since Richard Nixon, all US presidents have had energy plans, but with little effect. With rising oil import dependence the chances are that more energy plans will follow. The Middle East is likely to remain important for decades to oil importers, including the United States.

Throughout the twentieth century governments intervened in energy markets, regulating electricity and natural gas industries and sponsoring access to foreign oil. Before the First World War the UK government invested in an oil company, the precursor of BP, to secure access to oil from Iran for the Royal Navy. During the war, access to oil helped the Allies win. The dependence on oil caused the French government to embark on an interventionist policy to secure supplies.[46] After the war France and the United States struggled with the United Kingdom over the control of oil in the Middle East. Since then, the United States has pursued a decisive influence on the world oil market and a strong position in the Middle East.[47] The Second World War once more showed the military importance of oil. Germany, Italy and Japan suffered from scarce supplies, while the Allies had access to the bulk of the world's oil.

Between the Second World War and the early 1970s, a small number of multinational oil companies effectively controlled the international oil market and particularly the oil industries of the Middle East, North Africa and a few other important producers such as Indonesia, Nigeria and Venezuela. These companies operated in close co-operation with their home governments, whose interests apart from oil included military assistance and trade. Their control over oil permitted a steady increase in volumes extracted and consumed, much to the benefit of the North American, Western European and Japanese economies, which experienced decades of stable growth. The counterpart was an increasing dependence on oil imports, and especially on the Middle East, with a consequent vulnerability. The United States became the world's largest oil importer, while North Sea supplies have at least temporarily mitigated Europe's oil import dependence. Japan and the rest of East Asia have become the major market for Middle Eastern oil. The OPEC countries used their enhanced bargaining power to take control of oil supplies and prices and they have kept it, but they have not always been able to use their power.

Since the early 1970s, oil prices have been remarkably unstable, varying in constant 2001 dollars from $9 to $67 a barrel. High oil prices deter consumption and encourage the emergence of significant competition, harming Middle Eastern oil revenues. Low prices at first reduce Middle Eastern oil revenues, then encourage consumption and deter competition. Oil price volatility recurs because of cyclical swings in the market, Middle East politics and OPEC's recurrently imperfect responses to market trends. Unforeseen political and economic circumstances are inevitable recurring factors. Tensions in the Middle East have given rise to disruptions of oil supply and trading patterns, but they generally re-emerge, even at quite different price levels. Unless major changes should occur in the patterns of oil demand and supply, this cyclical pattern centred on the Middle East is likely to continue. At times, oil prices will be seen as too high for the consumers, at times as too low for the producers.

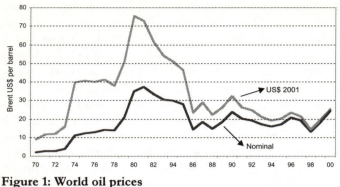

Figure 1: World oil prices
Source: Energy Information Association (EIA) 2001

The resilience of oil

Despite extreme price volatility, oil consumption and production continue to grow. Oil has proved to be a far more robust energy source than was generally assumed in the wake of the 1970s oil crises. Oil users have adapted to higher prices by efficiency gains, and oil producers have adapted to lower prices by cost cutting through reorganization and technology improvement, strengthening the competitive position of oil in the world energy market.[48]

Since 1973, the world economy has undergone a profound technological and structural change with information technology bringing a new division of labour, a transformation of work and the virtual space expanding for individuals and businesses.[49] Nevertheless, the world uses more and more oil, largely because people and merchandise still need to move. Put simply, the Internet provides information, but does not dematerialize goods and services.[50] Because oil remains essential to transportation, it matters to wealth and power, and to governments.[51]

For oil consumers, the good news is that the world is not about to run out of oil. More oil is being found and supply costs are declining. Progress in technology and organization more than mitigate resource depletion.[52] Middle East oil replacement costs have declined markedly.[53] Since the early 1970s, offshore oil development costs in the North Sea and the US Gulf of Mexico have been declining at a rate of about 3 per cent a year, measured in real terms on comparable projects.[54] The bad news is that alternatives to oil have not developed as expected. The bright future promised for nuclear power and coal never materialized.[55] Only natural gas, oil's sister fuel, is quickly gaining ground and the world remains as dependent as ever on oil from the Middle East.

For the oil exporters, the good news is that there is still a market for oil, and it is growing, increasingly concentrated on the transportation sector where there are few alternative fuels, so far. The bad news is that with few exceptions, they have not managed to diversify their economies and develop new sources of income.[56] They remain critically dependent on oil exports, fighting over oil prices and market shares, needing oil revenues more badly than ever because of a growing population. For many years, their per capita oil revenues have been declining in real terms.

The mutual dependence on oil supplies and oil revenues can provide interdependence, a common ground to enhance stability and avoid sudden and extreme oil price swings. The common ground is out of shape because of interest conflicts not only between oil importers and oil exporters, but also among both oil importers and oil exporters. Leading oil importers, such as the United States, China, France, Italy and Japan, obviously have a common interest in oil price moderation, but they are also rivals for supplies, trading positions and influence. The major oil exporters have a common interest in oil price stability, but at different levels and they are rivals for market shares.

The first major issue in international oil politics concerns the oil-importing countries' need for oil from OPEC, especially the Middle East, and at what price, as well as the impact of sudden oil price changes on the oil-importing economies, and their ensuing political interests. Historically, sudden price hikes have contributed to economic setbacks in oil-importing countries. Over time, the economic importance of oil seems to be diminishing, reducing the vulnerability of the oil importers, although sudden oil price movements still seem to have some macro-economic impact. The question is to what extent this relatively reduced economic significance of oil is leading to a corresponding decline in its political importance to consumer country governments, eventually making the Middle East less important in international affairs.

The second important issue concerns the political relations between the leading foreign oil-importing powers and the major Middle Eastern oil exporters, destined to influence their oil policies. Historically, the leading powers have secured their oil interests by political and commercial ties and at times military presence too, evidently not relying solely on market forces. Since 1970, the major oil exporters have asserted greater independence in all matters, especially oil policy, but they have in turn drawn on foreign powers to assert their interests against neighbours. Iraq developed close political and military ties with France and the Soviet Union that were broken off in 1990, but in recent years has been renewing contacts with China, France and Russia. Saudi Arabia maintained and strengthened close economic, political and military links with the United States. New major oil importers, such as China and India, will have to ponder commercial and political measures to secure access to Middle East oil.[57] The question is to what extent the quest for influence and rivalry among Middle East oil

exporters and foreign powers alike could lead to new alliance patterns with
a potentially destabilizing effect on the Middle East and the oil market.

The third major issue concerns capacity utilization to extract oil and
eventually to invest in capacity expansion in the Middle East. The outcome
essentially depends on internal politics and revenue needs. Iran, Iraq,
Kuwait and Saudi Arabia each has the geological potential to considerably
expand capacity to extract oil at low cost, but it is an open question how
much will be done and within what timeframe.[58] The primary objective of
any government is to stay in power, but the survival of Middle Eastern
regimes is often linked to that of governments because of the centralization
and personalization of power. Short-term political survival is more important than long-term economic strategy. The constant and immediate issue is
how to meet income requirements. The pivotal countries can increase
revenues by raising oil output, provided that other suppliers cannot or will
not do the same and demand expands. This was Saudi Arabia's situation in
the early 1990s. They can also increase revenues by cutting volumes,
provided that other suppliers do not raise theirs, or preferably also reduce
overall output, as has been the case in 1999–2001. The question is simply
under what economic and political conditions the major Middle East oil
exporters will decide to pump more or less oil.

The fourth important issue concerns taxes and duties on oil products
consumed in oil-importing countries as well as environmental taxes and
duties on emissions of carbon dioxide, aimed at curbing oil demand and
potentially harming oil exporters' revenues. The argument that oil product
consumption has an environmental cost and should be taxed has to be
weighed against the economic and social benefit of oil consumption,
especially in transportation. Restrictions on oil use and CO_2 emissions as
well as the trading of emission permits can put downward pressure on oil
prices. By taxing motor fuels for fiscal reasons, oil consumer governments
risk harming their own economies as well as oil exporter revenues.[59] The
question is the consumer benefit of using fuels weighed in the balance with
real or alleged social costs. Another question concerns the potential interest
of the OPEC countries in eventually taking part in a new climate treaty.

The fifth important issue concerns the new challenges to oil demand, oil
prices and oil exporters' revenues through oil company restructuring and
the rise of natural gas as a competitive fuel. Oil company restructuring
influences the bargaining positions of international oil companies and oil-
producing governments. The rise of natural gas represents an obvious
threat to oil demand and prices and a challenge to the Middle Eastern oil
exporters. The question is whether the leading Middle Eastern oil exporters
will take a more active part in oil industry restructuring and in natural gas
trade. The issue is linked to the overriding one of how much oil to extract
and at what price.

The importance of the Middle East

From the early 1970s to the mid-1980s, the Middle East was considered the economically most promising part of the world, in spite of its numerous political tensions and open conflicts. With oil income, the oil-exporting countries of the region had made an economic quantum leap. In some salient cases they went from dire poverty to extreme wealth within a decade. Their economic growth rates were exceptional and their relative position in the world improved remarkably.

Around 1980, Kuwait's per capita gross national product was higher than that of most European countries. By that measure, Iraq and Saudi Arabia were at the level of Central Europe. The Middle East had become an important market for goods and services. The region also had the economic resources to be a politically significant part of the world community. The general impression was that the oil wealth was reasonably well managed and that the oil-exporting countries of the region were making a transition into modern economies. The wise use of an important natural resource apparently could propel a group of countries into the modern world. They also gave the impression of having a sophisticated and visionary leadership combining wisdom and power.[60]

By the late 1990s, evidently the Middle East had slipped behind and is continuing to do so, although high oil prices in 2000 and 2001 provided temporarily high revenues. The need to create jobs is urgent. Youth unemployment is in many cases between 30 and 50 per cent. The need to replace foreign workers with locals, such as exists in Saudi Arabia, raises difficult issues of labour productivity and income distribution. Iraq has been the exception, as a welfare state with relatively good social conditions. This is no longer the case, because of the Saddam Hussein regime, the war against Iran, the Gulf conflict and the subsequent embargo. Average income is high by Western standards only in Kuwait, Qatar and the United Arab Emirates. Countries such as Oman and Saudi Arabia have an average income level about that of poorer European countries such as Greece and Portugal. Among citizens, income distribution is less unequal than among the working population, which includes a large number of foreign workers.

In other Middle Eastern oil-exporting countries, essentially Iran and Iraq, average income levels are much lower. The majority of the population has difficult living conditions by European or North American standards. The oil price decline of 1986 led to a serious drop in oil revenues for most oil-exporting countries and a subsequent and lasting deterioration of social conditions. Low oil prices in 1997–99 had a similar effect. Insofar as oil revenues are increasing less quickly than population and other sources of income are not sufficiently developed, the Middle Eastern oil-exporting countries are heading for economic decline. They are in a rush against time to develop and diversify their economies.[61] In the meantime they are caught

in a squeeze between high population growth and a critical dependence on
oil revenues.[62]

In 1970, the six leading oil exporters in the Gulf, namely Iran, Iraq, Kuwait, Qatar, Saudi Arabia and the United Arab Emirates, had a total
population of about 45 million. By 2000, it had more than doubled to about
110 million. Over the same period, their total oil output rose by about one-
half, from about 13 million barrels a day in 1970 to about 20 million barrels
a day in 2000, so that average per capita oil output almost halved, from 0.34
barrels a day per person in 1970 to 0.18 barrels a day per person by 2000.
Measured in constant 2001 prices, by the price of Saudi Light crude,
average per capita oil output value in the six countries mentioned was $653
in 1970. By 1985 it had more than tripled to $2075, but by 2000 it had
declined again to $1593. This latter figure is misleading as a rising propor-
tion of the oil is consumed locally at low prices; this is particularly the case
in Iran. Population growth and uncertain oil prices mean that per capita oil
revenues in the Middle East are far more likely to fall than to rise. The
revenue squeeze limits choice in oil policy, as a larger population requires
more money, to fend off the risk of social distress and political instability
with potential repercussions for the oil market.

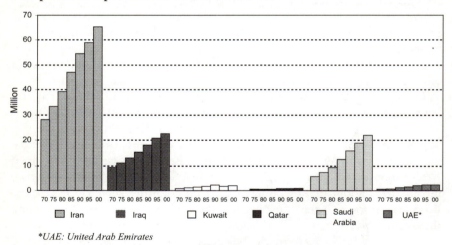

*UAE: United Arab Emirates

Figure 2: OPEC Middle East population 1970–2000
Source: The World Bank 2001

Since 1970, political events in and between the major Middle Eastern oil-
exporting countries have on several occasions caused sudden shifts in oil
supplies that resulted in significant moves in the oil price.

This has been the case in 1973–74, in 1979–80 and in 1986, and it was
repeated in 1990, 1991 and again in 1998 and 1999. Underlying economic
forces of supply and demand prepare the ground for oil price changes, but

the oil price discontinuities since 1973 have had a political trigger in the Middle East. In the early 1970s, Saudi Arabia had replaced Libya as the major oil exporter, but the rapid growth of Saudi oil extraction could not continue at the same pace, 25 per cent a year. The oil market was tense before the autumn of 1973 and OPEC had already demanded a significant price increase.

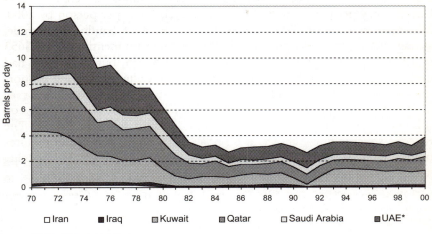

UAE: United Arab Emirates

Figure 3a: OPEC Middle East oil extraction per capita 1970–2000
Sources: BP Amoco Statistical Review of World Energy 2001; The World Bank 2001

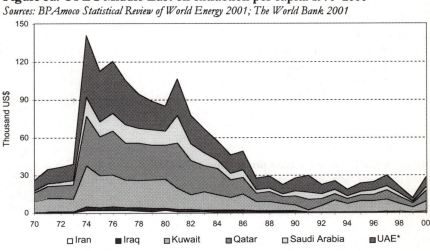

UAE: United Arab Emirates

Figure 3b: OPEC Middle East oil output value per capita 1970–2000
Sources: Energy Information Administration (EIA) 2001; BP Amoco Statistical Review of World Energy 2001; The World Bank 2001

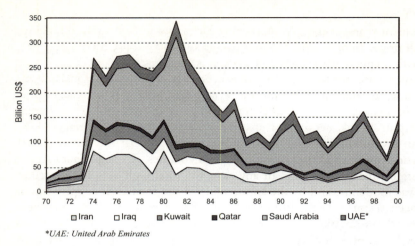

UAE: United Arab Emirates

Figure 4: OPEC Middle East oil exports 1970–2000
Sources: Energy Information Administration (EIA) 2001; BP Amoco Statistical Review of World Energy 2001

The first oil price shock of 1973 was essentially the result of a reduction of oil output by Saudi Arabia, Kuwait and the United Arab Emirates in October, November and December of that year. These three countries made up the essential force of the Arab oil weapon that was activated following the war between Egypt and Israel. Iraq did not participate officially, but reduced volumes in October, and subsequently benefited from the occasion to increase oil production and exports. Iran also abstained from any action. The net result was a cut in oil supplies from the Gulf of about 15 per cent during October, November and December, compared to September volumes. By January 1974, Saudi Arabia and Kuwait had again raised volumes. By February 1974, the action was called off, as Egypt had secured Israeli withdrawal, but by then oil prices had moved to a level about four times higher than a year earlier.

The new, much higher oil price stuck, despite the fact that oil supplies from the Gulf area were higher in early 1974 than early 1973, and with weaker demand. One reason was that the action took the market by surprise and created a psychological context supporting the much higher prices, regardless of the volume restoration. Even if there was some disagreement within OPEC on the new level of oil prices, especially between Iran and Saudi Arabia, there was sufficient consensus to stick to the new level and formalize an agreement.

The immediate effect of the oil price rise was a sudden transfer of income from oil-importing to oil-exporting countries, indeed an international transfer of resources of a magnitude that was unprecedented at the time. This led directly to a severe recession in the oil-importing countries in 1974 and 1975, with high inflation combined with high unemployment.[63] In the subsequent years, unemployment was reduced, but inflation stayed high and real oil prices were eroded as economic growth picked up in the late 1970s, and with it energy demand and in particular oil demand.

With a different twist, the oil price escalation repeated itself in 1979–80. This time, the absolute price rise was even larger, although the relative price increase was less. The oil market started to panic in January 1979 as Iranian oil output shrunk because of an oil workers' strike, which triggered the Iranian revolution. Spot oil prices shot up, regardless of the fact that both Iraq and Kuwait used the occasion to raise volumes, although Saudi Arabia moderately reduced volume. In any case, the total Gulf area supply reduction was moderate, and by the spring of 1979 the total Gulf supply volume had been restored to the pre-crisis level of December 1978. Nonetheless, oil prices were markedly higher and continued to rise. By May 1979, the nominal spot price for North Sea oil was twice the level of December 1978, although total Gulf export volumes were slightly higher.

Rising total Gulf supply volumes did not prevent oil prices from sliding slightly upwards during the summer of 1979. In the autumn, oil prices continued to escalate, disregarding Gulf supplies that were markedly higher than a year earlier. The market evidently then paid more attention to the Kuwaiti decision to restrain oil exports than to the higher volumes from both Saudi Arabia and Iraq, as well as the partial restoration of Iranian output.

After peaking in the late autumn of 1980, oil prices started to decline in the winter of 1980, with the slide continuing throughout the summer. At this point, however, total Gulf oil supplies did decline, as Iraq, Kuwait and the United Arab Emirates were cutting volumes to defend high oil prices, and Iranian oil exports were reduced because of revolutionary turmoil.

The 1979–80 double oil price shocks caused another sudden transfer of income from oil-importing to oil-exporting countries, this time of a yet greater magnitude. In the oil-importing countries, the result was, once again, a severe recession, with high inflation combined with high unemployment. This time, fighting inflation got a higher political priority than fighting unemployment, first through tight monetarist policies. The combination of expensive energy and expensive money caused a quick restructuring of the industrial economies, with the development of light industry, high technology and services, but with heavy industry scaled down or moved to countries with abundant and cheap domestic energy. This restructuring had been commenced under the impact of the first oil price shock.

The next critical event was Iraq's attack on Iran in September 1980. Immediate effects were reductions in both countries' oil output and oil prices rising again. The oil price escalation ended in early 1981. The trigger was a combination of oil inventory drawdown, reduced consumption and rising Saudi output.

In hindsight, the 1979–80 turbulence is the most protracted and most complex oil market crisis in modern times. Whereas panicky inventory build-up by consumers explains a good deal of the price escalation, the Gulf oil exporters' motives also deserve comment. Saudi Arabia had an important role in both starting and ending the crisis. At the outset of the crisis, as Iranian volumes fell, Saudi Arabia chose not to use spare capacity to offset the shortfall, but instead reduced its volumes. The motive was probably dismay at the United States and the Camp David agreement concluding a unilateral peace between Egypt and Israel. Only in the autumn of 1980 did Saudi Arabia call upon spare capacity to dampen the price escalation, as the oil price had risen substantially. It is equally significant that two well-off Gulf oil exporters, Kuwait and the United Arab Emirates, also cut volumes in late 1979 and throughout most of 1980, evidently to defend the oil price. In hindsight, there was evidently some consensus in the Gulf area that the oil price had been too low before the Iranian revolution.

An important contextual factor is that until the summer of 1980, the outcome of the Iranian revolution seemed undecided between a moderate, liberal faction and a radical, Islamist faction. Only the victory of the Islamist faction made Iran appear as an ideological and political threat to its neighbours, undermining the mutual trust that had permitted Iran, Iraq, Kuwait and Saudi Arabia to co-operate within OPEC and stabilize oil prices. The Islamist victory in Iran was an important factor in provoking Iraq's attack.

This time, total Gulf oil supplies were not restored to their pre-crisis level, but in the following years oil prices declined, partly because of lower demand resulting from substitution and conservation efforts set in motion by the first oil price rise, partly because of the ensuing economic recession, and partly because of rising oil supplies from new sources, not least the North Sea. The 1979–80 crisis marked the peak of both the OPEC and the Middle East market share for oil. The loss of market share was exacerbated by the effort in the early 1980s, essentially by Saudi Arabia and Kuwait, to defend the high oil price by cutting volumes.

The early 1980s effort to defend the high oil price was neither wholehearted nor successful. By 1985, the nominal oil price had fallen to $27–28 a barrel. In real terms, the oil price had been almost halved since the 1980 peak. Nevertheless, both Saudi Arabia and Kuwait experienced the situation as unsustainable, losing market shares and revenues. By the late autumn of 1985, the two countries alerted the other OPEC members to a change of oil strategy, aiming at market share instead of high prices. From January to July 1986, each country raised oil output substantially, with the United Arab Emirates following. All three countries could do so at low marginal cost because of spare capacity installed. Total Gulf oil supplies increased by more than 2 million barrels a day during the first six months of the year. Oil prices were more than halved, with the Brent spot price falling from $22 to less than $10 a barrel. This price decline was evidently too brutal, and during the second part of the year, total Gulf oil supplies were reduced almost to their initial level, but this time the effort was shared by the other Gulf oil exporters, including Iraq and Iran, which were still at war. Oil prices did not, however, rise to their previous levels.

In hindsight, the move was successful for Saudi Arabia and Kuwait, which no longer had to bear alone the brunt of being residual suppliers. Insofar as the aim was to stimulate oil demand, the price decline was a success. It is, however, open to dispute to what extent the oil price decline caused the subsequent increase in oil demand, or to what extent this was triggered by the positive impact on the level of economic activity by the oil price decline.

The 1973 oil price shock was more a trigger than a cause of the economic change, as tensions had been building up earlier, in the form of inflationary pressures and currency instability. The United States had already discontinued the dollar convertibility with gold in 1971. The two oil price jumps together forced through a profound restructuring of the Western economies during the 1980s, with a massive shift of labour and capital from older, energy-intensive activities to modern ones using less energy.

When oil prices declined again in 1986, the restructuring was too advanced to be reversed. Lower oil prices did not lead to a return to old investment patterns and the revival of heavy industry, but they did influence consumer behaviour, slowing the process toward greater energy efficiency. The oil price fall also meant a transfer of resources from oil-exporting countries to oil-importing ones, permitting the latter a higher level of economic activity than would otherwise have been feasible. The long-term effect of the 1986 oil price decline was to prolong the period of sustained growth in the Western economies that was commenced in 1982.

The next oil market crisis was provoked by Iraq's occupation of Kuwait in August 1990. Within a month, oil prices doubled as Kuwaiti oil production came to a halt and Iraq's output was reduced to a fraction of its earlier level. Even though Saudi Arabia raised output significantly, mobilizing spare capacity, and the United Arab Emirates raised output more moderately, the total Gulf oil supplies were not restored to previous levels until well after the crisis had ended. The difference was, however, essentially covered by rising output from Nigeria and Venezuela. As soon as the decision to attack Iraq and liberate Kuwait was made public, oil prices subsided.

The Gulf crisis was a salient example of how animosity, if not open conflict, between Saudi Arabia and Kuwait on the one hand, and Iran or

Iraq on the other, causes the former to raise oil output and lower oil prices. The need for outside assistance is important in this respect. The hostilities represented a huge drain on the Saudi economy as the country had to pay for part of the US military effort and at the same time increase its own military expenditure.

The oil price jump of 1990 following Iraq's invasion of Kuwait triggered an economic setback. By the summer of 1990, the United States had already moved into an economic recession, an indication of structural problems that would not be settled by low oil prices. Similarly, both Europe and Japan were heading for lower economic growth, although for different reasons. In Europe, where inflationary pressures were low in most countries, the combination of US recession and German high interest rates led to declining demand and activity. Because of the reunification process the German economy went through a difficult phase in 1991–92, and has yet, almost ten years later, to function as Europe's economic locomotive. Japan by 1990 needed to cool overheated financial markets. The effort was more than successful, so that Japan's problem now is economic stagnation, unrelated to oil prices.

From the oil exporters' point of view, the most recent crisis in the oil market was the 1998 price collapse. From October 1997 to August 1998, oil prices, Brent spot, fell by about 40 per cent, from $20 to $12 a barrel. In the autumn of 1998, oil prices were at a historical low in real terms, below the level before the 1973 oil price rise. In modern times, this is the second most brutal oil price decline, in magnitude surpassed only by the 1986 oil price collapse.

The 1998 oil price decline had composite causes, of which the East Asian economic crisis is an important one, but where political events and decisions in the Middle East have been crucial. Expecting significant oil demand growth in 1998, Venezuela increased output in the summer and autumn of 1997. Then OPEC raised quotas in the late autumn of 1997, but rather as an endorsement of output increases that had already taken place. In the meantime, the East Asian economic crisis had weakened oil demand and contributed to a depressed psychology in the oil market. This was further exacerbated by a mild winter simultaneously in Europe, Japan and North America, which further reduced oil demand and strengthened the pessimistic mood in the oil market. Finally, Iraq returned to the market with large oil exports, doubling output between January and August of 1998.

Every one of these factors would have been sufficient to put downward pressure on the oil price. Together they caused an exceptional price decline. Again, the supply side was the problem, as the oil market was oversupplied in relation to demand. With political resolve, OPEC would have been able to cope with the setback in Asian demand or the effects of a mild winter.

The outcome was that huge inventories continued to weaken oil prices in the late autumn of 1998. Even if Iraqi oil exports apparently subsided, rising Iranian volumes offset the market effect, so that the total Gulf oil supplies in October 1998 were at about the January level.

In bringing down oil prices, the Gulf suppliers were instrumental. OPEC, especially the Gulf countries, wanted a larger share of the oil market. The background was strife between Saudi Arabia and Venezuela over shares in the US market as well as a desire in the Gulf and in Iran to take positions before Iraq's eventual return to the oil market. By the autumn of 1997 practically all OPEC countries had budget and trade deficits and a need for higher revenues. The objective of the November 1997 decision to raise OPEC quotas was to keep the real price stable and let OPEC take most of the market growth. The assumption was that Iraq's eventual return to the market would be the subject of OPEC negotiation, but Iraq succeeded in returning to the market with a sizeable export volume without any OPEC bargaining, thanks to the United Nations and indirectly the United States. The deal with the UN meant that until late 1999 revenue targets, not volumes, determined Iraq's oil sales for food and medicine so that Iraq's export volumes and market share increased as a function of declining oil prices. The deal effectively removed the price risk from Iraq's oil policy. Iraq's oil output has since the summer of 1998 been above that of Kuwait, at least temporarily strengthening Iraq's position in the oil market and in the Middle East.

Low oil prices caused severe budgetary and balance of payments problems in most oil-exporting countries, not least in Iran and Saudi Arabia. During 1998 several attempts were made at a deal to cut volumes and raise oil prices, but only in March 1999 was agreement reached by OPEC, with the exception of Iraq, but supported by Mexico, Norway and Oman. The immediate effect of volume restrictions was to increase oil prices from about $10 a barrel to about $17. Strict adherence to quotas and buoyant demand made oil prices rise above $30 a barrel in the following year. The 1999 OPEC agreement was possible because Iraq could no longer expand oil exports, since Venezuela under a new government chose to co-operate with the Gulf oil exporters rather than compete for market shares and especially since Iran and Saudi Arabia experienced a common predicament and had a mutual interest in higher oil prices.

Experience since the early 1970s shows that timing is the essential factor in the interaction between the oil market and the world economy. The oil market is more vulnerable to disruptions when the world economy is booming. Without recessionary tendencies in the United States in 1990, the oil price rise could have been substantially stronger. The world economy is more vulnerable to oil price shocks when it has been booming for several years.

Table 1: Oil market chronology

Year	Event	Trigger	Underlying tension	Effect
1973	Oil prices quadrupling	War by Egypt, Jordan and Syria against Israel	Strong rise in oil demand	Lasting higher oil prices
1979	Oil prices doubling	Iranian revolution	Resumption of oil demand increase	Even higher oil prices
1980	Another oil price rise	Iraq's attack on Iran	Widespread concern with oil supply security	Historically high oil prices over several years
1986	Oil prices halved	Saudi Arabia and Kuwait changing oil policy	Strong rise in oil supplies from new provinces, particularly the North Sea	Low oil prices for several years
1990	Oil prices rising	Iraq's attack on Kuwait	Concerns about future oil supplies	Immediately higher oil prices
1991	Oil prices decline	Gulf War against Iraq	Saudi Arabia and other OPEC countries raise output	Lasting lower oil prices
1998	Oil prices decline by 40 per cent	Iraq re-enters the market as a big exporter	Weak oil demand because of East Asian economic crisis and mild winter	Even lower oil prices
1999	Oil prices double	Understanding between Iran and Saudi Arabia	Strong oil demand	Even higher oil prices

The demand for oil

Economic activity generally requires commercial energy. The consumers' capital stock and the level of economic activity condition energy demand. In most cases, the consumers' capital stock is set for using one particular technology and one choice of fuel. Changing fuels usually involves capital expenditure. Energy conservation by using more efficient technology also involves capital expenditure, the alternative being a lower utilization of the equipment in place. The impact of energy price changes on inter-fuel competition and the level of demand is conditioned by capital costs and the state of technology. Substitution of one energy source with another is generally a costly and slow process, so that the immediate impact of price changes on demand and supply patterns is limited, but increases over time as consumers and producers respond by replacing capital stock. Governments influence this process through taxes, subsidies and direct intervention.

At least since 1970, oil demand has been more sensitive than energy demand in general to changes in the level of economic activity. Oil still plays the direct or indirect role as an energy price leader, meaning that other energy prices tend to align themselves to the oil price, rather than the other way round.

Firms and households use oil and other energy forms for ulterior purposes. Using energy is a secondary or tertiary choice in accomplishing specific tasks. In this it is but an input factor purchased in the market to accomplish a specific undertaking, together with other input factors and time spent. The utility is determined by the ulterior objectives, and by the value to the consumer of the tasks to be performed. For most single tasks or purposes, whether production or consumption processes, energy represents but a small part of the total cost, hidden by fragmented purchase. Demand for energy is a derived demand, just like the derived demand by a firm for any factor of production.[64]

The economic gains from more efficient energy sources at lower costs are pervasive and have benefited consumers, who have been able to expand their habits of energy consumption at declining real cost. The historical trend is that efficiency gains in energy use in salient cases do not lead to lower demand, but to an expansion of the capital stock using energy as well as its increased utilization, representing a higher level of economic activity.[65] With engines that are more efficient, there are more cars on the roads. With more fuel-efficient planes, the cost of flying has declined and frequency has increased.

Historically, the use of commercial energy, at first coal, later oil, gas and electricity, has had a comprehensive qualitative impact on society. In the nineteenth century, the increasing use of coal in railways and shipping facilitated transportation, which opened markets and enhanced the division of labour, resulting in productivity gains and rising living standards. The replacement of horses with coal in transportation caused savings in time, labour and land that ultimately were far greater than the cost of coal. The gains included speed and the marketing of farm produce, land available for growing food for people instead of horses. In the twentieth century, oil and electricity had a similar economic effect. The subsequent replacement of coal with oil caused big savings in capital, labour and land, in addition to the environmental and health gains. Such gains are difficult to measure; they are not included in the monetary value of energy, but represent a consumer surplus. For this reason, the importance of oil is not reflected in its small share of the gross national product.[66] It nonetheless functions as a catalyst without which other inputs would be less effective.[67]

A transportation system uses capital, labour and land, together with technology and organization, but none of them would be of value without energy. It is energy, today mostly oil, that moves cars, airplanes, ships and trains, not capital, labour or land, nor technology or organization. Capital and technology transmit and depend on energy.

Using more capital, labour, land, technology or organization cannot make up for a sudden loss of energy.[68] Energy and capital are essentially complementary, although there is a limited substitution potential. Whether energy and capital are substitutes or complementary is an unsettled empirical and theoretical question.[69] A possible compromise is that energy and capital are partial substitutes when deciding investment in new capital stock, but subsequently complementary. Energy demand essentially depends on the utilization of the capital stock, the level of economic activity. A sudden loss of energy normally causes a loss of economic activity, a lower utilization of the capital stock, and a loss of welfare. The use of energy in the longer run is closely linked to the level of economic activity. Energy, or oil, becomes an issue only in times of sudden price rises, supply trouble or difficult trade-off with environmental concerns.

When energy prices rise and technologies improve, energy use declines. Capital investment, changing production processes and new product ranges reduce the use of energy so that capital substitutes for energy.[70] The use of the new capital stock requires less energy. Ample capital resources seem to accelerate this process, further reducing energy needs. This is why the general trend in manufacturing industry is toward declining energy intensity.[71] The overriding objective is to improve profit margins. Ultimately the capital market will be the judge of efficiency, with severe consequences for the laggards. Energy-saving technology reduces the cost of energy as an input factor, providing incentives to substitute energy for labour and capital.[72] Energy savings increase the consumer surplus, as well as providing gains in service. Historically, technological changes that cause a more efficient use of energy have often resulted in rising energy use.[73] In the United States economy between 1920 and 1969, the input of energy is estimated to have increased three times as fast as the input of labour.[74]

Since the early 1970s, manufacturing industry in North America, Western Europe and Japan has changed profoundly. The capital stock has been largely replaced to use less energy. Production processes are no longer the same and the range of products has altered markedly. The emphasis is now on light industry and high technology. The result is that with a much higher value added in the 1990s than 20 years earlier, manufacturing energy use has stabilized, showing substantial efficiency gains.[75] Between 1973 and 1989 manufacturing in the former socialist economies of Eastern Europe and the Soviet Union significantly expanded energy use with little progress in value added, indicating substantial efficiency losses. Since 1990, these countries have been increasingly engaged in the same process of industrial restructuring as the Western industrial countries have carried out since 1973. The potential for energy efficiency gains in manufacturing is still considerable, indicating that the level of energy use in this sector is unlikely to reach historical levels for a long time.

For households, the purpose of using energy is not to produce goods or services for sale in a competitive market, but to enhance convenience, comfort and enjoyment, according to micro-economic theory of individual and household behaviour.[76] Households' energy use and expenditure seem to be rising, even in mature economies such as the United States.[77] For household energy use, the relationship between time and money seems crucial.[78] Rising employment raises both income and time pressure. By double labour market participation, households' ambitions and real incomes increase, but their available time diminishes. Time, not money, gradually becomes the critical factor in household life, making time more valuable, measured in money or in opportunity cost, justifying rising expenditure to gain time, as by driving and using appliances.[79] In this process of gradually shifting energy use from manufacturing to households and services, the trendsetters are the rich societies of North America and Northern Europe. For oil demand, it means an increasing concentration on private motoring and airlines, more sensitive to income than to price. Gradually, many other parts of the world seem to be adapting to this pattern.

The arena of competition

The world energy market is an arena where different technologies co-exist and compete.[80] Although the world at any moment will use a number of different energy technologies and fuels, the trend is toward greater efficiency, cleanliness and convenience, as a result of a combination of technology, consumer preferences and policies. This is why animal power, dung, wood and peat were replaced with coal, which in turn was replaced with oil as the dominant fuel.[81] Apparently, the market share of oil has peaked in the late twentieth century, with natural gas advancing.

Oil has acquired a dominant position in the world energy market because of competitive qualities as a condensed form of energy that is easy to transport and store and suitable for both stationary and mobile uses. In addition, oil is an industrial feedstock. Availability at first gave oil an edge over whale oil in lamps. Subsequently, it could successfully compete against coal in transportation, heating and power generation because it is lighter in relation to energy content and cleaner. Simplicity of transportation and storage still give oil an edge over natural gas for many uses, even if it is less clean.

Experience shows that energy transitions, meaning moves into new fuels, take decades. New technologies have to be developed and become competitive. Infrastructure requires planning, investment decisions and implementation. Consumers have long lead times; it takes many years and much capital investment to change a society's stock of cars, boilers and power stations. Energy producers have to overcome initial technical, safety, environmental and cost hazards as they move from experimental to commercial operations.

The capital intensity of both energy demand and supplies means that effective competition involves huge investment and takes a long time. The impact of relative prices for the various energy commodities on demand and supply patterns is moderated by the cost of capital, the level of economic activity, lead times and by political intervention. Substitution of one energy source with another is a costly and generally slow process. The inertia translates practically into low short-term price elasticity for both demand and supply in the energy market. By contrast, the long-term price elasticities are much higher, because, as mentioned, consumers and producers respond as investors to price signals. The substitution is usually driven by a change of technology, where increasing energy efficiency is but one of several causes or motives in a wider industrial transformation.

The introduction of the automobile made oil the dominant fuel over coal. The combustion engine was a technical novelty that transformed the world, but it needed a new fuel. Natural gas is increasingly preferable in power generation, because modern gas turbines represent an economic advantage, with low capital and maintenance costs, short lead times and high efficiency, as well as environmental advantage through low emissions. Today, where natural gas is available, it is the preferred fuel in new power plants, but in most cases it is not economical to replace coal with gas in old thermal power plants. The rise of natural gas leaves oil use increasingly confined to transportation. Oil still keeps a position in decentralized heating systems and in small-scale power generation in remote areas, where it is difficult to bring coal or natural gas.

Oil is used as a variety of products, competing in distinctive arenas against different fuels, with specific demand properties. The long-term trend is that the proportion of gasoline, diesel and jet fuel increases, while that of fuel oil declines.

In the transportation sector, oil remains dominant, if not exclusive. Airplanes, cars, buses, trucks and ships use jet fuel, gasoline, diesel and bunker oil with hardly any alternative. The transportation sector is the prime market for oil, where demand generally has a high income elasticity and low price elasticity. Economic growth usually implies productivity gains through labour specialization and expanding markets, meaning that more goods are to be transported over longer distances, more often and at higher speed. Likewise, with rising incomes people also tend to travel longer distances more often, and if possible at higher speed, in conjunction with both work and leisure. Typically, airfreight and air travel seem to expand at a faster pace than economic growth. The lack of alternative fuels and the value added of the transportation services tend to make oil demand here fairly insensitive to price.

In space heating in homes, service institutions and industrial plants, fuel oil, whose quality will depend on local environmental standards, competes against electricity and natural gas, in some cases even coal. In this segment of the market, demand is less income elastic and more price elastic. Rising incomes do not necessarily lead to a preference for higher indoor temperatures, although in the longer run they will lead to expanding space that will require more energy to heat. With several energy sources available, users have the ability to choose the least expensive solution, but many will have equipment restraining the options.

In power generation, fuel oil competes against coal, natural gas, nuclear power and hydropower, where available, and increasingly new sources such as solar and wind power. This segment of the market has the highest price elasticity because the competition is so intense. Although economic growth is in most cases accompanied by a rising demand for electric power, the choice of oil as the generator is not obvious. In the 1950s and 1960s, increasingly inexpensive fuel oil made heavy inroads into power generation in most parts of the world. In the 1970s and 1980s high prices made power generators replace fuel oil with coal and nuclear power. Increasingly, natural gas, where available, is the preferred fuel in power generation because of its cleanness and efficiency.

The alternatives to conventional oil are heavy oil, tar sand and oil shale. The technology is available and resources are huge, but costs are generally high, apart from environmental hazards, through high emissions, especially of CO_2 and dust. Not yet competitive, but emerging alternatives, are fuel cells, based on oil products or natural gas.[82] In the longer run, natural gas appears to be the most serious competitor to oil. Any breakthrough in the use of fuel-cell vehicles is likely to enhance demand for hydrogen or methanol based on natural gas.[83] A breakthrough in the costs of conversion of natural gas to liquid fuels would significantly enhance its competitiveness in relation to oil, blurring the barriers between the oil and gas markets.[84] The essential effect would be to undermine the predominance of oil in the transportation sector.

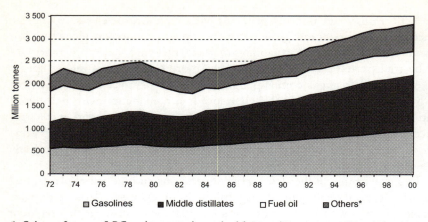

* *Others: refinery gas, LPGs, solvents, petroleum coke, lubricants, bitumen, wax, refinery fuel and loss.*

Figure 5: World oil product category consumption 1972–2000
Source: BPAmoco Statistical Review of World Energy 2001

In spite of high transportation, storage and distribution costs, natural gas is the fuel whose use is expanding the most quickly at the turn of the millennium. Natural gas has the advantage of being plentiful, with a geographically more dispersed resource base than oil as well as lower CO_2 emissions, apart from its flexibility and multiple uses.[85]

In any case, since the mid-1970s, the world's combined dependence on oil and natural gas has not diminished, in spite of supply shocks and price turbulence. In relative terms, the importance of oil in the world energy market has receded moderately, although world oil demand has on average increased by 1 per cent a year. This has been more than offset by the rising market share of natural gas. From 1975 to 1999, total world energy demand rose by 43 per cent, oil demand by 27 per cent, and natural gas demand almost doubled, increasing by 91 per cent.

The oil market in the new economic setting

For decades, oil has been the swing factor in global energy demand because it is indispensable to economic activity and at the same time liquid and easy to transport and store. When more energy is needed, oil is usually the first choice. Correspondingly, when the need for energy declines, oil is the first to suffer. Oil demand is highly sensitive to changes in the level of economic activity. This has been proved many times since 1970. For example, oil demand rose quickly in the mid-1990s as a result of high economic growth in East Asia. Likewise, in the late 1990s, when economic growth subsided in the region, oil demand was severely hit. Oil demand tends to fluctuate more sharply than energy demand in general.

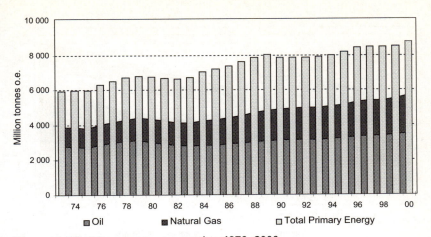

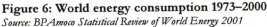

Figure 6: World energy consumption 1973–2000
Source: BP Amoco Statistical Review of World Energy 2001

The increasing concentration of oil use on the transportation sector does not make it less indispensable. Indeed, in a modern society, economic growth is based on an ever-advancing division of labour and specialization as a prerequisite for productivity gains, as well as expanding markets, nationally and across borders. Adequate transportation is a necessary condition for economic growth. Access to oil is a necessity for a modern society to function and provide rising living standards and levels of welfare for its citizens. For this reason, with the concentration of oil on the transportation sector, where it meets little, if any, competition, the price elasticity of demand has apparently declined, so that oil use has tended to become less sensitive to price changes insofar as no substitutes are available.

Oil users show its importance by their willingness to pay extremely high prices during times of crisis when supplies appear to be scarce. Nations have gone to war to defend their oil interests, most recently in the Gulf in 1991. Even if the overriding concern for the individual users of oil is availability, which means secure supplies, the price risk is a major concern for the oil-importing countries. They generally aim at securing both supplies and prices.

Measured by value, oil is the world's most important traded commodity. Oil is probably the only commodity whose price movements can have a macro-economic impact. Low short-term price elasticities of oil demand and supply mean that price changes influence inflation rates and trade balances rather than volumes traded, so that adjustment can be painful. As a result, the economic and political stakes linked to crude oil prices are huge.

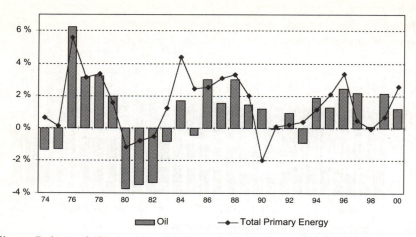

Figure 7: Annual changes in oil and total energy demand 1974–2000
Source: BPAmoco Statistical Review of World Energy 2001

Indirectly, oil price movements tend to influence interest rates and economic activity. As a result, the oil price also has repercussions for economic
stability and the survival of governments in the oil-importing countries. For
example, in the United States, an oil price shock has apparently preceded all
but one economic recession since 1945.[86] The importance of oil to the oil
importers' trade balance and inflation rates and to their economic stability
is such that they cannot be indifferent to the actions of the oil exporters.
Secure supplies and stable prices are the priorities.

The turnover in oil trade is enormous. For most oil-importing countries,
oil is still a major item on the trade balance. For example, in 1999 the
United States' total imports were $1059.44 billion, of which crude oil and
oil products accounted for $67.2 billion. Including crude oil and oil prod-
ucts, the US 1999 trade balance had a deficit of $357.34 billion. Excluding
crude and products, the 1999 United States trade deficit was $290.14
billion. The generally low short-term price elasticity of oil demand gives the
oil price a macro-economic feedback, with repercussions for trade balances,
inflation rates, purchasing power and levels of economic activity.[87] Since
1970, the world has been reminded of the close relationship between the oil
market and the world economy on a number of occasions. The reason is
that for many purposes oil is difficult to substitute immediately and that oil
to some extent acts as a price leader for other energy sources. It is important, however, to distinguish between short-term and long-term effects.
The short-term effects concern immediate consumer behaviour and the
transfers of income between energy exporters and energy importers. The
long-term effects concern investment choices and the repercussions on the
capital stock and the pattern of economic activity in the world and the

different regions, as well as the way energy price moves trigger off other economic changes, where tensions have been building up.

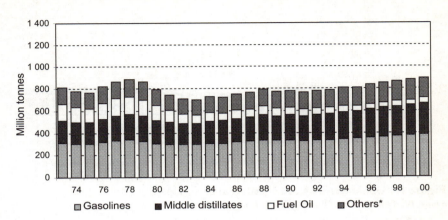

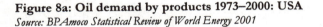

* *Others: Refinery gas, LPGs, solvents, petroleum coke, lubricants, bitumen, wax, refinery fuel and loss.*

Figure 8a: Oil demand by products 1973–2000: USA
Source: BPAmoco Statistical Review of World Energy 2001

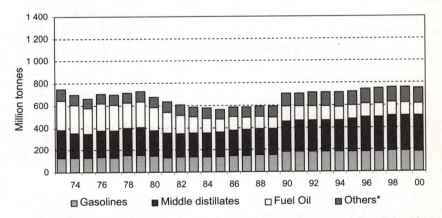

* *Others: Refinery gas, LPGs, solvents, petroleum coke, lubricants, bitumen, wax, refinery fuel and loss.*
**From 1980, including Eastern Europe.

Figure 8b: Oil demand by products 1973–2000: Western Europe**
Source: BPAmoco Statistical Review of World Energy 2001

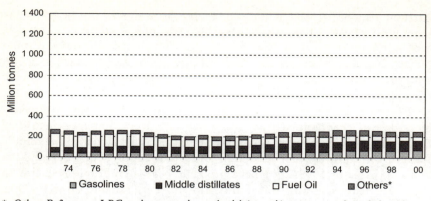

* *Others: Refinery gas, LPGs, solvents, petroleum coke, lubricants, bitumen, wax, refinery fuel and loss.*

Figure 8c: Oil demand by products 1973–2000: Japan
Source: BP Amoco Statistical Review of World Energy 2001

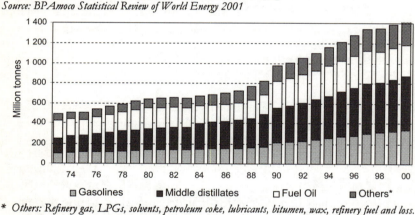

* *Others: Refinery gas, LPGs, solvents, petroleum coke, lubricants, bitumen, wax, refinery fuel and loss.*

Figure 8d: Oil demand by products 1973–2000: rest of the world
Source: BP Amoco Statistical Review of World Energy 2001

As we have seen, the 1973–74 and 1979–80 oil price jumps together forced through a profound restructuring of the Western economies during the 1980s, caused by recessions triggered by the sudden transfers of income from oil-exporting to oil-importing countries. The higher the dependency upon imported energy, the stronger the pressure for changing the pattern of activities. With some hiccups, growth managed to remain reasonably substantial.

The oil price jump in the summer and fall of 1990, following Iraq's invasion of Kuwait, led not so much to a transfer of resources as to an end of the sustained growth mentioned above. The long-term effect was more important than the short-term one. Oil prices remained high for less than six months, and part of the incremental Saudi revenues were spent on the US war effort. After Iraq's defeat and the return of low oil prices, prospects for the US economy were less than bright, with the combination of inflationary pressures, budget and trade deficits, plus rising unemployment. Similarly, both Europe and Japan were heading for a cooler economic climate, although for different reasons.

The oil price decline of 1997–98 helped the United States maintain a high level of economic activity, offsetting the adverse impact of the East Asian recession on the world economy, but it had a high cost to the Middle Eastern oil exporters, not least Iran and Saudi Arabia. Subsequently, the high oil prices of 1999–2001 have probably been a contributory factor to economic activity slowing down in North America and later on in Europe. Low oil prices in 1997–99 stimulated demand, at least through the macro-economic responses, being helpful in stimulating economic growth in East Asia, with the high oil prices in 1999–2000 having an opposite effect. Low oil prices also hit oil company earnings and their exploration and development activities, which essentially take place outside the Middle East. The 1998 oil price decline prepared the ground for a subsequently tighter oil market in 1999 and 2000, enhancing the bargaining power of the leading Middle Eastern oil exporters and consequently triggering another oil price rise.

The cost of economic restructuring between the 1970s and the early 1990s has been sluggish economic growth and high unemployment. The benefit has been a reduced energy intensity in the economies and less dependence upon oil, together with new activities based on technology that is more modern. This is not a continuous evolution, but a historical process marked by discontinuities and uneven development. In hindsight, the basic restructuring, setting the new pattern, was accomplished during the period from 1980 to 1985, under the impact of oil prices that in real terms were exceptionally high by historical standards. By comparison, the pre-1973 pattern of economic activities was established in the immediate post-Second World War period, during the years 1945–50, under the impact of low oil prices. It was brought to an end only by two sudden energy price shocks and a deep recession.

From a historical perspective, for the industrial countries with a market economy, the 1980s mark a transition from one economic structure to another, with a profound impact on investment patterns and energy use. Such profound changes, with a high social cost, do not occur often. They require a certain maturity of economic structures, with new technologies and new activities ready to take over from obsolete ones.[88] The importance for the future is that in the industrial countries with a market economy, the present pattern of economic activities, with a stronger emphasis on services and modern technology, is historically young and likely to persist for a long

time. Countries that are becoming more or less advanced market economies will increasingly adopt these patterns of economic activity and energy
use. Salient cases are Russia, South Korea and Thailand. Present patterns of
energy use are likely to persist, as they are structurally determined. In this
respect, it is important to distinguish between the effects of the first and
the second oil price shock.

The first oil price shock of 1973–74, followed by low real interest rates,
stimulated extensive investment in other energy sources, first coal and
nuclear power, that could replace fuel oil in electricity generation. The
results appeared in the oil market in the early 1980s, as reduced demand,
especially for fuel oil.

The second oil price shock of 1979–80, followed by high real interest
rates and a severe economic recession, did not lead to any similar investment in energy output, but rather in energy conservation and the cutback of
energy-intensive industries, or their transfer to developing countries with
cheap indigenous energy sources. Capital was attracted to services and light
industries based on modern technology, not to the energy sector, as
demand for energy was seen as declining.

The new economic structure, established in the early 1980s, with high
oil prices, is far from mature. The real capital in the expanding sectors is
new and can reasonably be expected to stay in place for a long time. The
lack of investment in other sources of energy since the mid-1980s, with the
exception of natural gas, means that oil use is likely to increase rather than
decline as the world economy grows. The restructuring of economic
activity that took place in the early 1980s, with the subsequent energy
conservation in the industrial countries, is unlikely to repeat itself, regardless of the level of oil prices. Instead, macro-economic performance will be
affected, with oil price jumps leading to setbacks and oil price falls permitting expansion of activity. For this reason, the oil-importing industrial
countries have an interest in moderate oil prices. This is also the case with
the United States, which today is less than 40 per cent self-sufficient in oil,
and whose oil import dependency increased markedly during the 1990s.
The countries embarking early on the transitions were rewarded by the
1986 oil price decline.

In the developing world oil demand is growing vigorously. As was the
case in Japan, North America and Western Europe in the 1950s and 1960s,
the developing countries, as an aggregate, are in a phase of energy-intensive
growth. Here, economic growth particularly leads to higher demand for oil
products. The trend is for increasing differentiation, with the energy
intensity of economic growth levelling off among the most developed of
these countries. Still, demand for oil is likely to continue growing. Population growth leads to higher oil demand, so the most effective way of halting
the growth of oil demand would be economic stagnation, but with a high

social cost. These countries' interests in relation to oil prices are split, depending upon whether they are energy exporters or not. Oil demand growth in the developing countries seems likely to strengthen the bargaining position of the Middle East oil exporters.

The situation in the formerly centrally planned economies is of less importance from a global perspective. These countries have had a particularly energy-intensive pattern of economic activities. In Eastern Europe and the Soviet Union, contrary to China, there was a considerable potential for energy conservation. In Eastern Europe, after the economic restructuring, the result is nevertheless likely to be greater dependence upon oil. In Russia and other parts of the former Soviet Union, oil-exporting regions, there is a potential for maintaining or even moderately increasing exports, as domestic demand is reduced. In the longer run, depending upon the outcome of economic reforms and conditions given to foreign investment in the oil industry, there could even be a potential for increasing output and exports. The time involved would be long, however, and investment requirements huge, so that Russia has an interest in high oil prices.

The special role of the United States in the oil market deserves mention. The major difference between the United States and most other industrialized countries is in the historical background and present oil consumption patterns. The United States has a history of regulation and protection of domestic oil interests. It currently has some of the world's lowest taxes on oil products. Domestic output has a rising marginal cost, causing increasing dependence on oil imports. The large domestic consumption and the rising import dependence have important foreign policy consequences. Defending oil interests abroad is an important priority for US foreign policy. In relation to the oil-exporting countries, especially those of the Middle East, the United States is, however, meeting increasing competition from the large developing countries, such as, for example, China and India.

In the new economic setting, the concentration of oil use in the transportation sector enhances sensitivity to changes in the level of economic activity, but increases robustness to price changes. During the economic recession of the early 1990s, oil demand was stagnant. Oil consumption worldwide was only 1 million barrels a day higher in 1993 than it had been in 1989. After 1993, however, the world's demand for oil rose by almost 7 million barrels a day, reaching 73.7 million barrels a day in 1997. The East Asian economic crisis that started in 1997 had a serious effect on oil demand. In 1998, East Asian oil demand growth, which had averaged 5.6 per cent annually between 1990 and 1996, slowed sharply. Since then, oil demand in the developing and industrializing Asian countries has resumed growth, although not at historical rates.

Overall, oil demand in the industrialized countries is likely to grow slowly. Although oil is still the most important energy source in the majority of industrialized countries, its share of total energy consumption is falling in Europe, Japan, North America and other countries. Here, newer technologies use oil more efficiently, and natural gas and other energy sources replace oil for many uses. Oil demand growth in the industrialized economies is essentially for motor fuels in transportation, without any substantial competition. In developing countries, oil demand is likely to increase quickly over the next 20 years. The major impetus for growth is expected to be Asia.

The growth of oil demand and the increasing concentration on motor fuels, for which there are few, if any, substitutes, means that the end-uses of oil will increasingly be in segments of the market where price elasticity of demand is low, but income elasticity is high. Bargaining and taxation for the division of economic rent will be fierce, possibly with rising price volatility. Anyway, the prospects for economic growth in developing countries indicate that the social rent, the macro-economic benefit from oil use, is likely to increase significantly. Oil is likely to remain economically and politically important.

In times of supply crises, real or perceived, consumers are willing to pay far above usual market prices for energy. As already stated, from the consumer point of view, the most expensive energy is often the energy that is not available. The generally low price elasticity of energy demand indicates that for most uses, consumers pay energy prices well below the threshold of pain, that is a price level at which they would discontinue important habits of energy consumption, which is an indicator of the social rent from energy. In normal situations, consumers pay energy prices well below the social value of energy, so that they largely benefit from the social rent. In strict economic terms, this indicates a loss of efficiency, with consumers getting energy at prices that are too low, but in social terms consumers benefit from a welfare gain. Low energy prices may induce consumers to use more energy than is strictly necessary, although that level is difficult to define, but they also provide them with budget discretion and freedom of choice.

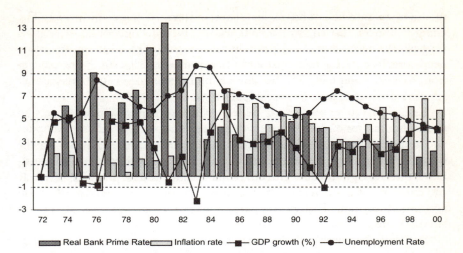

Figure 9a: US economic repercussions 1972–2000
Source: Energy Information Administration (EIA) 2001

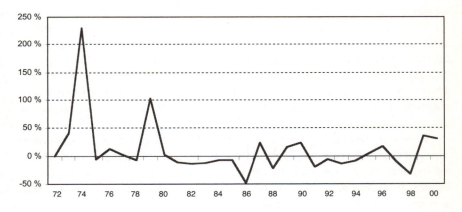

Figure 9b: North Sea oil price increase (real) 1972–2000
Source: Energy Information Administration (EIA) 2001

The politicization of oil

The question is often raised whether governments should intervene in oil and other energy prices, but the question is redundant as governments do intervene, regardless of ideology and pronounced economic preferences. The question is rather why this intervention takes place and how governments should go about it. The energy industry needs government. In many cases the energy industry operates with a government licence, giving it a privileged access to resources or markets, but also giving the government the right to intervene and to levy special taxes to share the profit. The energy industry and energy markets cannot function without a regulatory framework, dependent on governments and politicians. Energy investors need security to recover capital and often preferential treatment or protection against competition. The energy industry also needs government support when operating in foreign countries.

Energy is too important to be left to market forces alone. Access to energy is a matter of military strength and national security. Energy supplies and prices are matters of economic stability and welfare. Citizens usually consider energy supplies and prices to be a matter of government responsibility, directly or indirectly. Governments and politics set the price of crude oil, the energy price leader, in the world market, whether OPEC is in agreement or not. Energy supplies, transportation and use affect the environment.

Since the beginning of the twentieth century governments have intervened in energy markets. At times the objective is a direct price impact, at times an indirect one. All countries in some way or another regulate their electricity industries and consequently power markets and prices to secure investment or to safeguard consumer interests, depending on the maturity of the industry.

The oil and natural gas industries essentially operate on government land with a privileged access. The United States, including Texas, has a long and varied record of government intervention in electricity, natural gas and oil, regulating investment, returns, markets and prices. In 1990–91 the United States went to war over oil supplies and prices. The leading European powers have actively pursued their oil interests abroad, largely in North Africa and the Middle East.

In dealing with energy, especially oil, political considerations overwhelm and governments respond to pressures. Politicians usually give a priority to re-election over economic rationality. With elections approaching, consumer interests gain in strength. In the United States, with biennial elections, consumer interests often prevail.

In the relationship between government and energy, short-term opportunistic considerations often win over long-term economic rationality. Governments often neglect to secure the proper functioning of markets and to let price signals work throughout the system. Yielding to vested interests, governments often neglect to enhance competition by facilitating the access of newcomers, to cut up integrated structures and to regulate transmission networks by independent authorities. The neglect to secure transparency of prices and access conditions is even more serious.

The balance of benefits and costs of government intervention in energy markets throughout the twentieth century is an open question as concerns electricity, natural gas and oil. For oil, the question also concerns the balance of benefits and costs of intervention abroad, including the Gulf War and more discreet moves to convince or compel oil exporters to increase supplies to moderate world oil prices. Throughout the twentieth century, government policies manifested a disbelief in the ability of market forces and private initiative alone to secure energy supplies. The counterpart is that the energy industries use governments to promote their own interests. This is not least the case with the oil industry.

The risks involved for the consumers make oil a matter of state interest, even in times of apparent oil market stability. For this reason, there is a close interaction between energy use, the oil market and international politics. The experience that for consumers the most costly barrel is the one that cannot be obtained makes the Middle East important to the world and causes governments to intervene.

The major issue is the importance of energy in general and of oil in particular in the economy. No modern economy can function without a regular supply of commercial energy. Economic growth requires energy, besides capital and labour. Historically, there is a strong correlation between economic growth and the growth of energy demand. Until now, all economic progress has entailed rising energy consumption. Until substitutes are developed on a large scale at competitive costs, a regular supply of oil is a necessary condition for the functioning of a modern transportation system and for the division of labour in the modern economy.

Throughout the twentieth century, oil trade was marked by a close relationship between economics and politics. Two world wars have shown that oil is a strategic commodity, with great economic importance in peacetime, and a significant military value in times of war. For this reason, trading conditions and the division of economic rent are closely linked to the relationship between oil-importing and oil-exporting countries.[89] Decisions to permit exploration for oil and gas and extraction are discretionary whether the landowner is private or the government.[90] They are subject to immediate concerns for revenue and to long-term concerns for markets. Finally, total oil supply in the market is in the last instant subject to producer or exporter government discretion, and as such heavily influenced by politics. Unusually close relations between companies and governments have marked the oil industry. Oil trade is often subject to special regulations and taxation as well as special government protection. Throughout most of the twentieth century, many oil-importing countries made active attempts to secure their oil supplies, considering that in the longer run, the market and private enterprise were not sufficient. In oil-exporting countries oil policy has been a central issue, with national control of the resources and the major industry advanced as a top priority.

The reference is a presumed imperfect competition in the oil industry, implying a risk of facing an oligopoly or a cartel.[91] The oil industry is special because of capital intensity and high risk. It has its own economics, where price and marginal cost may vary considerably over long lapses of time, and its own politics, where joint ventures and mutual understanding are accepted means to reduce the common risk. The barriers to entry of high risk and high capital requirements, with a potential for huge losses and huge gains, lead to an imperfect competition, which again provides some leeway between the imperatives of the market and the decisions of the major actors. They have both incentives and resources to pursue long-term strategic objectives as well as their political interests. The political aspect of the oil industry is to a large extent explained by these factors: the capital intensity, the risk and the long time horizons for investment projects, and the imperfect competition.

Control of oil supplies is widely, and with reason, seen as a key to economic and political success.[92] The presence or the absence of domestic coal determined the patterns of industrial development before 1914. In the nineteenth century, oil was mostly used for lighting and did not compete with coal. Since then, oil has essentially been a fuel for motion and power generation. In brief, access to domestic oil is a major comparative advantage, even when the price is low. Several oil-importing countries try to make up for the lack of domestic oil reserves by controlling foreign supply sources, so that oil policy is essentially foreign policy: government business, whether the tools and companies are in private, public or semi-public ownership. Focus has generally been on the Middle East. In this way, oil also becomes a political instrument.[93] Indeed, in the twentieth century, wars were fought over, or even decided by, access to oil.

For oil, market forces are considered insufficient to cope with problems of overriding national interest.[94] In many countries, for example the United States, the government involvement in oil matters has traditionally been indirect, through regulations to protect domestic production or home consumers, and the government defending the interests abroad of nationally based private oil companies. In other countries, government involvement in the oil business is direct through public investment in a national oil company. Salient examples are Argentina, Algeria, France, Iran, Italy, Kuwait, Mexico, Norway, Saudi Arabia and Venezuela.

For countries such as the United States, the UK and France, control of or access to oil abroad, in most cases meaning the Middle East, has been an important objective of foreign policy, the projection of power as well as the defence of national economic interests. For the imperial powers, oil and foreign policy have been inextricably linked. The economic foundation of the British presence in the Gulf region was the oil investment, which also motivated the military presence. Likewise, the current US military presence in the Gulf region is clearly motivated by the need for access to oil. For the resource-rich countries, such as, for example, Argentina, Mexico, Norway,

Iran or Venezuela, the control of domestic oil has been a key aspect of the assertion of national economic and political independence. It is no coincidence that Latin American countries were early to establish national oil companies in order to assert their independence in relation to foreign interests, especially US and UK interests.[95] Likewise, in the 1970s and 1980s, the take-over of the oil industry was an important aspect of the assertion of independence of African, Asian and Middle Eastern countries.

For oil-importing countries, even minor disturbances in oil supplies cause considerable economic hardship. The oil shortages in Western European countries caused by hostilities in the Middle East in 1956 and 1973 provided an ample proof, as did the gasoline lines in the United States during the summer of 1979. Sudden oil price rises cause major economic disruptions through a deteriorating trade balance and inflationary pressures. The oil price shocks of 1973 and 1979–80 contributed heavily to economic setbacks in the oil-importing OECD countries. Even the temporary oil price rise during the Gulf conflict of 1990–91 triggered the turn of the business cycle. High oil prices in 2000 and 2001 may have had a similar impact, although on a more moderate scale.

For many governments of oil-importing countries, access to oil is considered a matter of national security. In two world wars in the twentieth century, access to oil played a critical role.[96] Insufficient oil supplies compromise national security. The US Reagan administration, which on most matters professed a strong belief in the market, made an exception for oil, stressing that vulnerability to oil supply disruptions affect military preparedness.[97] There is a remarkable parallel between present US concerns for secure oil supplies and corresponding UK concerns on the eve of the First World War. The US Congress has continued to vote money for the Strategic Petroleum Reserve even in a weak oil market, on the explicit assumption that in an emergency the market forces will not necessarily serve American interests in relation to oil. The US military engagement in the 1990–91 Gulf conflict was in many ways the ultimate demonstration of government resolve to secure access to oil at stable prices.

For oil-exporting countries, foreign dominance of their oil industry implies a technological and commercial dependence, so that foreign interests take decisions of crucial economic and industrial importance, and they are more responsive to consumer interests than to those of the producers, compromising national sovereignty in economic matters. For many oil-exporting countries, especially the member countries of OPEC, the nationalization of the oil industry was an assertion of national independence and a logical follow-up of decolonialization. A national oil company has traditionally been regarded as the most appropriate instrument to develop the relevant technical and commercial expertise, partly in order to enhance the bargaining position in relation to the international oil industry.

The issues considered by governments of oil-exporting countries are complex and concern national economic and industrial development related to oil when facing an industry where competition is supposedly imperfect. Matters to be considered include the rate of depletion, the division of the economic rent accruing from oil, and spin-off effects such as industrial development, for example goods and services for the oil industry or refining and petrochemicals. Insight into the technological and commercial details of the oil industry is also seen as a valuable asset. On these points private capital may be unwilling or unable to fulfil political objectives. Domestic capital may be insufficient or reluctant to take the risk; foreign capital may only be available on terms judged unacceptable. For reasons of competition and bargaining power, the perception may be that it is essential to concentrate the national effort. The answer, again, is often to establish a national oil company, as is the case in the principal Middle Eastern oil-exporting countries.

Oil and international power

The uneven distribution of the world's oil reserves means that some major powers are dependent on a few small countries for their oil supplies. Some small countries, such as Kuwait, Norway, Oman and the United Arab Emirates, are major oil exporters because of accidents of geology. Many oil suppliers enjoy an economic and political importance disproportionate to their demographic weight. For example, Saudi Arabia, which has 0.3 per cent of the world's population, in 1999 accounted for about 12 per cent of total oil output. Norway, with 0.07 per cent of the world's population, the same year had more than 4 per cent of total oil output. The contrast is the United States, which in 1999 had about 4.5 per cent of the world's population, about 10 per cent of total oil output, but more than a quarter of total oil consumption.

With few exceptions, essentially Canada, Norway, Russia and the United Kingdom, the rule seems to be that oil and natural gas import dependence rises with industrialization and economic development. In 1999, United States imports of crude oil and products accounted for more than 13 per cent of all oil supplied. The same year, Middle Eastern crude oil and products exports accounted for more than 25 per cent of total supplies. Likewise, by 1999 the world's proven oil reserves represented about 41 years of forward output, but the figure for North America including Mexico was 14 years, for Europe including the North Sea only eight years, but for the OPEC member countries 77 years and for the Middle East 87 years. This does not mean that North America will run out of domestic oil in 14 years or Europe in eight years, but that oil output is likely to decline and become more costly unless major new finds are made.

The uneven distribution of proven oil reserves is significant for long-term bargaining power only insofar as oil remains an important fuel and no major discoveries are made outside the OPEC member countries. Both conditions are partly dependent on oil prices. This puts the OPEC countries and especially the major Middle Eastern oil exporters in a dilemma over oil policy. By limiting output and raising prices they give incentives to developing alternatives to oil and to exploring for oil in new areas, compromising future revenues. By raising output and lowering prices they deter the development of alternatives and oil exploration in new areas, but lose present income, as the volume rise in most cases will not make up for the price decline. The high cost of competing for market shares was acutely evident for OPEC during the years 1997–99. The dilemma also splits OPEC.

The critical position of oil in the world's energy balance and the uneven distribution of reserves give oil an exceptional economic, strategic and political importance. The control of supplies is the key to the oil price, but they are potentially conflicting political issues. In addition, oil becomes linked directly or indirectly to other issues. Since most countries are net importers of oil and rely heavily on oil imports for total energy supplies, the price of oil and its control can have direct implications for their freedom of action in economic and foreign policy. Oil is accordingly linked to such matters as the rate of economic growth, the level of employment, the rate of inflation, trade policy, and general foreign policy orientation. Matters relating to oil have a high priority in the industrial, economic, trade and foreign policies of both oil-importing and oil-exporting nations, whether they are developed or developing economies.

Oil prices influence the international distribution of power. The best example is provided by the Arab oil-exporting countries, which in the 1970s dramatically improved their ability to pursue foreign-policy goals. Another example is the United States, which by organizing the Western industrial oil-consuming countries in the International Energy Agency, IEA, hoped to offset any loss to its own position as leader of the Western world, inflicted by the new conditions in the oil market. The structure and organization of the world oil market not only serve purposes of rationality and efficiency, but are also in part mechanisms of political control.[98] In hindsight, the oil exporters, through their selective embargo and price rises, were more successful than the Soviet Union ever was in inflicting economic and political damage on the United States. The United States was not successful in making the IEA a counter-cartel to OPEC under its own control, but it was successful in defusing attempts at a common European energy policy that would have made the then European Community, EC (now European Union), a more serious competitor in the Middle East.

The origins of the IEA are to be found in the 1973 oil embargo. As a response, in the winter of 1974 the US government under the direction of then Secretary of State, Henry Kissinger, called for the oil-importing industrial countries to organize to defend their interests in the oil market and to push oil prices down. The Energy Co-ordinating Group, ECG, was established to develop an energy emergency programme.[99] In November of 1974 it became the IEA. France and Norway abstained. The US objectives were both economic and political, aiming at lower oil prices, development of new energy sources and to confront OPEC's emerging power, seen as a challenge to Western, especially US hegemony. The economic objectives were contradictory, as the development of new energy sources generally had costs above prevailing oil prices. The political objectives met with resistance from Western Europe and Japan, which did not want to compromise their relations with the OPEC countries. In hindsight, the IEA has failed in its original objectives.[100] It developed emergency plans for sharing oil supplies in case of a severe disruption, set at 7 per cent, but they were never activated, not even during the 1979–80 or 1990–91 oil crises. Apart from the crisis planning, the IEA essentially remains an agency for compiling data and making forecasts on energy markets.

Another purpose behind the IEA was to preserve the position of US-based multinational oil companies in supplying OECD countries with oil. An extensive network of bilateral deals between the other OECD countries and the oil producers would probably have affected the structure of the international oil trade, reducing the role of the multinationals and benefiting the national oil companies of the producing and oil-importing countries. It would obviously have reduced the influence of the United States in the Middle East. The solution for the United States, to defend its interests, was to attempt to speak for all the industrialized consumers. This in part explains why the United States, which at the time was much less dependent on imported oil than Western Europe and Japan, at least verbally, took a much more aggressive attitude toward OPEC.

The Iranian revolution of 1979 was seen by the United States not only as a challenge to immediate oil interests, through the shortfall of oil supplies, the ensuing oil price rise and the nationalization of oil assets, and as a security policy issue, as the country was the barrier between the then Soviet Union and the Gulf, but essentially as a political threat because of Iran's potential ideological influence in the Middle East and possibly wider damage to US interests and positions in the region. For the United States, the ultimate risk was being marginalized by Europe and Japan striking separate deals with radical Middle Eastern oil exporters. Similar considerations were among the motives for the United States to go to war against Iraq in 1990–91. There is a potential for such concerns to reappear.

For both oil-importing and oil-exporting countries there can be internal conflicts over priorities related to oil and other social, economic, trade and foreign policy goals, creating difficult choices. Restricting or expanding oil imports can directly affect the trade balance, inflation rates and domestic political goals in oil-importing countries. Conversely, the world's oil exporters are concerned about the rate of depletion of their finite resources. Many oil-exporting countries are concerned about sustaining output levels, and others may prefer to keep the major national asset in the ground, deferring income to future generations. The way they exploit their oil plays a decisive role in determining how and when they influence the market. Securing supplies and controlling demand are of primary importance to the governments of consumer countries, and the management of reserves is critical to the governments of the oil-exporting countries if they seek to maximize their income or promote other political goals. As a result the production, distribution and consumption of oil are traditionally to a large extent subject to government intervention and regulation.

Traditionally the international oil industry had an oligopolistic structure dominated by a limited number of private international and state-owned oil companies.[101] Their long-term interests and policies often determined their short-term behaviour. In addition, the oil companies and the governments normally had close relations of consultation and co-operation. The wave of nationalization of the upstream oil industry by OPEC countries in the 1970s and 1980s broke up the integrated circuits of oil trading. Instead, oil trade was fragmented, and upstream nationalization paradoxically enhanced competition and transparency, essentially through the rising importance of spot and futures markets. The most recent wave of mergers again moves the international oil industry in the direction of oligopoly, especially in downstream operations. In the longer run, the downstream consolidation could affect the distribution of economic rent accruing from oil.

The major agents in the international oil market are still a limited number of companies and governments, often with clearly defined long-term interests. The patterns of oil production, distribution and consumption are less the result of market forces than is the case with many other commodities. Instead, political intervention and strategic considerations have a greater impact, and governments are more important, also when oil companies are private.

Some of the political crisis dimensions that appeared in the early 1970s are still present. The oil crises of 1973–74, 1979–80 and 1990–91 demonstrated the complexity and wider political significance of the oil market. The Western-dominated system of relations between oil-importing and OPEC countries, and with the Third World, was shaken, first in 1973–74 and again in 1979–80. The 1973–74 Arab oil embargo was explicitly linked with the conflict in the Middle East and with the position of the Western countries toward Israel. This in turn directly affected relations between the United States and Western Europe. The co-operative policy of the European Community toward the Arab and the Mediterranean countries was in conflict with the Atlanticist policy of consolidation of the United States.

The 1979–80 oil crisis, triggered by the Iranian revolution, showed a potentially precarious position for Western interests in the Middle East, and particularly so for the United States, facing regional forces of nationalism and Islamism. To contain Iran became imperative for US oil interests in the Middle East. Iraq's attack provided the easy solution, which at the time was in the interests of the United States. The alternative would have been to leave the rest of the Middle East exposed to the ideological and political influence of the Iranian revolution, with great risk for oil supplies and prices, and also for the US position in the region. The sad irony is that the 1990–91 oil crisis was triggered by Iraq's attack on Kuwait, and this time the United States chose to roll back Iraq by war, not only to liberate Kuwait, but more importantly to prevent Saudi Arabia and the other Gulf States from being dominated by Iraq, which would also have represented a great risk to oil supplies and prices. The alternative would have been to abandon US positions in the Gulf, possibly in the entire Middle East.

On both occasions, Europe and Japan were tempted to strike oil and trade deals with regimes not palatable to the United States. More than ten years after the Gulf War, the risk for the United States is that UN sanctions against Iran and Iraq will start to be eroded and other countries' oil companies will move in before US companies are permitted.

Another dimension is the split within the Western world over how to respond to Middle Eastern oil concerns about Israel, even after the 11 September 2001 attacks on the United States. The United States has consistently supported Israel in the Middle East and in 1973–74 was reluctant to back down simply because of the oil embargo. The other OECD countries have tended to deal with the Arab oil producers more easily. France's support for the Palestinians and bilateral arrangements with Arab countries are probably the best example of this type of response. Just as the Atlanticist policy was in the best interest of the United States, the co-operative policy of the EC was likewise a response of self-interest. The then relatively low dependence of the United States on foreign oil allowed it to continue its support for Israel while the Europeans, with a greater dependence on Middle East oil, preferred to avoid confrontations with the Arab oil producers. The Europeans also knew that the United States was not going to abandon Israel. In this context they could use their softer stance in an attempt to placate the Arab oil producers and make bilateral deals with them to help provide for their own immediate energy needs. In the future this split could have dramatic consequences for the political cohesion of the OECD area, especially in the event of a new war or if prolonged tension in the Middle East, especially over Israel and Palestine, should threaten the stability of oil supplies. Such an eventuality could drive a wedge between the United States and Europe.

The relatively reduced economic significance of oil, so far, does not seem to have led to a corresponding decline in its political importance to consumer-country governments. The Middle East remains prominent in international affairs. Since the 1970s, there has been a certain repetitive pattern in international oil politics, with the United States balancing poor or hostile relations with some oil exporters, such as Iran, Iraq or Libya, with close relations with Kuwait, Saudi Arabia and the United Arab Emirates. The paradox in US foreign oil policy is that increasing reliance on foreign oil is matched by hostility towards some of the major oil exporters. This carries a risk of US oil interests being ignored in some salient countries. The US double containment of Iran and Iraq was no success. Instead, the United States and its main regional ally, Israel, were isolated in the Middle East. By the summer of 2001, the renewal of the Iran–Libya Sanctions Act and secondary reprisals against third-country oil companies doing business in countries under US embargo revealed serious inconsistencies in US foreign oil policy and Middle East policy.

CHAPTER TWO

FOREIGN POWERS AND MIDDLE EASTERN OIL

Fighting for oil

Essentially the United States fought the Gulf War in 1990–91 over oil.[1] It saw an immediate need to safeguard Saudi oil reserves and supplies, to keep them from Iraqi control, because Kuwait, then occupied by Iraq, bordered on the oil-rich eastern province of Saudi Arabia.[2] The United States also wanted to prevent the emergence, from the fusion of Iraqi and Kuwaiti assets in the ground and in the financial markets, of a strong Iraq that would dominate the Gulf and eventually the Middle East.

The Gulf crisis was not only a US-led response to Iraqi aggression, but equally a Saudi act of defence against a military and political threat from a hostile neighbour. The crisis concerned the oil supply pattern from the Middle East and the oil price, as well as the regional balance of power. During the 1980s, Western powers, especially the United States, and the conservative Gulf monarchies had bolstered and armed Iraq as the bulwark against allegedly aggressive Islamist Iran. The war against Iran strengthened Iraq's military and political position in the Middle East, but Iraq was left with a huge army and huge debts, with Kuwait undermining oil prices and Iraqi oil revenues.[3] The Gulf War cut short Iraq's attempt at establishing a regional hegemony, which would have endangered the oil supply pattern.[4] This has split the Arab world. The main beneficiary was Turkey, the most important US ally in the region, with a pivotal role in the US strategy to bring Caspian oil to the world market. Since the Gulf War, the United States has had a dominant role in the Middle East as the protector of Saudi Arabia, Kuwait and the United Arab Emirates. The reward was for several years stable oil supplies and moderate oil prices.

The constellation of powers that emerged in the Middle East from the Gulf War is changing. China, France and Russia pursue their own Middle East policies in conflict with the United States. Germany and Japan operate more discreetly, but are expanding trade, particularly with Iran. The US policy of dual containment, isolating Iran and Iraq, has been a failure and has backfired so that the United States, with Israel, has isolated itself. Iran is rejoining the world, actively building economic and political relations with other countries, except the United States, so far. Since 1997–98, relations between Iran and Saudi Arabia have improved spectacularly. Iraq is improving ties with some Arab countries as well as with China, France and Russia. The risk for the United States is to be left behind in Iran and Iraq, with Europeans and Asians getting access to the oil, trading opportunities and political influence.

This changing constellation means that Saudi Arabia, the leading oil exporter and the linchpin of the oil market, has to pay more attention to the Middle Eastern context, at the expense of relations with the United States. This reorientation of policy has become more urgent because of the worsening conflict between Israel and the Palestinians, making unilateral US support for Israel a heavier burden on US–Saudi relations.

The outcome in 2000–1 has been unexpectedly high oil prices and a firm Saudi refusal to pump oil at full capacity, at least until the autumn of 2001, in spite of repeated US requests, because of Saudi income requirements and opposing views on the oil market. The political message given by restraining oil output and keeping oil prices high is that for Saudi Arabia, the Middle East, especially Iran, has gained in importance relative to the United States. The potential for the United States to gain in leverage with Saudi Arabia by more actively contributing to settling the Israeli–Palestinian conflict has been more visible since the September 2001 terrorist attacks.

Governments and oil companies in Middle East policy

For the United States, the UK and France, control of oil abroad has been and remains an important foreign policy objective. The economic foundation of the British presence in the Gulf region was the oil investment, which also motivated the military presence. Likewise, the current US military presence in the Gulf is motivated by oil. International oil relations are mercantilist, with nation-states and oil companies acting together.[5] The objective is to secure positions in foreign countries to procure natural resources and trading privileges, seeking economic rent and excess profits through political dominance, with decision making across the institutional boundaries between governments and companies.

Western dominance of the Middle East can be seen as imperialist interests colluding with corrupt and despotic local leaders lacking legitimacy and buying foreign support for their positions through oil.[6] Another perspective is that throughout much of the twentieth century, a desperately poor region, although the victim of foreign intrigue, also had an urgent need for foreign investment and knowledge, as well as for protection by foreign powers against hostile neighbours. For decades, the various Middle Eastern countries were competing for foreign oil investment and for oil market shares, more or less regardless of the political orientation of their governments. Even the nationalist Iranian Mossadegh regime only nationalized the oil industry after having been pushed to extreme limits by UK oil interests. From a dialectical perspective, foreign oil investment improved the bargaining position of the Middle Eastern oil-exporting countries, enabling them to better assert their interests in relation to the Western countries that needed their oil, and still do so.

For resource-rich countries, such as, for example, Argentina, Mexico, Norway, Iran and Venezuela, the control of domestic oil has asserted national economic and political independence. Latin American countries were early to establish national oil companies in order to affirm their independence in relation to foreign interests.[7] Likewise, in the 1970s and 1980s, the take-over of the oil industry was an important aspect of the assertion of independence of African, Asian and particularly the Middle Eastern countries. The take-over of the oil industry and the gradual replacement of foreign specialists with nationals historically represent a decisive step in the emancipation of the Middle Eastern oil producers from foreign dominance.

Foreign powers are politically active in the region, using Middle Eastern governments and groups for their own purposes. Various Middle Eastern interests invite and use foreign powers for their own protection and strength. Oil is the common ingredient in the multiple relationships between foreign powers and Middle Eastern interests and an essential factor in the pattern of regional conflicts, but not the only one. The combination of regional dispute and foreign intrigue has caused an extraordinary level of tension in the region, with recurrent open conflicts as well as a multitude of latent national, ethnic and territorial discords. Indeed, since the end of the Cold War, the Middle East has been the world's most conflict-ridden and militarized region.

The political instability of the Middle East is partly caused by domestic factors, such as the general absence of democracy and accountability of rulers, as well as an excessive centralization of power, with the military in most cases being the ultimate arbiter. Reasons are also to be found outside, in the intrigues of foreign powers that have been playing the Middle Eastern countries off against each other, supporting strongmen and autocratic rulers who could advance their interests. On both counts, oil is responsible.[8] In the Middle East, oil has been a substitute for democracy, insofar as oil revenues have permitted rulers to remain autocratic, being exempt from accountability toward a tax-paying population.[9] It is no coincidence that Middle Eastern countries with little or no oil, such as Egypt and Jordan, have been advancing more quickly in a liberal direction, economically and politically, than countries with much oil, such as Iraq, Kuwait and Saudi Arabia. Correspondingly, oil has been the major attraction for the foreign powers making intrigues in the Middle East, seeking access to oil and to oil revenues through exports, preferably of arms.

In the twentieth century practically all the major powers sought positions in the Middle East, with varying degrees of success. In this process, they also sought allies and partners, largely autocratic rulers and the military, which could be relied on to keep order, the oil flowing and the arms purchases continuing. For this reason, the foreign powers, without exception, have had no interest in promoting democracy in the Middle East.

The link between Saudi Arabia and the United States has been the most salient constant in the Middle East. Since the terrorist attacks of 11 September 2001 it has also been under unprecedented stress. Oil is the backbone of this relationship. Apparently, Saudi Arabia with the US link represents stability in the Middle East, but it is often under challenge. Another constant is the French quest for a position in Iraq. Oil is the attraction. This has manifested itself continuously since the 1920s, and again in the late 1990s. More often than not, the French support has strengthened Iraq in the region, at the expense of Saudi Arabia. A third constant is Kuwait's and the United Arab Emirates' need for an outside protector. Oil is the incentive. This is as evident in the early twenty-first century as it was in the early 1920s, as the United States has replaced Britain.

By contrast, Iraq's and Iran's relations with outside powers are variable and a source of instability. Iraq's shifting of alliances is one key to the region's instability and it affects the oil market. Iraq's position in its rivalry with Iran and Saudi Arabia influences the supply of oil from the Middle East and the world market oil price. Iran also represents a factor of regional instability, because of internal unrest and shifting relations with outside powers. The Russian, previously Soviet, positioning in the Middle East, through alliances with Egypt, Yemen and in particular Iraq, is a variable source of regional instability. Finally, in the 1990s after the end of the Cold War, Turkey seemed to make a re-entry on the Middle Eastern stage, possibly taking up former Ottoman ambitions of influencing Middle Eastern affairs. The history of foreign intrigue in Middle Eastern affairs throughout the twentieth century can throw a light on the structural problems of the region relating to oil and instability.

Since the first decade of the twentieth century, oil has motivated foreign powers to seek positions of influence in the Middle East. The Western powers, France, the United Kingdom and the United States, have not only struggled to keep other intruders, essentially Germany and the Soviet Union, out of the region, they have often contested each other. There is a long history of competition between French and British oil interests in the Middle East. In the 1920s, France sought to limit US oil interests in Iraq.[10] The United States aims to keep French oil interests out of Iran and Iraq as long as the US oil industry cannot take positions. Motives are the desire to secure oil supplies and the perceived need to gain influence and markets to offset the cost of oil purchases. The fear of running out of oil has been a continuous driving force, providing a rationale for seeking privileged positions and denying access to rival powers.[11] As has already been said, control of Middle East oil has also been a crucial factor in the outcome of two world wars.

At the beginning of the twentieth century, oil was struck in Iran by British explorers, backed by the UK government. The discovery immediately prompted a more ardent interest in Iran's internal affairs by the United Kingdom. The first secular, democratic Iranian state after the revolution of 1905–11, aiming at parliamentary rule, private property and capitalist development, became the victim of British and Russian intrigues. British oil interests were already predominant. Britain took the defence of the conservative forces in Iran and soon came to represent the imperialist arch-enemy for Iranian democrats and nationalists, explaining the Iranian sympathy for Nazi Germany during the Second World War.

Just before the First World War, a joint British–Dutch–German oil company was set up to explore for oil in the then Turkish Iraq. British oil interests were decisive for the dismemberment of the Ottoman Empire and the ensuing political fragmentation of the Arab lands.[12] Local rulers, such as the Hashemites in Hedjaz, were Ottoman governors, in principle loyal to the Sunni Caliphate and Sultanate, but opposed to specific policies.[13]

The First World War caused the end of Turkish rule in Iraq, Hedjaz and Palestine. Britain and France divided the area according to the Sykes–Picot agreement of 1916, with Iraq and Palestine getting British rule, Lebanon and Syria French rule. The outcome for the Arab population was not independence, but a transfer from Turkish to European suzerainty. To enlist the Arabs as allies against the Turks, Britain had promised Arabic independence and an Arab nation-state. Instead, efficient British and French masters replaced an inefficient Turkish sultan. At the end of the First World War, oil had become a major factor in the Western powers' interest in the Middle East. The essential part of the carve-up of the Ottoman Empire was the separation of Syria and Lebanon under French rule and the establishment of Iraq as a new, artificial entity under British rule.

In theory, the alternative could have been an independent Arab nation-state, covering the Fertile Crescent, comprising Lebanon, Syria and Iraq, in addition to Hedjaz and present Jordan, with ports on the Red Sea, the Mediterranean and the Gulf. Eventually, this would have made a country with a large population and ample resources, including agricultural potential and much oil. It would have been ethnically and religiously mixed, but the large Arab Sunni Muslim population could have contributed to political stability. It is questionable whether Kuwait and Saudi Arabia without Hedjaz would have been able to stay outside such a large Arab nation-state. Such a consolidated Arab political entity was contrary to the British strategy of fragmentation.[14] Control of oil was the British motive, not ethnic homogeneity. Political legitimacy has always been a serious problem in Iraq. Among the spoils of victory, oil in Mesopotamia was the prize, especially in the Kurdish-speaking province of Mosul.[15] At a late stage during the First World War, the area was transferred from the French sphere of interest to the British one, in return for a British recognition of a French stake in Mesopotamian oil.[16] The British joined the Kurdish-speaking Mosul province with the Arabic-speaking Basra and Baghdad provinces to make the new state of Iraq. The majority of the Arab Iraqi population is Shia, but the political power has in modern times usually been Sunni.[17]

In Iran, oil finds had already caused a strong British involvement before the First World War. In 1921, Britain supported a *coup d'état* in Iran, but was soon antagonized by the new rulers. US oil interests moved into Saudi Arabia, unhampered by any British or French competition, laying the foundation for a close relationship. In hindsight, this relationship has been more lasting and more successful than any other between a European power and a Middle Eastern or North African oil producer.

The British and French rule in the Middle East between the two world wars had some salient common features, whether the lands were colonies, mandates or protectorates. The new masters sought alliances with the most conservative parts of these societies. They were especially large landowners and Bedouin sheikhs with claims to tribal land. In return for tax relief and more land, these groups had to safeguard the established order and if necessary manipulate elections that could not be avoided in the mandatory areas.

In Iran, the economic effects of the nationalist military coup in 1921 and the subsequent Pahlavi Empire, from 1926, were essentially the modernization of the administration, investment in infrastructure and the beginnings of a timid industrialization. Oil revenues were crucial to the investment plans of the regime, which soon clashed with British oil interests. In 1932 the Iranian government declared the British oil concession invalid. It was renegotiated the next year, under duress according to the Iranian point of view. The political effects were a centralization of power and a brutal dictatorship. Iran had already in the 1920s developed the dichotomized society that has later characterized many Muslim countries. The modern part of the society was small. The oppression of the traditional society was correspondingly brutal. This oppression also hit most of the merchant class. The military had an important role as supporters of the public sector technocrats and the emerging industrial capitalists.

Within the Arab world, Saudi Arabia represents the only country that has kept its independence for centuries and the only one to keep its original institutions. Saudi Arabia's peripheral geographical position, originally Nejd, the central desert, made the country of little interest to the Ottomans. After the First World War, British oil interests largely ignored Saudi Arabia in favour of Iraq, giving US oil interests a chance. In the 1930s, US companies found oil, enabling the Saudi king to play off the United States against Britain to maintain independence. Relations with the oil industry and with the United States developed in a far less conflictual way than was the case with Iran's and Iraq's relations with Britain. Modern Saudi Arabia was created in the 1920s and 1930s after the Wahhabite Al-Saud family had driven the Hashemites out of Hedjaz. It is closely linked to the development of the oil industry under US control. Subsequently the royal family has enlarged its political base through marriages with all the important tribes and families. All Saudi leading families are related to the royal family, strengthening the legitimacy of the regime, in contrast to Iran and Iraq.

The Second World War again highlighted the strategic importance of Middle Eastern oil. In Iraq in 1941, anti-British forces staged a *coup d'état*, provoking war with Britain, followed by a British occupation. In 1941, shortly after the German attack on the Soviet Union, British and Soviet forces in turn occupied Iran. At stake were strategic and oil interests. The objective was to secure British oil interests and the Soviet oil fields in the neighbouring Caucasus from the advancing German army. After brief resistance, the occupants compelled the shah to co-operate. They forced him into abdication and exile in 1944. The next shah, the previous shah's son, started out as a British favourite, but in a weak political position, so that he was unable to rule in an autocratic way by himself. The outcome was political instability within a democratic and parliamentary framework.

The Second World War had reconfirmed the military and strategic importance of oil. The Middle East had become an even more prominent target for the economic and strategic policies of the major powers. Only at this time did most Arabic countries achieve full independence. Britain remained a power in the Middle East until around 1970. The United States has later become a leading power in the region. The stake is still oil. In practically all cases, authoritarian governments took power. The transitions of power in most cases were effected by means of natural death, murder or coups, not by elections. Political power was reserved for a small minority, often with a heavy representation of the new landed aristocracy. The autocratic rulers usually had the support of the West, whose motives were security concerns and oil. Fear of Soviet advances was a strong motive for Western policies on the Middle East. Soviet advances in Egypt, Iraq, Syria and Yemen were seen as undermining the Western hegemony in the region, inciting Britain and the United States to support the traditional autocratic rulers who were seen as guaranteeing access to oil.

During the 1950s, 1960s and early 1970s, oil production in the Middle East rose dramatically as the result of investment carried out by US and European companies. The economic and strategic importance of the Middle East increased markedly. Until 1970–71, taxation of the oil companies was moderate. The Libyan revolution in 1969 was a turning point in international oil relations, strengthening the bargaining position of the oil-producing countries. The oil price increase of 1973–74 followed by the large-scale nationalization of the oil industries provided the oil producers with a sudden influx of revenues, stimulating ambitious development plans. With both oil and money, the Middle East became more important than ever to both Western powers and the Soviet Union. At this time, Iran and Saudi Arabia had close relations with the United States, Iraq had close links with France and the Soviet Union, while Kuwait appeared more neutral, although there were close historical ties to Britain.

High oil revenues continued into the early 1980s after the second oil price increase of 1979–80, but soon oil revenues started to decline. The absence of democratic institutions in a situation of social and economic duress is apparently an effective way to undermine political legitimacy.

In Iran in 1950, parliament effectively stripped the new shah of his powers. A radical nationalist government in 1951 nationalized the British-controlled oil industry. In spite of major economic difficulties and a British blockade, the democratic Iranian regime managed to resist British attempts at subversion. The Mossadegh government also attempted to launch wider reforms, making the shah a constitutional monarch without political power, reducing the military budget and improving social welfare, but not introducing land reform. The reform policy also produced considerable resistance. Only a US-organized coup in 1953 put the shah and a pro-Western government back in power. This also signalled that Iran had moved from a British to a US sphere of influence, until the revolution of 1979.

The combination of Iran's oil reserves and strategic position was the chief reason for the US involvement in the coup in 1953 to reinstate the shah. Conservative forces in Iranian society supported the coup, but large parts of the population identified the second shah's regime with foreign dominance. From the outset it suffered from serious problems of legitimacy. The United States provided extensive assistance in the development of the armed forces, the police and the administration. The regime never managed to improve its legitimacy through democratic reforms, but consolidated its position through a vacillation between attempts at reform and direct repression of opponents. Its political basis was also shifting. In the beginning, the political basis was powerful conservative interests, such as big landowners, including rich urban merchants and the priesthood with landed interests.

Iran's oil revenues were necessary for an autocratic regime to survive for a generation without making serious compromises with private economic interests. For this reason, the oil revenues were also the cause of the regime's ability to overlook for decades the vital interests of important groups and isolate itself politically. The shah's regime moved politically from limited pluralism to authoritarianism as opposition gained strength in the 1960s. In economic matters it moved from a limited liberalism to state capitalism. The shah had throughout his reign an important foreign protector and ally. He had oil and represented the major bulwark against Soviet expansion to the warm waters of the Persian Gulf and the Indian Ocean, threatening oil supplies from the Gulf. The Soviet invasion of Afghanistan less than a year after the shah's departure indicates that this threat had some reality.

The United States had a crucial interest in the shah's political survival, regardless of his shortcomings. It short-circuited the indigenous political processes in Iran. The motive was oil and the strategic position of Iran. With less oil in Iran, it is questionable whether the United States would have bothered to put the shah back in power in 1953 and later backed him until the late 1970s. The United States took some moderate political distance from the shah's regime only in the late 1970s, when it was already cracking. Subsequently in 1979, the collapse of the shah's regime also represented a severe setback for US oil and strategic interests in the Middle East. The Iranian revolution occurred during a hostile phase of the Cold War, stimulating US fears that the new regime might eventually develop closer links with the Soviet Union, apart from representing an ideological, political and possibly military threat to the Gulf States. This can explain the intense US hostility to the new regime in Iran, which did not preclude secret arms deals. At the end of the Cold War, by 1990, Iran was economically exhausted after eight years of war against Iraq.

In Saudi Arabia, the oil discoveries in the 1930s had caused substantial American investment, but for a long time the country kept a distance from American political interests in the Middle East. In 1955, Saudi Arabia, Egypt and Syria began an economic and military co-operation. It was a counterpart to the American-dominated Baghdad Pact, consisting of Iran, Iraq, Pakistan and Turkey. In 1957, however, Saudi foreign policy changed, starting a close co-operation with Iraq and Jordan, against Egypt. The reason was probably a combination of domestic social and political unrest and fears of Egyptian foreign policy ambitions, backed by the Soviet Union. Co-operation with the United States was also enhanced. During the 1960s, the last British protectorates in the Gulf were terminated. Kuwait got full independence.

In Iraq, during the monarchy, until the revolution of 1958, common economic interests united Shia and Sunni landowners, making the social conflicts overshadow the ethnic and religious ones. The country's secular tradition also reduced the importance of religious cleavages. The British nevertheless remained the masters of the country, controlling most of the oil industry.

The 1958 revolution transferred political power to an alliance of radical technocrats and young military officers, supported by the small merchant class. Practically the entire economic surplus came from the oil industry. After the revolution, ethnic, religious and social conflicts undermined the attempted democratic institutions, causing chronic political instability and making military coups a permanent feature of Iraqi political life.[18] In the 1960s and 1970s high and rising oil revenues financed the growth in public administration. This included a comprehensive effort in education and health, besides the growth of the armed forces. A comparably high level of education enabled the country to staff its own oil industry. Successive nationalist and military regimes have aimed at nationalizing the basic industries.[19] By the early 1970s, most industrial production and employment was in large nationalized enterprises. Yet the smaller private firms often proved more efficient and more vigorous.[20] Indeed, Iraq has known the typical Middle Eastern and North African industrial dichotomy. The large capital-intensive industries were until recently state owned and usually in a monopoly position. Smaller labour-intensive plants are private and operate in the home market.

The long-range objective of Iraqi economic policy in the 1960s and 1970s was to develop industry, diversify and reduce dependence on oil.[21] The objective was not reached, essentially because of the first oil price rise that raised the share of oil in the overall output. For several years Iraq did, however, keep its oil production below capacity and output did not expand during the years immediately following the first oil price rise. Iraq also had the ambition to keep oil production and its revenues at a level that the country could absorb, preferably in investment projects with a reasonable return.[22] Military needs soon overshadowed the civilian priorities.

The coup of 1978 brought Saddam Hussein to power. Since then, political power in Iraq has become increasingly personal and militarized. Repression has reached heights and intensities hardly equalled even in the Middle East. The regime is also totally Sunni dominated. Of Iraq's three constituent parts, only one controls the political structure. The result is a pitiless war against both Kurdish opponents in the north and Shia Muslim Arabs in the south. This was the case as much before the Gulf War as it is now. Iraq's national unity was put under threat by Kurdish and Shia Muslim separatism at the end of the Cold War, which coincided with the Gulf War.[23]

Since the Second World War, the United States has gradually replaced Britain as the dominant outside power in the Middle East. On the military front, the historical watershed was the British withdrawal from east of Suez in 1971. On the economic front, the essential factor is oil company positions. Here, the shift has been more gradual. The trend has been that US oil companies have gradually got access to areas that have been the domain of British and French companies, without any reciprocal opening of traditionally US-dominated areas to oil companies from other countries. Saudi Arabia remained an exclusive domain for US oil companies, whereas the latter also got positions in Iran and Iraq. It was after the coup in Iran in 1953 that US oil companies got access to Iran, putting an end to the exclusively British oil concessions. Subsequently US oil companies got concessions in the United Arab Emirates and in Kuwait, and extended concessions in Iraq. In contrast, British and French oil companies never got concessions in Saudi Arabia.

In the 1970s, the large Middle East oil exporters with the exception of the United Arab Emirates nationalized their oil industries. British interests have since largely withdrawn. The United States has asserted itself in the position of military protector and leading trade partner for the Gulf States, which has given it a higher political exposure. The Gulf War, which as already stated coincided with the end of the Cold War, proved the uncontested dominance of the United States in the Middle East. This was due to a unique coincidence of historical circumstances and events. The terrorist attacks on New York and Washington represent a crunch for US Middle East policy, showing as they do local resentment against US hegemony and the need for the United States to ultimately defend salient interests more forcefully or to withdraw. The attacks show the risks linked to a more lasting US hegemony in the Middle East.

Soviet interference in the Middle East between 1945 and 1990 was variable in the intensity of its attempts to gain footholds, in the choice of potential positions and in the rates of success or failure. Because of self-sufficiency in oil, the Soviet Union did not seek control of the Middle East. Iraq was the only major oil exporter with which it developed close relations. In hindsight, it seems that Soviet attempts to gain influence in the Middle East met with increasing difficulty over time, as the colonial or semi-colonial past became more distant. The various Middle Eastern leaders wanted to use the Soviets for their own purposes, just as they were using Western powers, but they were even more reluctant to experience Soviet dominance.[24] The Soviet objectives were evidently to gradually gain ground in the Middle East, particularly through military co-operation, and to counter or reduce US influence, at least until the 1979 invasion of Afghanistan. This invasion may have been an immediate response to a domestic political crisis. It could also have been part of a deliberate strategy to gain a foothold on the Hormuz Strait to menace oil shipments from the Gulf and eventually to secure both political leverage and economic advantage through high oil prices.

The Soviet Union evidently had a direct interest in Middle Eastern oil policies. Contrary to the oil-importing Western powers, the Soviet Union as a major oil and gas exporter benefited greatly from the oil price rises in 1973–74 and 1979–80. The importance of oil and gas export revenues for Soviet hard currency earnings was such that it could be argued that the oil price hikes provided additional lifetime for an inefficient and otherwise exhausted economic system. The collapse of the Soviet Union occurred a few years after the 1986 oil price decline.

After suffering a setback in Egypt in the early 1970s, the Soviet Union gave the highest priority to Iraq. Here, the Soviet assistance was almost exclusively limited to military co-operation. The Iraqi Baathist regime, in power since 1968, balanced Soviet assistance, particularly with French aid. Over time, the Soviet share of Iraq's foreign trade fell, to the benefit of principally France and Japan.[25] The Baathist government combined the call for Soviet assistance with a deep suspicion of Soviet political intentions, repressing the Iraqi communist party at the same time as it received Soviet military assistance.

Middle Eastern oil and the absence of regional hegemony

The crisis provoked by Iraq's invasion of Kuwait focused attention on the short-term movements of the oil price. The crisis also, however, revealed some important features of the oil market and of Middle Eastern oil supplies. A closer analysis of these fundamentals is useful in discerning potential long-term trends in the oil market. The defeat of Iraq invited attempts at seizing the hegemony in the Middle East, but with no lasting success. Siding with the winning alliance against Iraq did not help Syria play a stronger political role in the Arab world. Saudi Arabia emerged for some time as the winner, but the alliance with the United States has been a political liability that has caused the country to develop closer links with Iran. Therefore, by early 2002, the historical pattern prevails, as relations between Iran, Iraq and Saudi Arabia oscillate between hostility and co-operation. This is evidently pertinent to the oil market.

The absence of strong regional co-operation, democratic governments and a regional hegemonic power impede political stability in the Middle East. Intrigues by foreign powers advancing their interests enhance instability. The various states and regimes have competing and conflicting interests that complicate a mutually responsive regional co-operation. Partly, this is linked to the positions of individuals and ruling groups, which are a result of the absence of stable democratic institutions. Since the collapse of the Ottoman Empire, no single state has been able to dominate the Arab Middle East, to exercise hegemony through a combination of geography, population, economy and organization. On the ruins of the Ottoman Empire, Britain and France established political entities out of their own economic and strategic interests, regardless of those of the local population.[26] These entities were to become the present Arab Middle Eastern states; in most cases they have yet to become nations. The political fragmentation has divided the region into separate markets, with trade impeded by tariffs and other barriers, leading to a commercial disintegration that has contributed to economic stagnation.[27]

The separation of Iraq and Syria has split the Arab world and remains crucial to the Middle East power balance. Internal instability and border disputes impede co-operation. In the northern Gulf, Iraq's border disputes with Iran and Kuwait are relevant to oil supplies.[28] The absence of hegemony or close political co-operation aimed at regional economic and political integration through common institutions, as is today the case in Europe, necessarily means instability and temptations to establish dominance. Any attempt at establishing hegemony has an impact on oil supplies and oil prices, as was demonstrated by the 1990–91 Gulf crisis. It has also provoked foreign intervention.

With a weak Iraq, the Middle East is split and unstable. After Iraq's defeat, Iran is no candidate for hegemony, even with a large population and lack of foreign debt. Liabilities are political instability and rising income requirements. Pressing financial constraints could make Iran again a potential source of instability in the Middle East.

Egypt, the most populous Arab state, is poor and geographically distant from the Gulf, but plays an important cultural role. Poverty prevents a leading political role. Saudi Arabia is the wealthiest state in the region, but is highly dependent upon US support, as was apparent during the 1990–91 Gulf crisis. As the economic heavyweight of the Middle East, Saudi Arabia has considerable political clout.[29] The fact that it has the leading role in Muslim affairs also gives it political weight in the Middle East, but the opaque nature of the family-based regime, restrictions on political debate, fundamentalist influence on Saudi society and close ties to the United States prevent Saudi Arabia from assuming the role of regional cultural and political hegemony.[30]

Iraq is geographically, economically and culturally the heartland of the Arab Middle East and has been the closest candidate for regional hegemony, through the combination of a central geographical position, a sizeable population, the potential for a diversified economic basis, a high level of education and a comparatively efficient administration. Apparently, this was realized by France and the Soviet Union as they chose Iraq as their essential partner in the Middle East.

Iraq had strong economic motives for invading and subsequently annexing Kuwait. Even if Iraq is a rich country, notwithstanding the foreign debt and the massive military build-up, the country was in a desperate economic situation. Before the August invasion, the immediate economic outlook for Iraq was dismal, with a huge foreign debt and high expense for the imports of food and investment goods.[31] Iraq did not have the means to service the foreign debt and feed its population, let alone make new investment and maintain the military hardware. During 1989–90, Iraq had attempted to renegotiate the foreign debt and to defer interest payments. With a few minor exceptions, these attempts failed, as Iraq's creditors had little confidence in the ability of the regime to improve its financial performance and at the same time were alienated by the regime's continued military build-up. Military imports could have been reduced only at the risk of alienating the regime's domestic basis, the armed forces. Reducing civilian imports could have led to social unrest. In the spring and early summer of 1990, Iraq was quickly approaching bankruptcy. In this situation, the physical survival of the Iraqi leadership was at stake, and to avoid a collapse a leap forward was seen as necessary.

Richer neighbours had frustrated Iraq's desire for higher oil prices, and it had practically no capital to invest in additional capacity, but there were apparently ways out. Neighbouring Kuwait had for a long time been seen as provocatively countering Iraqi oil price interests, by the policy of producing above OPEC quotas.[32] In addition, Kuwait was Iraq's major creditor, having equally large oil reserves, but a tiny population. Combining the oil reserves of the two countries with Kuwait's port facilities and small number of people had to appear as an attractive proposition to an economically beleaguered Iraqi regime. In the early summer of 1990, Iraq had made explicit threats to Kuwait of what it would do unless the latter agreed to enforce higher oil prices. Iraq also wanted part of its debt to Kuwait, at least $15 billion, to be waived.[33]

Put together, Iraqi and Kuwaiti oil revenues should have been more than enough to provide the regime of Greater Iraq with a comfortable economic situation. Greater Iraq would have been a regional economic power, in addition to its military power, making it the indisputable leader of the Gulf area. From this perspective, Iraq would not have needed to invade more countries in order to dictate the oil policies of Saudi Arabia and the United Arab Emirates, so that oil prices could stay at a level desirable to Iraq. A plausible Iraqi motive, not only for invading Kuwait, but also for embarking upon a strategy of achieving regional hegemony in the Gulf area, was to influence the future oil supply pattern from the Middle East. The objective was evidently to acquire both a larger market share and a higher economic rent.

The Saddam Hussein regime has also had its foreign allies, but since the revolution of 1958 Iraq has never been dependent upon a single foreign supporter. Britain was the major loser at the fall of monarchy. The new republic at first developed close links with the Soviet Union; later France became the preferred partner. Both the Soviet Union and France found large arms markets in Iraq. By contrast, relations with the United States were at a low level throughout the 1960s and 1970s.

The Iranian revolution of 1979 and the termination of US influence in Iran suddenly increased the political value of the Iraqi regime for both the United States and the conservative Gulf States. The Iranian revolution appeared as an ideological threat to political stability throughout the Middle East. It was in the interest of both the United States and the conservative Arab regimes to topple the new regime. It is an open question to what extent Iraq in September of 1980 went to war against Iran entirely on its own initiative, or whether there had been US and possibly Arab encouragement. As it turned out, the war was an economic catastrophe for Iraq, although there was no clear-cut military winner or loser.[34] The subsequent attack on Kuwait was an Iraqi attempt at compensation, winning both a military and an economic victory.

Any discussion of Iraq's future is speculative. The regime and Saddam Hussein have managed to survive, in spite of or because of the sanctions and isolation. The country has immense problems of reconstruction and is burdened by huge foreign debts and war reparations, unless these should be waived by its creditors, essentially Kuwait and Saudi Arabia. There is anti-Western sentiment caused by the isolation and ensuing hardship of the population during the 1990s. The political balance between the different ethnic and religious groups in Iraq remains unsettled, and ultimately Iraq's integrity could be at stake. The invasion of Iraq by US-led UN forces in 1990 provoked revolts by both the Shia and the Kurdish population. The traditionally close links between the Shia Iraqi clergy and the Iranian clergy represent a potential for closer political relations. This would eventually have an impact on regional politics in the Gulf region as well as on internal politics in the Gulf States. Iraq nevertheless risks facing more adversity, even if relations with Iran are less hostile.

Neighbouring Syria, a long-term rival to Iraq, has a chance of playing a stronger political role. If Syria should in any way be closely linked to Iraq, the political fundamentals in the Middle East would change. Even without much oil, Syria has a geographical position with the potential of being a power broker in the Middle East, through shifting alliances. Since gaining independence after the Second World War, Syria has had conflictual relations with all its immediate neighbours, namely Iraq, Israel, Jordan, Lebanon and Turkey. By contrast, Syria has had more friendly relations with Iran and Saudi Arabia, which are the neighbours' neighbours. Syria's alliances show the complexity of Middle East power politics, which also influence the flows of oil from the region. For Syria, ties with Iran and Saudi Arabia are useful to counterweight the menacing Iraqi neighbour. Correspondingly, both Iran and Saudi Arabia find political benefits in close links with Syria, not only to offset Iraqi challenges and threats.[35]

For most of the time since 1945, Syria's relations with Iraq have been hostile, causing the interruption of transit for Iraqi oil to the Mediterranean. The reason is partly that Iraq and Syria have competing and rival regimes, issuing from different parts of the Baathist party, which distrust each other.[36] The two countries have nevertheless avoided going to war. During the Cold War, both Iraq and Syria had close links with the Soviet Union, receiving Soviet arms. Syria benefited from the end of the Cold War to improve relations with the West, taking part in the coalition against Iraq in 1990–91. Repeated wars and the loss of the Golan Heights have marked Syria's relations with Israel. Syria has suffered severe economic damage from the hostile neighbourhood, and an eventual peace with Israel would bring considerable economic benefits. For Syria, Jordan is an unfriendly neighbour, who has moved ahead in normalizing relations with Israel. Syria's relations with Lebanon are now those of de facto overlord, with both countries fearing Israeli military might, but also sharing the potential benefits of peace. In the meantime, the Syrian and Lebanese economies have become closely integrated, supposedly to the greater benefit of Syrian interests.

Syria's relations with Turkey are tense, threatening to become more so because of disputes over borders and water as well as military issues.[37] Syria's good relations with Iran and Saudi Arabia make sense. With Iran, there is an old relationship based on religion, as a result of the common Shia heritage. For Iran, close ties with Syria and Lebanon represent a counterweight to Iraq as well as a connection to the Mediterranean. Saudi Arabia has for years been Syria's benevolent paymaster, financing part of a persistent budget deficit. For Syria, close links with Saudi Arabia also represent political support against Iraq and Jordan, as well as Israel and Turkey. For Saudi Arabia, Syria represents a useful counterweight to both Iraq and Jordan. For both, the link also demonstrates an Arab unity, potentially useful to both countries' security interests.

Syria has the potential to play a pivotal role in reshaping the Middle East alliance pattern in a way that could affect the flows of oil from the region. One possibility is that improved relations with Iraq could lead to the reopening of the pipelines to Syrian and Lebanese ports, facilitating an expansion of Iraqi oil exports to the Mediterranean. Another possibility is that a threat from Israel and Turkey, perceived or real, could cause a new alliance of Syria, Lebanon and Iraq, with a considerable economic and military potential. This would be a much belated realization of the concept of Arab unity based on the Fertile Crescent. Iran could eventually join such an alliance, which would represent an important and independent political force in the Middle East. Most likely, such an entity would weigh on Saudi Arabia, Kuwait and the other Gulf States, potentially also influencing their oil policies.

As a military power with a large population and an economic potential, Turkey has the ability to exert greater political influence in the Middle East. By repeated incursions into northern Iraq, Turkey demonstrates that it is back as a military factor in the Middle East, for the first time since the Ottoman Empire. The Turkish concern is evidently to take an active part in any political reorganization of the region if the Iraqi state should disintegrate. An eventual separate Kurdish entity in northern Iraq could threaten Turkish territorial integrity by inciting the secession of the Turkish Kurds. As an oil importer with large and rising energy needs, Turkey could benefit and raise self-sufficiency by controlling oil and gas in the present northern Iraq.

Iran is in a different situation. The country's assets are a large population, considerable oil reserves and a geographical position on the Gulf, together with limited foreign debt. Historically, Iran has played an important role in international oil politics. This is likely to be the case in the future also, even if future Iranian oil exports are likely to be lower than they were in the 1970s. Political moderation has led to Iran gradually renewing relations with outside powers and opening up for international trade. Its reintegration into the international community means that Iranian interests and problems will have a greater significance for Middle Eastern politics. Nevertheless, in spite of improved relations with the rest of the world and high oil revenues during 1999–2001, it seems to be heading towards domestic political instability, as the forces of change clash with the guardians of the Islamic republic.[38]

The major problem of post-revolutionary Iran was isolation and continued economic stagnation. Although this is no longer the case, effects linger on. The isolation caused technical and organizational stagnation, rising costs and loss of competitiveness. The Iranian oil industry suffers from technical obsolescence caused by the US embargo. The development of agriculture and manufacturing suffers from obsolescence and the isolation of the country. Overcoming the obsolescence will be necessary if employment, food and industrial products are to be provided for a rapidly increasing population. This in turn will require overcoming the isolation, implying more open contacts with the outside world, not least Europe and North America. Iran's isolation is partly a result of US pressures that often have causes in domestic politics. Mounting domestic social pressures in a strained financial situation could in the worst case lead to an isolated regime representing a rising risk for more prosperous neighbours. The US moves to isolate and weaken the Iranian regime have backfired.

In 2001, Iran and the United States had a mutual interest in removing the Taliban regime in Afghanistan, and Iran was an active, although discreet backer of the US-led military campaign. The renewal of US economic sanctions remains an obstacle to closer co-operation. In making US policy toward Iran, pro-Israeli lobbies worried about Iran's support for the Hezbollah in Lebanon, and alleged plans to acquire nuclear weapons have more weight than economic and political interests related to oil and the US need to find new friends. In Iran, the US sanctions strengthen the conservative clergy that opposes liberal evolution and portrays the United States as the arch-enemy to maintain its own economic and political power, weakening the liberal forces and contributing to the present stalemate, whose outcome is uncertain.[39]

Political instability in Iran has potential repercussions not only for the neighbouring countries, but also the world oil market. Even if the present Iranian regime represents no threat to its neighbours, it may lose power. One alternative is rapid reform, more or less discarding the ideology of the past 20 years and aiming at restoring a market economy and international trade. Another alternative is a backlash to a fundamentalist regime that could present an ideological and political threat to the neighbouring countries, given the large Shia populations in Iraq, Kuwait and Saudi Arabia. In the first case, Iran could contribute to stabilizing the Middle East, in the second case to unsettling the area. For example, political unrest in Iran, leading to a fundamentalist government in Teheran, could inspire a similar political development in Iraq, or parts of Iraq. By contrast, a successful reformist regime in Iran, leading to a market economy and subsequently democracy, could also inspire a corresponding trend in Iraq.

The Gulf States, namely Saudi Arabia, Kuwait, Oman, Qatar, Bahrain and the United Arab Emirates, possess enormous riches as oil and gas in the ground and assets invested abroad, but they cannot defend themselves against the poorer and more populous Iran and Iraq. They attract hostile attention, as was evident during the 1990–91 Gulf crisis, and they have to rely on foreign protection.[40] Interests are reciprocal, with the Gulf States needing to settle a security problem and the outside protector getting compensation through access to oil. Since the British withdrawal from the Gulf, the protector has been the United States.

Throughout the 1980s, rising security concerns made the Gulf States more attentive to US oil interests. They had to exchange US protection for other favours. With Iraq or Iran, or both, representing a military or political threat, the Gulf States provided incentives to the United States to protect them. Their means were oil policy, investment and military purchases. Against this backdrop, Saudi Arabia, Kuwait and the United Arab Emirates

had a security policy interest in the United States needing their oil, directly
for physical supplies or indirectly to stabilize the market. Since 11 September 2001, this no longer seems to apply as much to Saudi Arabia.

For Saudi Arabia and Kuwait the major risk is to be caught between US
and Iraqi interests, or eventually a coalition of Iraqi and Iranian interests.
This would directly affect Saudi oil policy and eventual capacity expansion.
Historically, Saudi Arabia has had a strong interest in maintaining a US
commitment to the defence of the country. The best incentive to a continued US commitment, as acceptable to the US public as to Congress, has
been to present willingness to expand capacity in order to meet future
United States oil demand. In practice that has meant increasing supplies at
stable prices. The combination of improved relations with Iran and domestic political pressures makes Saudi Arabia less eager to please the United
States by keeping oil prices stable. Indeed, in early 2002, for the first time
since 1973, there have been calls in the closely monitored Saudi press for
reducing oil supplies to induce the United States to put pressure on Israel.[41]

For Saudi Arabia, the major issue is for the regime to survive facing
military, political and economic threats. Iraq still represents a military threat.
Even as Iraq was forced to disarm after the Gulf War, there is a legacy of
distrust. It is in Saudi Arabia's long-term interest to improve relations with
Iraq, as has happened with Iran, and not to provoke either by an oil policy
that neglects their income interests. Indeed, if it follows US interests in its
oil policy, Saudi Arabia might after some time find itself in the same
position as that of Kuwait in the early summer of 1990, but exposed
politically rather than militarily. The obvious way to avoid arousing Iraqi or
Iranian anger would be for Saudi Arabia to comply with their oil interests,
defending a high price by restraining output and refraining from any major
capacity expansion. With more critical views of the United States among
the Saudi public, this would help to stabilize the domestic political situation.[42]

Middle Eastern oil since the Cold War

Since the end of the Cold War, the Middle East has been the object of
intense competition between the major powers for political influence and
economic positions, whether for oil investment or arms sales. With the
collapse of communism around 1990, the Soviet Union disappeared from
the Middle East arena, leaving the space open for the US hegemony since
the Gulf War. In the new world order, the United States apparently enjoys
supremacy, able to command oil supplies from the Middle East as it needs
them. Recently there has been a strengthening tendency for the United
States to balance its energy problems abroad.[43] In the face of failure to
implement an effective oil conservation policy and of the gradual depletion
of domestic oil, the answer has been strongly rising oil imports. Consumers

have benefited, at the expense of a rising trade deficit and increasing dependence on Middle Eastern oil, directly and indirectly. The Middle East has a direct importance to the United States as a source of oil, and an indirect importance in securing low prices.

This dependence on the Middle East is problematic insofar as the US supremacy in the Middle East and the international economy is contested. The attacks on New York and Washington demonstrate the economic and political risks for the United States as challenges to US supremacy mount. Such challenges are building up internally in the Middle East. Arab nationalist and Islamist forces resenting the US dominance represent a risk of renewed attacks. Iran and Iraq still represent major political risks to their neighbours and to the United States. In addition, other outside powers challenge the US supremacy. French oil interests are present in the Gulf and Iran. France has also been actively promoting the termination of the embargo on Iraq and the opening of Iraq to foreign oil investors. Chinese, French, Japanese and Russian oil interests have also been positioning themselves in the Middle East.

The Middle East and North Africa are often seen as the 'near abroad' of the European Union, EU, as a legitimate sphere of interest.[44] This view is especially prevalent in Latin Europe, France embodying the imperial and colonial tradition that lives on in strong commercial and political interests in the region. Italy and Spain also have important commercial interests in the Middle East. France nevertheless represents the best-organized oil interests with the strongest political backing and the longest tradition in taking economic and political positions in the Middle East, if necessary in conflict with the Anglo-American oil companies.[45] There is an evident potential for rivalry with US interests in the Middle East, not least over access to oil and weapons markets.

France has for years openly challenged the positions of the United States and of the major US and UK oil companies in the Middle East. Iraq has been the focus of French attention since the 1920s, and again in the 1970s. France has been the champion for European interests, often in direct competition with the United States. However, even with a common currency, Europe is no match for the United States in the Gulf. Europe has little political weight in the Middle East, although France in particular followed by Italy and Spain have ambitions for more influence.

Europe has its distinctive commercial and financial interests, different from and competing with those of the United States. With a common currency, Europe will presumably be in a much stronger position to defend its own interests also in international markets. Western Europe has good reasons to challenge the US commercial and financial advantages that emerge from the leading role of the US dollar. For the US private sector, the advantage of the dollar hegemony has been the shelter it gives from currency risks and the ability to hedge costs. The leading position of the dollar also gives political advantages to the US government as well as commercial advantages to US businesses. These advantages increasingly attract the jealousy of Europe.

In dealing with the Middle East, Europe has distinct advantages over the United States in geographical proximity and a less close relationship with Israel. Because of the proximity, stability and peace in the Middle East are even more important to Europe than to the United States. With increasing integration, Europe also develops stronger interests in trade with the Middle East. Europe's long-term concept is the development of a free trade zone encompassing not only the European Union and associate countries, but also the countries of North Africa and the Middle East.[46] One objective is to secure economic development and political stability in North Africa to furnish markets for European industry and, through rising employment, prevent an undesirable influx of immigrants. Another objective could be to secure privileged positions for European investors, including in oil. On the first count, there is little reason for a clash with US interests; on the second one there is a considerable potential for conflict. A free trade zone could be a vehicle for European oil investors to gain advantages over their US competitors, helped by a common European currency.

The new Russia, emerging in the 1990s, was for several years passive in Middle Eastern affairs. Since 1997, Russia has shown more interest in the Middle East, particularly in renewing links with Iraq. Russian diplomacy has actively tried to mediate between Iraq and the United Nations, together with France and China. Russian oil companies have been negotiating investment opportunities in Iraq. Russia's interests and capabilities in relation to Middle Eastern oil are uncertain. As an oil exporter, Russia has an interest in co-operation between the Gulf exporters to stabilize oil prices. Russia evidently lacks both the capital and technology to play a major part in the development of the Iraqi oil industry. On the other hand, the new Russia no longer presents an ideological challenge or military threat to the Middle East regimes. It has the potential to represent an alternative political support for Middle East countries seeking to reduce dependence on the United States or Europe, or both. Unless Russia seriously mismanages its own oil industry, it should not need oil from the Middle East.

Nevertheless, Russia sometimes acts as if it is at least considering the possibility of having to import oil. Russian oil companies are evidently seeking positions in Iraq. During recent confrontations between Iraq and the United States, Russian diplomacy had an active, mediating role. Russia could have a long-term interest in seeking allies in the Middle East to improve the bargaining position with the United States and Europe.

The energy needs in Asia are rising quickly. East Asian oil demand growth averaged 5.6 per cent annually between 1990 and 1996 because of an energy-intensive pattern of economic growth. In South Korea, for example, oil consumption grew at an average rate of 13.5 per cent per year from 1985 to 1995, and in 1995 the country's annual oil consumption was 16.5 barrels per capita. During the 1990–96 period, the total energy demand for ten East Asian countries, China, Hong Kong, Indonesia, Japan, Malaysia, the Philippines, Singapore, South Korea, Taiwan and Thailand, grew at an average rate of 5.5 per cent per year, compared to the world average of 1.5 per cent per year. The average annual increase in energy consumption for these ten countries as a group exceeded their combined average annual economic growth rate.

As the East Asian economies recover from recession, they embark on a growth pattern that is less capital and energy intensive, but still causes a quickly rising need for Middle Eastern oil. China's oil consumption and imports are likely to multiply during the first decades of this century. China is already seeking investment opportunities in Middle Eastern oil. The Chinese oil strategy evidently also includes building tankers to transport oil from the Middle East. China seems set to become an increasingly important buyer of Middle Eastern oil, but distance reduces its potential to intervene militarily in the Middle East.

India's energy needs are also rising quickly.[47] The Middle East is the immediate source of oil for India. Likewise, Pakistan's energy needs are likely to rise quickly, also implying a rising call for Middle Eastern oil. Both countries are potential markets for gas from the Middle East, from Iran as well as the Gulf States. For both India and Pakistan, rising energy imports risk compromising the trade balance. Against this backdrop, the possibility of military threats from India and Pakistan cannot be excluded, in which case the Gulf States would need US protection even more.

The Middle East in the US oil strategy

The United States deserves a special mention, not only because of its vanguard role in the 1990–91 Gulf conflict, but also as the world's major market for oil and the home of the bulk of the oil industry. Indeed, at least since the First World War, the United States has defined oil as a strategic commodity.[48] The reasons were fears of exhausting domestic supplies as well as a realization of the economic gains to be made from oil. Even if the United States never established a national oil company to secure oil supplies, unlike, for example, Britain, France, Italy and Spain, the US government has consistently supported its private oil industry in seeking a foothold and advantages in foreign oil provinces.[49] This is even more true now than it was in the 1920s, essentially because of the dependence on oil imports. There is a persistent symbiotic relationship between US foreign policy and US oil interests. Access to foreign oil supplies has repeatedly been defined as a security concern for the United States.[50]

The US interest in Middle Eastern oil dates back to the end of the First World War. The spread of automobile transportation caused concern that domestic oil supplies would be insufficient. New discoveries and rising oil production in California, Texas and Venezuela subsequently dissipated this fear. The fear of oil scarcity again surfaced during the Second World War. After 1945, the bulk of the world's oil production moved from North America to the Middle East and North Africa. This shift was accompanied by gradually declining oil prices from 1945 to the early 1970s and by an equally gradual rise in US oil imports.

US oil imports continued to rise quickly even after the first major oil price increase in 1973–74, reaching their first peak in 1979. The reason was partly the low domestic oil prices in the United States, which were regulated to benefit consumers, but which were detrimental to output. After the deregulation of the US oil market and under the impact of the economic recession, US oil imports declined in the early 1980s, reaching in 1985 about the same level as in 1973. Since the mid-1980s, US oil imports have risen steadily, in 1993 passing the previous historical peak. They are still rising and set to continue rising, possibly for decades, depending on US economic performance and the supply of competing domestic fuels.

With Mexican exports declining, Venezuela has appeared as the next immediate oil supplier to the United States. Venezuela has provided increasing oil supplies and has the potential to supply rising volumes of oil at low cost. Regardless of Venezuelan or other Atlantic oil supplies, the United States will need the Gulf, especially Saudi Arabia, to stabilize the oil market.

Any Iraqi domination of the Gulf area would have jeopardized the world's oil supply system, as it exists today and as the major oil importers, first of all the United States, would like it to exist in the future. Saudi oil policy could have been the principal casualty of any effective Iraqi domination of the Gulf area. Because of the growing dependence on Middle Eastern oil, the US interest is in political stability in the area on its own terms, securing price-elastic oil supplies, meaning steadily rising volumes at constant prices. This is contrary to Iraq's interests, but compatible with those of some other Middle Eastern oil exporters.

With the prospects of rising oil import dependence, the United States will need increasing oil supplies from the Middle East to balance the market. The positive effects for the domestic oil industry of high oil prices will count steadily less and the consumer interests correspondingly more. Therefore the outlook is for stronger US political involvement in the Middle East, but US interests are likely to be increasingly torn between considerations for Israel and oil interests in the Arab countries, with prospects that relations with Saudi Arabia will become more tenuous. For the United States, this development has a risk potential.

Iraq's economic distress and political interests in dominating the Gulf area led to an open confrontation with the United States, whose vital interests in relation to oil were threatened.[51] The United States not only has an interest in moderate oil prices today, but increasing access to oil at moderate prices in the future. This is the strategic issue for the United States. The key is control of the Middle East, essentially Saudi Arabia.

This explains the immediate and massive US response to Iraq's invasion of Kuwait. Indeed, Iraq left the United States with no choice but to respond militarily, given the interests at stake. For the United States, the issue was not Kuwait, but the future position of Saudi Arabia, with an estimated quarter of the world's oil reserves. US oil companies have essentially developed Saudi oil and there are today close economic links between the two countries. As mentioned, there has been a close historical relationship between US oil imports and Saudi oil production. In the future, the projected growth of US oil imports will reasonably have to be matched by a rise in Saudi oil production: a massive rise in US oil imports, as has happened in the 1990s, did have a counterpart on the supply side and did not trigger off a major price rise. With Iraqi dominance of the Gulf, Saudi co-operation would have been less likely for the United States. This crucial aspect of US oil interests is unlikely to change over the next few decades.

In relation to the population or the economic output, energy demand and oil demand are considerably higher in the United States than in Western Europe or Japan. For example, in 1997 the per capita energy use was more than twice as high in the United States as in Western Europe. Energy demand in relation to nominal gross domestic product, GDP, was roughly 50 per cent higher in the United States than in Western Europe. Roughly the same differences apply to oil consumption. At the same time, the United States is one of the world's largest oil producers. The United States apparently has complex and even contradictory interests in relation to oil prices, balancing concerns for consumers and domestic producers.

In relation to economic output, measured as nominal GDP, the United States had a markedly less efficient use of energy. This is particularly the case for oil use. For example, in 1997 the United States' per capita oil consumption was about twice that of Western Europe. In relation to employment it was about two-thirds higher. Finally, when measured in relation to economic output, nominal GDP, oil use was about 50 per cent higher in the United States than in Western Europe. These data indicate that even if the US has an economic output per capita and per person employed on average above that of Western Europe, it is less efficient in its use of energy.

The Reagan administration was attentive to the interests of the domestic oil industry. The 1986 oil price decline severely hit US oil producers. As oil prices hit $10 a barrel in the summer of 1986, there was rising concern in Washington over domestic oil and the long-term supply security. Then Vice President George Bush travelled to Saudi Arabia, apparently with a message that oil prices should stabilize at a level closer to $20 a barrel, which was seen as more convenient to US interests. Within a matter of days, oil prices actually doubled to about $16–17 a barrel. This can be seen as a sign that for the United States, open competition had its limits in the oil market and that a certain floor price should be respected for the sake of the US oil industry.[52] This is but one example of how state interests interfere in the oil market, even under ideologically liberal governments. Nevertheless, even with higher oil prices, US oil production continued to subside slowly but continuously throughout the 1980s.

The 1991 oil strategy change had been under preparation for several years, but it was enhanced by the Gulf crisis. Since 1991, US oil policy has been to reduce the economic weight of an inevitably increasing physical flow of oil imports. Barring effective measures to curb US oil consumption, which, as mentioned, is in relation to economic output about 50 per cent above the Western European level, the United States has an interest in low world market oil prices. Insofar as the US dollar remains the world's leading currency, the United States does not need to worry about trade and payments deficits as do other countries. As long as the United States can contract debts and pay for imports in its own currency, which it can print at will, the competitive advantage of cheap imported oil over more costly domestic oil strengthens. This facility also favours oil imports over costly and politically unpopular energy conservation measures.

Since the mid-1980s, the United States has increasingly perceived its oil interests as those of a consumer and importer, although it is also one of the world's largest oil producers. With rising oil consumption and imports, the domestic upstream oil interests have steadily lost political influence. US oil policy has increasingly favoured low oil prices and market stability through risk diversification by a large number of oil suppliers to the world market. The focus of US oil policy is increasingly on the stability of the world oil market, not narrowly on US importer interests, although defending the investor interests of US oil companies in foreign upstream activities has a high priority. This change of oil policy focus can explain salient aspects of US foreign and energy policies that otherwise would appear peculiar, for example the heavy commitment toward the new states of Central Asia and the Caspian region.

For this reason, the change of US oil strategy in 1991 was less a radical break with the 1980s practice than an adaptation to the new world order as it then appeared after the collapse of communism. After the collapse of the

Soviet Union and the defeat of Iraq by a US-led coalition, the major threats to Middle East oil supplies seemed to have been removed. The Soviet Union had represented a continuous political threat to US positions in the Middle East as an alternative supplier of arms and supporter of regimes, limiting the US freedom of action in the area and posing a permanent risk to oil market stability. The Soviet Union, as a major oil and gas exporter, had oil price interests opposite to those of the United States, the world's largest oil importer, and could profit economically from political instability in the Middle East, as during the oil crises of the 1970s. The Soviet collapse around 1990 removed an immense threat to US oil interests in the Middle East and made it easier for the United States to deal with the Iraqi challenge.

In 1991 the Bush administration presented the new oil policy. It largely reflected the advanced oil province maturity of the United States, with declining exploration success rates and field sizes and rising costs. Emphasis was on oil market stability, stressing that even with physically secure oil supplies, the United States economy had suffered from the past sudden and sharp oil price rises, as in 1973–74, 1979–80 and most recently in 1990. The sudden oil price shocks were identified as much more harmful than gradually rising oil prices, even if the long-term average price were identical. The US economic vulnerability to oil price shocks was seen as a reflection of its dependence on the world oil market, independent from the volumes or proportions of oil imported into the United States.[53] The oil price shock sensitivity was defined as a function of the overall oil dependence of the US economy. This is not only an issue of oil consumption, but also of the ability to convert to other fuels, oil stocks available in the United States and the world, and the spare oil production capacity quickly available in the United States and the world. The conclusion was that oil prices mattered for the United States, but not import dependency, because US consumers would be affected by any increase in oil prices, even increases outside the United States, regardless of the cause. To avoid shocks the United States' interest was in a competitive and well-functioning oil market, with diversified supplies, avoiding any excessive reliance on a single source of oil.

Oil import levels were defined as irrelevant to the oil price risk. This also represented a distinct policy shift in favour of US oil consumer interests, to the disadvantage of US oil producers who would eventually benefit from high oil prices. The policy shift also amounted to the US government explicitly defending oil consumer interests worldwide, not only those in the United States. It is a recognition of the interdependence of the US and world economies. This can be seen as a sign of the globalization of United States policies on a pivotal issue, an aim to manage global problems, recognizing that the world's problems also affect the United States. The position could also bring political advantages to the United States, allowing it to appear as the leader of the world's oil importers, as during the Gulf crisis of 1990–91.

Iraq had represented the most consistent opposition to US dominance in the Middle East. Contrary to most other oil exporters of the region, Iraq had never had close economic or political ties with the United States. The Iraqi oil industry had been developed largely by British investment. At a later stage, in the 1960s, 1970s and 1980s, Iraq had established close links with France and the Soviet Union. Both countries were important arms exporters to the different Iraqi regimes. French oil interests were particularly active in Iraq, offering an alternative access to capital and technology. Through money, weapons and skills Iraq became a leading regional military power, although not a dominant one. Iraq nevertheless represented a threat to all its neighbours as well as to Israel and US oil interests. At least since the time of the 1958 revolution, relations with Syria were mostly conflictual, with Iran hostile and with Kuwait tense. Over most of the period, until the Iranian revolution in 1979, Iraq and the United States were not on friendly terms, as witnessed by the absence of diplomatic relations.

The Iranian revolution soon provided Iraq and the United States with a common enemy. For secular Iraq, the Islamist revolution in neighbouring Iran represented an ideological and political threat as well as a chance to settle a historical border conflict affecting Iraq's access to the sea. For the United States, the Iranian revolution likewise represented an ideological menace as well as a political threat to US positions in the Gulf and to oil supplies. For the Carter government, the occupation of the Teheran embassy and the ensuing sequestration of embassy personnel in late 1979 caused political damage, prompting decisions to intervene in Iran, with the aim of liberating US diplomats as well as overthrowing the revolutionary regime. The aborted incursion by US commandos into Iran in the spring of 1980 showed that the Carter administration was prepared to settle scores with Iran by force if necessary.

The subsequent attack by Iraq on Iran in the autumn of 1980 served US interests, whether or not Iraq received actual US encouragement. At this time, the Carter administration was desperate for re-election, with their chances suffering from high oil prices and humiliation in Iran. The hope could have been that an Iraqi attack would lead to the collapse of the Iranian regime, with the ensuing liberation of the hostages and possibly an end to the Iranian oil workers' strike. The oil flow would resume and prices decline. This combination of factors would assure President Carter of reselection. Events turned out otherwise. Even in revolutionary turmoil, Iran showed remarkable ability to resist the Iraqi attack and did not disintegrate. President Carter was not re-elected, but replaced by Ronald Reagan. Oil prices did not come down, but the US oil market was deregulated and integrated into the world market. Iraq did not get a quick victory, but was caught in an eight-year war with a more populous neighbour, causing financial ruin.

The corollary to the preference for cheap imported oil is an active policy to stabilize world oil prices at a comfortable level. This comprises close bilateral links with salient oil exporters, preferably, but not exclusively, the Gulf oil producers, to enhance their attentiveness to US oil interests, as well as an active involvement in opening new oil provinces for private investment to secure the diversity of oil supply sources. It also includes a policy for keeping spare oil production capacities that can be quickly activated in emergencies, again preferably in the Gulf, as well as keeping a huge domestic strategic petroleum reserve. Furthermore, the policy also includes measures to enhance conservation of energy, especially oil, by more efficient use, and to develop substitutes for oil.

The corollary to rising oil imports is the military capability to intervene to defend oil supply sources abroad. The United States has an evident interest in having close allies neighbouring the oil exporters. Turkey has a double function in US oil strategy, representing transit routes as well as a military potential, and has proved a close ally of the United States, against the Soviet Union during the Cold War and against Iraq during the Gulf War. Turkey's problems with the European Union strengthen ties with the United States.

Pipelines link the oil fields of Northern Iraq with Turkish ports on the Mediterranean. For the United States, as will be discussed later, Turkey for a number of reasons represents the politically preferable transit route for Caspian and Central Asian oil, although a costly one. With strong armed forces, Turkey represents a military capability that can supplement or even substitute for US forces in the Middle East. Turkish military incursion in Iraq has become a persistent feature of Middle Eastern politics. Turkey also represents a potential threat to Syria, particularly in view of its military alliance with Israel. Finally, Turkey has a potential for eventually intervening in the Caucasus to defend oil transit routes. With this array of assets, Turkey is an exceptionally valuable partner for the United States in the Middle East.

Turkey also represents a risk for US oil interests. The lack of fully fledged democratic institutions exposes politics to instability.[54] In spite of vigorous economic growth, the country suffers from endemic inflation and widening social disparities. The Kurdish problem could also compromise the security of oil transit routes as well as the political integrity of Turkey.

Russia represents both a temptation and a risk for US oil interests. Successful privatization has channelled investment capital to the oil industry and output is increasing. Against this backdrop, Russia appears as a more appealing place for US oil companies, in spite of regulatory and fiscal problems.[55] On the other hand, Russia's attempt at opening and integrating with the West does not seem to have overwhelming domestic support. Apart from armament limitation agreements revoked unilaterally by the United States, NATO extension, Central Asia and Iraq represent potential points of discord.[56] Against the backdrop of potentially sour relations, increasing US reliance on Russian oil carries a political risk.

For consumers, the new US oil strategy has been remarkably successful. The Clinton administration evidently adopted the Bush oil policy, but with an even stronger emphásis on the consumer interest of oil market stability at reasonable prices. During the Clinton administration, with rising oil consumption and imports, the definition of reasonable oil prices seems to have been defined downward. From 1990 to 1997, US oil consumption increased by 9 per cent, whereas domestic oil production decreased by 7 per cent, so that oil imports rose by 28 per cent over the period. The rate of oil self-sufficiency sunk from 55 to 47 per cent. The United States' share of world oil consumption stayed even at 25 per cent, but US oil imports by 1997 made up 13 per cent of the world oil market, against 11 per cent in 1990. The rise in US oil imports has accompanied a generally downward oil price trend as well as a steady growth of the US economy. The September 2001 attacks were a reminder of the foreign political risk accompanying the domestically easy solution.

During the 1990s, the US economy made huge annual savings by using relatively low-cost imported oil rather than more expensive domestic energy sources.[57] The substitution of oil imports with domestic energy would have benefited some sectors and some regions of the United States, but at a high cost and with a substantial burden to the rest of the economy. Insofar as oil prices in the United States are aligned with those in the world market, higher oil self-sufficiency would not have given any additional protection to the US economy, only higher energy costs.

The exposure to supply disruptions and oil price shocks nevertheless remains a serious risk for the US economy, but their low frequency means that the annualized cost has been limited, so far at least. The short-term insurance policy against oil price shocks comprises the Strategic Petroleum Reserve, which the US government can unleash to counter rising oil prices caused by a supply disruption. US oil supply security also includes a spare oil production capacity abroad, essentially in the Gulf States, and even at home, in an oil production capacity that is price elastic, as well as the military capacity to intervene to defend US oil interests. The United States' oil import dependency also carries military costs that are more difficult to measure.

The long-term insurance policy against oil price shocks has for decades included a research and development effort to improve technology and provide new energy sources, especially in the transportation sector, to reduce oil dependency. Likewise US policy has for many years aimed at opening up new oil provinces around the world. From this perspective, the US interest in Central Asia and the Caspian region appears sensible. The Clinton government's commitment to curb greenhouse gas emissions and its benevolent interest in the Kyoto Protocol also fitted into this picture. The domestic supplement, high taxes on oil product consumption, as in Europe, to curb oil demand, has been politically unacceptable in the United States so far, although eventually it would put downward pressure on oil import prices. The weight of oil consumer interests in Congress has prevented such measures. An international treaty, such as the Kyoto Protocol, could eventually provide political reasons for raising oil product taxes in the United States, but the rejection of the Protocol by the George W. Bush administration shows that this is not on the current political agenda, even after the September 2001 attacks on New York and Washington.

The gradual erosion of real oil prices during the 1990s was in the economic interests of the United States and a sign of a successful implementation by the Clinton administration of an oil strategy designed under Reagan and Bush. The oil price decline of 1998 reduced inflationary pressures in the United States, facilitating a relaxation of monetary policy. Lower oil prices also provided valuable assistance to the crisis-ridden East Asian economies, reducing inflationary pressures and improving trade balances. The responsiveness of international oil prices to the macroeconomic needs of the United States and other leading oil importers appears to be the ultimate success of the US oil strategy.

This apparent success also reveals the contradictions and weaknesses of the strategy. As the United States is the world's oldest and most mature oil province, oil production there is the most sensitive to price movements. High average lifting costs and reduced exploration imply a risk that domestic oil supplies will decrease quickly. With low oil prices, both consumption and especially imports of oil are likely to grow over the next few decades, unless high oil product taxes are introduced, which does not seem likely. With low oil prices, the policy of diversifying foreign supply sources by opening up new oil provinces meets its limits. Oil from Central Asia and the Caspian region, for example, to which the United States gives much importance, has high transportation costs. Low oil prices also mean serious economic strains on even the richer oil exporters, such as Saudi Arabia, Kuwait and the United Arab Emirates, with a risk of social tensions. Ultimately the apparent recent success of the US oil strategy risks undermining the political stability of the very oil exporters that are the linchpin of the strategy.

These contradictions imply not only that the success of the US oil strategy is historically conditioned, but also that serious problems are latent and may herald instability. Whereas the objective of the US oil strategy is to stabilize the oil market at prices comfortable to the importer and consumer through competition from diversified supply sources, the immediate outcome seems to be heavier dependence on a few suppliers, essentially the Gulf producers. It also means rising exposure to the political risk of oil price shocks, which the strategy was designed to reduce.

Apart from the political risk in conjunction with the dependence on a few oil suppliers, the United States is also meeting increasing competition for positions in the Middle East and the favours of the Middle Eastern oil exporters. The competition is about access to oil, access to markets and selling arms, as well as money. The first criterion for the continued success of the US oil strategy is the continuation of the special relationship with Saudi Arabia as well as Kuwait and the United Arab Emirates. Another criterion is the absence of a serious competitor among the major powers offering the same array of services as the United States, namely a huge market for oil, a financial market that can absorb investment from occasionally large oil revenues and finally, military protection. A third criterion is the continuation of the facility to use US dollars to pay for oil, giving little weight to trade and payments balances. So far, the US position seems unrivalled, but serious competition is building up, especially from Europe.

Caspian and Russian oil in US strategy

During the 1990s, oil in the Caspian region and Central Asia figured prominently in US policy. High oil prices in 2000 and 2001 have renewed US interest in Caspian and Central Asian oil.[58] Since September 2001, reduced trust in the Middle East has also caused greater interest in Russia and prepared the ground for closer co-operation in the Caspian region and Central Asia. Stakes for the United States are not only access to the region's oil and gas, but also trade and political positions. The campaign against Afghanistan following the September 2001 terrorist attacks has for the first time provided the United States with a military presence in Central Asia, in Uzbekistan. For the United States, fighting terrorism in this way can go together with securing oil interests.[59] In the mid-1990s, US interests were actively pursuing pipeline projects to bring oil and particularly natural gas from Central Asia, in particular Turkmenistan, through Afghanistan to Pakistan and eventually India.[60] At the time, US oil companies were on speaking terms with the Afghan Taliban regime. Central Asian oil and natural gas provide motivations for the United States to secure a position in Afghanistan, although the outcome is uncertain and there is competition with Chinese and Russian interests.

If the Caspian region and Central Asia had not been landlocked or had freely available transit routes, the region would be one of the world's most favourable oil provinces.[61] A reasonable bet is that the geological potential is underestimated, so that the region may contain much more oil and gas than generally anticipated today. The potential is for a rising output of oil and gas at declining costs. The prospect is for huge profits, but their division remains an open question, linked to the transportation issue. The development of Caspian oil and its eventual access to the world market will have a profound influence on the Middle East power balance, with direct stakes for Iran and Turkey, or Russia.

The political risk involved in developing the oil and gas resources of the Caspian region and Central Asia and in bringing the oil and gas to the market is enormous. The risks involved should be analysed from at least three angles: the transportation problems, the great power involvement, and the potential instability of the regimes in place. These three dimensions interlock. The transportation problems invite interference from neighbouring states for both economic and political reasons. The solutions affect the great powers involved. The potential instability of the regimes in place in Azerbaijan, Kazakhstan, Turkmenistan and Uzbekistan makes them seek allies outside the region. The internal politics of the new states of the Caspian region and Central Asia also affect the great powers, especially the United States and Russia, besides Iran and Turkey. These interlocking dimensions of political risk make the region perhaps the world's most complex environment for the oil industry. Nevertheless, the stakes are enormous.[62]

From a petroleum point of view, the region's salient cases are Azerbaijan, Kazakhstan, Turkmenistan and Uzbekistan. These countries have autocratic governments of various degrees of harshness. They all face fundamental political problems. They have a higher level of education than the oil exporters of the Middle East and North Africa. Autocratic governments may be less stable, especially if they do not deliver economic progress. The very survival of these regimes may depend upon their ability to attract oil investors. The political risk should induce oil investors to apply a higher than usual risk premium when assessing investment opportunities in the region. This risk premium, in addition to the cost of transportation, could mean that oil and gas development in the region is economically less attractive than it appears from the geological potential.

The new countries in the Caspian region and Central Asia are at a different stage of development from the Middle East and North Africa.[63] The region is politically important because it may have the geological potential to become a leading new oil province. The political entities are new and immature. Their oil industry is in most cases young. Like Iran, Algeria and Saudi Arabia, they lack democratic traditions. So far, their institutions are only nominally democratic.

Throughout the region, the democratic process, timidly begun in 1991, seems to have stalled. Insofar as these countries develop substantial oil and gas exports, they have good chances of not only developing rentier econo-

mies, with detrimental effects on other industries, but also rentier states.[64]
This would make their emerging private sectors parasites upon the oil state.
The chances are that the distribution of wealth and income will become
more unequal, so that mounting conflicts over distribution will push the
new rulers toward more repressive methods to stay in power. The new
rulers may even choose to secure their positions with new alliances with the
old colonial power, Russia. In some cases, they are already actively seeking
alliances with outside partners.

The attraction of the Caspian region and Central Asia is simply huge oil
reserves in countries whose governments are in need of revenues, investment and trade. The international oil industry apparently has a favourable
bargaining position. Oil and gas development has the potential to significantly help the new republics to economic prosperity as well as political
stability and independence. Indeed, the essential economic assets of
Azerbaijan, Kazakhstan, Turkmenistan and Uzbekistan are oil and gas
reserves.

The difficult outlets to world markets compromise the value of these
assets. The land-locked position of the countries mentioned severely limits
the choice of markets. In principle, the region's oil and gas could be
exported by pipeline to the growing markets of China, India and Pakistan,
but the capital cost would be extremely high, and some transit routes, for
example through Afghanistan, would mean a risk of disruptions caused by
political strife. An alternative transit route would be through Iran to the
Gulf. At least for the region's oil this may be the most economical outlet.
From Iranian ports, the oil could then be shipped to the growing Asian
markets. Such a solution would, however, strongly reinforce Iran's position
in both the world oil market and in the political context of the Middle East.

A route through Turkey is in the planning. The project is for an oil
pipeline for Azeri and eventually Kazakh crude through Georgia to the
Turkish Mediterranean port of Ceyhan.[65] The point is to avoid Armenia,
Iran and Russia, all of which are actually or potentially on less than good
neighbourly terms with Azerbaijan. The capital cost for the 1700-kilometre
line is estimated to be at least $2.5 billion, possibly much more. This is the
most costly way out for Azeri and Central Asian oil. It is justified by
political considerations rather than by economics. Turkey and its regional
rivals Iran and Russia see the control of pipeline routes as an important tool
for strengthening their influence in the Caspian basin. The United States
supports this route as this apparently would reduce Russia's influence and
as it avoids Iran. It would also strengthen Turkey, which is an important US
ally.

This benefit may be more apparent than real. Georgia remains a weak
link. The route proposed would have to pass fairly close to the Armenian
border. Armenia has comparatively strong armed forces, being Russia's

traditional ally in the region. Armenia also received support from Iran during its conflict with Azerbaijan. Georgia is, by contrast, a weak state on both political and military accounts, although its democracy seems to be consolidating.[66] Even as a post-Soviet independent country it is subject to heavy Russian pressures. The pipeline proposed would run the risk of interruption by Armenian forces, directly or by proxy, should Armenia desire to cut Azerbaijan's revenues. For such a purpose, Iran or Russia might also act through an Armenian proxy.

An alternative, less costly and politically less risky route has been proposed by Russia, requiring tankers to load Azeri and eventually Central Asian crude from Black Sea terminals for shipment through the Bosphorus to markets in the west. Turkey opposes any increase in oil tanker traffic through the straits, pointing to serious safety and environmental dangers. Turkey, evidently, also wants to avoid any shipment through Russia. In addition to complex risk factors because of foreign policy, there is also the potential problem of internal instability in the countries concerned.

The potential economic gain and the strategic importance of the Caspian region and Central Asia cause the interest of outside powers, whether they are neighbouring or not. Indeed, the great game of the nineteenth century between Russia and the United Kingdom over the control of Central Asia seems to be reappearing over oil at the turn of the twentieth century. This time, however, the United States appears to be Russia's chief contender, with Iran and Turkey in secondary roles.

These four external powers have a similar and competing interest, that is access to and control of the region's oil and gas, but their means are not equal. The United States has a disadvantage because of remoteness and needs a partner for the transit of the oil. Russia and Iran have an advantage because of proximity, adjacent markets and easy transit. Turkey is at a disadvantage because of costly and potentially vulnerable transit routes. Furthermore, Armenia, a traditional ally of Russia and Iran, is in the important position of representing a potential threat to both Azerbaijan and Turkish oil interests. So far, the United States has chosen Turkey as a partner, but this is insufficient, as Russia or Iran or an alliance of the two could upset any Turkish transit route. Investment in new pipeline systems may not be sufficient to secure outlets and the free flow of oil and gas. This enhances the economic risk for the oil investors.

In addition, the regimes in place in the Caspian region and Central Asia are all potentially unstable.[67] Their post-Soviet political life has striking similarities with Soviet times, indicating a remarkable continuity in social relations, in spite of spectacular formal and institutional changes. Common features are the smooth transition of the local Soviet power elites into nationalist ruling elites, with ideology changing rather than substance or methods, as well as an extreme centralization of power, often with authority vested in a single person.[68] Such political systems are inherently unstable. They have no mechanisms for dialogue and compromise. Authority vested in dispensable and mortal individuals is more fragile than the authority of more lasting and solid institutions. This point is of critical relevance to the region and to the oil industry.

Lessons from other oil and gas exporters are that petroleum revenues easily lead to a distorted economic development.[69] In many oil- and gas-exporting developing countries there is a propensity for autocratic regimes with an extreme centralization of power that hampers gradual adjustment and over time leads to political instability and discontinuities.

Even if there is reasonably little risk of nationalization of oil and gas facilities, there is a considerable risk of difficult operating conditions as a result of deteriorating political circumstances. The situation in present Algeria or in Iran in the late 1970s is a relevant reference. In the Caspian region and Central Asia the monopolies of the Soviet times have been replaced by patron–client relationships, which because of their discretionary and selective character bear little resemblance to open markets. This is a real problem for oil investors, who risk betting on the wrong horses or even the wrong riders. It is an open question to what extent the immediate post-Soviet regimes in these countries represent a transitory phase or a more lasting solution. This is also pertinent to the interests of the great powers.

The great game over Central Asia is being continued at the beginning of a new century, this time with the United States replacing the United Kingdom. In this game, Russia is a constant factor, seeking to regain both economic and political control of the region. Oil is evidently the important factor. Iran is a new factor in the frame. It is emerging as an independent actor, seeking economic and political control, trade and transit for the oil. In this game, Turkey is essentially an old outsider, seeking trade and transit for the oil. Turkey apparently also has an ambition to exercise economic and political control of the region, but with more limited means than either Iran or Russia. The United States is a newcomer to the region and an outsider. It is seeking economic and political control as well as oil and gas. In this new version of the great game, there are essentially two distinct rivalry dimensions: the United States versus Russia for control of the oil, and Turkey versus Iran for the transit routes.

Russia's interests are, in short, a preferential access to Central Asian oil and gas and regaining economic and political control of the region. As Russia's economic development accelerates, it is likely to need more natural gas in power generation. Russia is the world's second oldest oil province after the United States. The Russian natural gas industry generally suffers from mismanagement and high costs, in addition to an outdated technology and generally poor management. Output in the large West Siberian oil fields has peaked. The most favourable geological sites have been explored and developed. For Russia, getting oil from Azerbaijan and Central Asia could be a good alternative to expensive development in Eastern Siberia or in offshore Far Eastern Russia. Azerbaijan and Central Asia are connected to European Russia by oil and gas pipelines. Russia's economic interest is to capture part of the economic rent from the region's oil and gas through preferential access, prices below those of the world market and eventually through transit fees.

Russia's political interest in relation to Azeri and Central Asian oil and gas seems to be to deny other external powers control of the region.[70] This does not mean barring access to foreign oil investors, provided Russia keeps a large stake. Indeed, by first giving the new countries some leeway to negotiate directly with Western oil interests and then reasserting some dominance of the region, Russia seems to be following a devious strategy. It may seem to be attracting Western capital and technology to modernize the Azeri and Central Asian oil industry, but to some extent this is for its own benefit. A proof of this point is that Russia has put fairly blunt pressure on Kazakhstan to choose an oil transit route through Russia rather than Turkey and to get a share in the Azerbaijan oil consortium, apparently without payment.[71] Correspondingly, Russia has the means to foment troubles and put pressure on Georgia, through ethnic minorities and factional groups. Against this backdrop, the desire to control the pipeline for Azeri oil to the Black Sea may explain Russia's ferocious fight against the Chechen secession. Because of oil, this war may not be over, in spite of the truce in force.

Russia has an interest in controlling Caspian and Central Asian oil and gas exports to improve its own bargaining position with Western oil investors. The stakes are access to capital and market power. The oil and gas export pipelines are the instruments giving Russia a political leverage.[72] This is regardless of the fact that for the populations and political elites in Azerbaijan and Central Asia, nationalism is on the agenda, not any new subservience to Russia.[73] Russia apparently also has the means to obstruct or disturb any oil or gas transit through Georgia and maybe in practice any transit route through Turkey. Russia's connection with Armenia is important in this respect, but this is not its only means of pressure.

The United States, as Russia's chief contender in the region, has less vital interests. It nevertheless has universal interests as the world's only superpower. As the world's leading oil importer harbouring the major part of the world's oil industry, the United States has a persistent interest in a stake in and preferably a control of the world's major oil provinces, wherever they are. It has an interest in Caspian and Central Asian oil reaching the world market and in investment opportunities for US oil companies.

On this basis, the United States has an evident interest in getting an economic and political foothold in Azerbaijan and Central Asia.

US policy has been to avoid any understanding between the region's oil and gas exporters and Iran, to prevent the latter from serving as a transit point. Since the end of the Cold War, the United States has viewed Iran as one of the major adversaries. For years the US policy towards Azerbaijan and Central Asia has apparently been aimed at isolating Iran, if necessary by complying with some of Russia's interests. For example, in 1995 the United States government vetoed any Iranian participation in the Azerbaijan oil consortium, but accepted Russian participation. With Russia asserting its interest in the region's oil, the US position will be under increasing pressure to change. The dilemma is that the United States seems to have an over-riding concern to avoid the oil from Azerbaijan and Central Asia reaching the Gulf.

The interest of the United States is apparently to get the Azeri and Central Asian oil to the Mediterranean instead. The reason seems to be partly to put a downward pressure on Atlantic crude prices, partly to reduce the overall supply and price risk in the world oil market caused by dependence on the Gulf.[74] Should the US position in the Middle East and especially in the Gulf weaken because of the protracted breakdown in the peace process between Israel and Palestine, the US interest in an alternative route for Central Asian oil to that of the Gulf is likely to strengthen.

The US interest also seems to be to assist Turkey economically by getting transit revenues and eventually to help Israel get secure oil supplies from a nearby Turkish port.[75] The United States in any case has formidable means to play a role in Azerbaijan and Central Asia through its oil industry, technology, capital and trade opportunities. In this respect, the US oil companies in the region, such as, for example, Chevron and Unocal, are also political actors, with an increasingly important role in the region.[76] The problem for the United States is that the partners chosen for the oil transit route, Georgia and Turkey, may be in a weak position to deliver.

Among the second-rank external actors, Iran has got little attention, in spite of the recent success of the Turkmen gas transit. Iran's interests are, briefly, to get the Caspian and Central Asian oil to the Gulf and establish close political and economic ties with the region. First, Iran has a desperate need for foreign exchange and would benefit from oil and gas transit fees. Second, with oil and gas transit, Iran would be in a better position to develop trade with the region. Central Asia could eventually become an important market for Iranian manufactured goods. In turn the combination of oil and gas transit and trade could establish Iran as a regional power in Central Asia. Third, with oil transiting from Central Asia to Iranian Gulf ports, Iran would strengthen its position in the Gulf, essentially in relation to Saudi Arabia, potentially also in relation to Iraq. Emerging as a Central

Asian power would also reinforce Iran's position in relation to its Gulf neighbours.

Iran's relations with Azerbaijan merit special attention. The present republic of Azerbaijan was part of the Persian Empire until conquered by Tsarist Russia between 1796 and 1828. It shares its language and religion with the neighbouring Iranian province of Azerbaijan. The number of Azeri speakers is probably much higher in Iran than in Azerbaijan, although estimates differ. Relations between Azerbaijan and Iran are nevertheless troubled.[77] Iran has consistently supported Armenia in the war against Azerbaijan. Azerbaijan, in turn, in the early 1990s under a nationalist government, made fairly overt claims for a unification of the two parts of the Azeri-speaking region, amounting indirectly to a territorial claim on Iran, although there is hardly any record of Azeri separatism in Iran. Finally, Azerbaijan in 1995 under pressure from the United States cancelled the Iranian participation in the Azeri oil consortium. From the Iranian perspective, Azerbaijan appears at best as an unreliable partner, at worst as an adversary and a threat to Iran's integrity. Potentially, an economic success in Azerbaijan could make the country a greater risk for Iran. Against this backdrop, controlling the flow of oil from Azerbaijan would help Iran. Instead, Iran has sought to develop close relations with Turkmenistan. For Iran, Turkmenistan represents the bridgehead to Central Asia for trade and political links.

Iran's means are favourable transit deals and trade. By choosing an Iranian outlet, as opposed to the Georgia–Turkey route or any easterly route to China, India or Pakistan, Azerbaijan and the Central Asian oil exporters could keep more of the economic rent. This fact enhances Iran's position. Turkmenistan evidently realized this when it signed the deal on the gas pipeline through Iran. For Azerbaijan and Central Asia, Iran also represents the outlet that is the most secure from Russian interference and pressure. Both Azerbaijan and Turkmenistan have a common border with Iran. Turkmenistan could eventually transit Kazakh and Uzbek oil and gas to Iran.

Iran's final trump-card would be closer relations with Russia. Iran and Russia have together supported Armenia against Azerbaijan. They now share influence in Turkmenistan. Iran and Russia have a common interest in excluding outside powers from exercising a political influence in the Caspian region and Central Asia. They could also have a common interest in preventing an alliance of the Turkic-speaking countries of the region, ultimately supported by Turkey.

Turkey's interests are, briefly, political and economic ties with Central Asia as well as transit revenues and access to oil and gas. A major preoccupation for Turkey is to reduce the dependence upon Arab Middle Eastern oil.[78] This is the reason why Turkey apparently buys any quantity of oil delivered to the Georgian port of Batumi. Turkey's quickly rising energy needs also mean that the country is a large and expanding market for gas from Central Asia. Turkey's means are less favourable transit routes, trade and the support of the United States. As already pointed out, the transit route through Georgia and Turkey is both costly and politically vulnerable compared to an outlet through Iran.

Turkey evidently aims at developing the Caspian and Central Asian markets for its industrial goods and in the longer run to become a major investor in the region. Even if a certain religious and linguistic community undeniably favours economic and political links, Turkey is in some respects in an ambiguous position.

For Turkey, trade with Russia and the Ukraine is too important to be compromised by open attempts to cross Russian interests in remote and poor Central Asia.[79] Cultural links between Turkey and Turkic Central Asia are weak and may remain so because of Central Asian ambitions of a distinctive cultural and linguistic development. Likewise, in Azerbaijan linguistic links with the Azeri minority in Iran compete for priority with linguistic links with Turkey. In this part of the world, language is politics, although religion and ethnic background often blur the issue. Only nearby Azerbaijan has some real affinity with Turkey, but even this link is weakened by differences in religion and history. So far, Turkey has been unable to exert much influence in Central Asia.[80] The Turkish transit of Caspian and Central Asian crude might perhaps be compromised by Turkey's Kurdish problem. The proposed pipeline from Georgia through eastern Turkey to the Mediterranean will not only traverse difficult mountainous territory, it will also cross Kurdish land that might cause occasional problems. The southeastern part of Turkey has been in a state of insurrection for many years. Kurdish guerrilla fighters have on several occasions attacked pipelines carrying oil from Iraq, although so far never with any lasting damage.

If the Azerbaijan oil consortium backed by the US government has its way, the oil pipeline through Georgia and Turkey is likely to be built, regardless of cost and political risks. Should the United States push for a transit route through Georgia and Turkey for Caspian oil, it could provide ground for at least a tacit alliance between Iran and Russia. When Iran was excluded from the Azerbaijan oil consortium in 1995, there were signs of an understanding between Iran and Russia.[81] Subsequently, Iran and Russia have co-operated in arms deals, and trade between them is expanding. Turkmenistan has joined these projects to a certain extent. The recent gas pipeline deal with Iran is a sign that for the moment Turkmenistan has no objection to closer ties with Iran, nor with Russia, which remains an important transit country for Turkmen gas.

There is an evident risk of oil and gas transit politics splitting the region into two camps, one with Azerbaijan, Turkey and the United States, the other with Iran, Russia and Turkmenistan, possibly also Kazakhstan and Uzbekistan. Such a division would put Azerbaijan and the outlet of Azeri oil at great political risk. There should be little doubt of Russia's incentives and abilities to defend its interests in the region. Russia's and Iran's potential manoeuvres for disturbing the flow of Caspian oil to the Mediterranean are legion, using proxies such as Armenia, Georgian dissidents or Kurdish guerrillas. In addition, should the region divide along the lines indicated, the internal political stability of Azerbaijan could also be at risk. If Russia could help unseat the preceding Azeri regime, as it did, it could eventually also make the position uncomfortable for the present one.

The new version of the great game over Central Asia is likely to go on for years, possibly for decades, until a balance of power emerges that can secure oil and gas investment as well as transit routes. Should the US-backed route from Azerbaijan through Georgia and Turkey prove to be an inadequate solution, because of high costs and political risks of disruption, the United States as Russia's and Iran's main antagonist in this game will face a difficult choice, whether to favour Iran or Russia.

By accepting a transit route through Iran, the United States would not only be recognizing Iran as a major power in international oil politics, in the Gulf and in Central Asia, but also renouncing its ambition to get the Azeri and Central Asian crude to the Mediterranean. The position of the Gulf in the world oil market would be reinforced, also strengthening the supply and price risk. For oil supplies and prices the United States would face an even more significant Gulf, but with a stronger Iran.

By accepting a stronger Russian stake and eventually the transit route through Russia to Central and Western Europe, the United States would achieve its objective of diverting the Azeri and Central Asian crude from the Gulf. This would, however, also strengthen Russia's position in the world energy markets and imply at least a tacit acceptance of the return of Russia as the dominant power in the Caspian region and Central Asia. Russia's position would be further strengthened by the combined control of the Caspian and Siberian oil resources. To sum up, for oil supplies and prices, the United States would face a more resourceful and more self-confident Russia.

Until these issues are settled, the risk is that many oil investors will lose much money in the region. The geology indicates the potential for a handsome return on oil exploration and development, but this is hardly sufficient as long as safe and inexpensive outlets are not available. Participating in the oil game around the Caspian and in Central Asia seems suited to only a small number of oil companies. Only those with a solid capital base, the ability to bear losses for years, a diversified international upstream portfolio as well as a solid experience of operating in unusually complex and difficult political circumstances are likely to remain in the region. To hedge their bets, oil companies investing in the Caspian region and in Central Asia might be well advised to improve their relations with both Iran and Russia, ultimately through investment.

On the political level, the United States remains the arbiter of the situation, but with the uneasy choice between recognizing the constant of Russia's dominance in the region or Iran's position as a rising regional power. A protracted US hesitation could even lay the ground for a closer understanding between the two. By sharing the control of Caspian and Central Asian oil and gas, Iran would still be a stronger regional power and Russia would recover some of the position lost by the collapse of the Soviet Union.

The West, first of all the United States and the oil industry, should be careful not to identify too closely with autocratic regimes whose economic success and political survival may be doubtful.[82] The West should realize that the present regimes are not necessarily the most stable partners. Indeed, the West could help its own cause by encouraging economic and political reform that would help stabilize the regimes. At the geopolitical level, the struggle for influence and investment in the Caspian region and Central Asia does not have to be a zero-sum game. Indeed, any apparent victory for the West would be more durable should Russia and eventually Iran be partners. The issue should be less one of exclusive options than of multiple ways for transporting Caspian and Central Asian oil and gas to the markets. It is also in the long-term interest of the Caspian and Central Asian oil and gas exporters to eventually balance close relations with the West with links with neighbouring Iran and Russia.

Since the events of September 2001, the prospects are, at least for some time, that a decade of rivalry between the United States and Russia over the control of Caspian and Central Asian oil and gas will be replaced by co-operation. Politically, the United States and Russia share an interest in stabilizing the region and curbing Islamic fundamentalism. Economically, they have a mutual interest in finding quick and cost-effective solutions for oil and gas development, including transportation to the markets. Already by 1999, Russia had scored an important victory by the new oil pipeline from Kazakhstan to Novorossiysk on the Black Sea. The prize is transit revenues and control of the flows. More recently, a new oil pipeline from the Ukraine to Poland has further strengthened Russia's position.[83]

For Russia, one prize extracted for supporting the United States in the 2001 Afghanistan campaign seems to be control of the oil and gas flows from the Caspian region and Central Asia.[84] Transiting oil and gas gives Russia revenues as well as leverage with volumes and market. Combining its own volumes and those of the Caspian region and Central Asia makes

Russia emerge as perhaps the world's leading oil power, exceeding Saudi Arabia in volume.[85] Russia is already the world's leading producer and exporter of natural gas. Even if the costs of extraction and particularly transportation are higher in Russia than in Saudi Arabia, the Russian economy is somewhat less dependent on oil revenues. It is in the US interest to see Russia emerge as a leading oil exporter, preferably competing with OPEC over market shares. Consequently, Russia's re-emergence as a leading oil exporter seems likely to enhance oil market instability, with price wars alternating with periods of co-operation with OPEC. Even if Russia, the Caspian region and Central Asia should export larger oil volumes, Saudi Arabia, the other Gulf States and eventually Iraq have the resource base to significantly raise volumes at lower costs. From this perspective, it would be in the interest of the United States to give priority to good oil relations with Russia and not to promote pipeline projects that compete with Russian interests. The first victim may the Baku–Ceyhan project to bring oil from Azerbaijan to Turkey. The incentive is access to Russia's vast oil and gas resources, even at high costs and under difficult operating conditions.

For the new states in the Caucasus and Central Asia, political and economic conditions have changed markedly since September 2001. A joint campaign against Islamic fundamentalism gives Russia and the United States an evident interest in the political stability of the new states.[86] The practical outcome is economic assistance, investment and military aid. Understanding between Russia and the United States also limits the freedom to manoeuvre in foreign policy for the new states.[87] The implicit deal seems to be that Russia tolerates an American economic and military presence, with Russian participation. Russia in this way becomes a more dominant neighbour, with US blessing.[88] Oil policy freedom may be an early victim.

Deferring the Baku–Ceyhan pipeline project weakens links between Azerbaijan and Turkey, constraining Azerbaijan into a closer relationship with Russia.[89] Consequently, Azerbaijan's position in relation to Armenia also suffers. Without an imminent pipeline project, the conflict between the two over Nagorno-Karabakh is of no major interest to the great powers.[90] Because of close relations with Armenia, both historically and currently, Iran is no obvious ally for Azerbaijan, although improved relations should be in both countries' interest. The impression is therefore that after 11 September 2001, Russia is, in co-operation with the United States, regaining historical positions in the Caucasus and Central Asia. Oil and natural gas are essential ingredients in this process, as Russia has the large volumes, but also the higher costs.

The US–Saudi alliance under stress

The September 2001 terrorist attacks on New York and Washington have put the US–Saudi alliance under unprecedented stress. Mounting distrust between the United States and Saudi Arabia is not linked to disagreement over oil, but to internal politics in both countries since September 2001. Strengthening pro-Israeli sentiment in the United States embarrasses Saudi Arabia and induces US politicians to distance themselves from Saudi Arabia, in spite of huge US economic, military and political stakes. Likewise, strengthening anti-Western sentiment in Saudi Arabia, particularly among the youth, embarrasses the Saudi rulers and induces them to distance themselves politically from the United States, in spite of common interests that include the survival of the Saudi regime. The fact that a possible US military withdrawal from Saudi Arabia can be mentioned indicates that profound changes in the relationship may be taking place.

The US–Saudi alliance is historically conditioned, like all other alliances, but for the United States, Saudi Arabia has usually appeared an exceptionally solid and lasting ally. The alliance has been based on oil, money and security. The history of Aramco, the Saudi national oil company, is largely also that of Saudi Arabia. It began in 1933, as King Abdul-Aziz ratified the first American oil concession.[91] The alliance was reinforced by a military dimension at the meeting of King Abdul-Aziz and US President Franklin D. Roosevelt at the Suez Canal in February 1945, which gave the United States an air force base in Saudi Arabia. Britain and France had disregarded Saudi Arabia, which opened up the country to US interests. Historical experience has tied the Saudi elite to the United States, contrary to the case in Iran and Iraq. Over decades, the United States and Saudi Arabia have had complementary interests in oil, finances, defence and Middle Eastern affairs. Saudi financial reserves and the flow of capital to the United States are mutual interests that make a strong link. The United States and Saudi Arabia are the dominant actors in the oil market. In oil matters, there has been a remarkable complementarity between the new US oil strategy and Saudi policy. Indeed, interests have been reciprocal, with the United States needing more oil at stable prices and Saudi Arabia needing outlets for incremental volumes. To stabilize the oil market, Saudi Arabia has systematically invested in excess capacity, to be able to raise output at short notice. This has been the return for the US security guarantee. Saudi Arabia still has the option to invest in capacity expansion. Also, to finance incremental investment, Saudi Arabia in 1998 declared its willingness to open the oil industry to foreign investors. So far this opening up has not materialized, but agreements on gas investment have been signed with foreign countries.

For the oil market, the linchpin is the relationship between US oil imports and Saudi production. In the late 1970s, after the first oil price rise, Saudi oil output continued rising, but less than did US oil imports. From

1973 to 1978, US oil imports corresponded to a rising proportion of Saudi oil production, with a fairly good match between the two. During the crisis years of 1979–81, Saudi oil output stayed at a high level despite quickly declining US oil imports, indicating a Saudi interest in lower oil prices. In the following years, Saudi oil production declined quickly, matching the US imports level in 1985. This indicated a Saudi policy of defending the oil price. The turn-about came in 1986, when both US imports and Saudi output started to rise again. The next change came in 1991, with a substantial increase in Saudi output to make up for lost oil production from Iraq and Kuwait. During the 1990s, both US oil imports and Saudi output have risen more or less continuously, but US oil imports until 1997 increased somewhat more than Saudi output.

Historically, the Gulf States and the United States have had corresponding interests in low prices.[92] The US concern for oil supply security matches well with the Gulf concerns for secure oil markets.[93] Saudi Arabia in particular has had an interest in providing the market with increasing volumes of oil at stable prices, if necessary through foreign participation in its oil industry. Saudi moves to invite in foreign oil companies, at least for natural gas exploration and development, seemed particularly targeted at US oil companies, aiming at further strengthening the bilateral Saudi–US relationship that has been the backbone of the oil market.

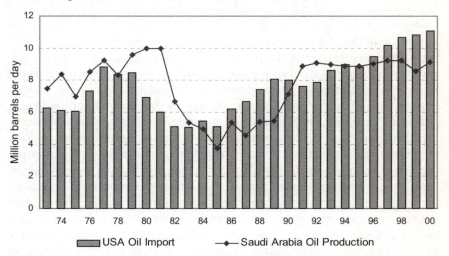

Figure 10: US oil imports and Saudi oil production 1973–2000
Source: Energy Information Administration (EIA) 2001

The Saudi regime has had a prominent foreign ally and protector in the United States. The United States has always had vital economic and strategic interests in Saudi Arabia. These interests have been growing in importance as US oil imports have risen over the past decades. Large-scale

US assistance in the development of the oil industry, the infrastructure, the armed forces, the police and the public administration has given the United States wide possibilities to influence Saudi policies. This has happened without making the Saudi state subordinate to US interests. The Saudi regime has to balance US interests against its own and also against considerations for its Middle Eastern neighbours. This is especially important in oil policy. This balancing has become much more difficult since the Gulf War and in particular since September 2001.

The close link between the Saudi monarchy and the United States carries a risk for both parties if pursued too narrowly. The problem has obviously become more acute since the September 2001 terrorist attacks. Insofar as the United States has a stake in the continuity of the Saudi monarchy, it could also be an obstacle to change. The United States does not import much oil directly from Saudi Arabia, but it is vitally dependent upon the Saudi policy of moderating oil prices, which helps keep the US oil import bill low in spite of rising volumes. The United States is also dependent on large Saudi armament purchases to offset parts of the oil imports bill and to secure jobs in the weapons industry. For the United States, a Saudi government pumping out less oil and driving oil prices up, but not buying weapons, would be highly undesirable. The United States not only has an interest in the survival of the Saudi monarchy, but even more in the continuation of present oil and arms procurement policies. For the United States, overlooking the Saudi record on democracy and human rights appears a modest payment for low oil prices and large arms sales.

Against this backdrop, the interest of the United States in the development of a constitutional monarchy in Saudi Arabia is doubtful, because democratic institutions could threaten both the oil policy and military expenditure. This may be short-sighted and in the longer term may backfire, but US politics with other countries suffer from notoriously short time horizons and equally short memories. The United States seems to have considered Saudi Arabia a limitless supplier of cheap oil and an equally limitless market for arms, regardless of the internal situation in the country. Insofar as the United States has political influence in Saudi Arabia, it has because of its economic interests tended to oppose change rather than promote it. This creates a risk of pressures building up, eventually leading to political discontinuities of which the September 2001 attacks may be a forerunner. Even US influence is unable to moderate the population pressure and the gradually deteriorating social conditions.

Being associated with political stagnation compromises the United States with an emerging Saudi opposition and possibly later Saudi governments. Since September 2001, this is a more acute issue. Competitors for Saudi oil and Saudi markets are aplenty in both Europe and Asia. For the Saudi government it is equally risky to end up in a political stalemate, seen as the dummy of US interests, even more so since September 2001. The Islamist opposition would benefit. From this perspective, the Saudi monarchy might benefit from taking some political distance from the United States, which it seems to be doing. The question is to what extent this means strengthening Islamist fundamentalist forces of opposition.[94]

Politics in Saudi Arabia take place at two distinct levels: within the royal family and between the royal family and the rest of Saudi society. Within the royal family, factions form on the basis of clans, personal ambitions and ideological orientation. Between the royal family and the rest of Saudi society, politics concern allegiances, privileges and promises. The distribution of power, wealth and income becomes increasingly thornier as population grows faster than oil revenues. Even if Crown Prince Abdullah has shown an astute sense of popular Saudi sentiments, cutting down on excessive expenditure and establishing closer links with Iran, it is an open question to what extent the Saudi royal family realistically understands the need for reform and the giving up of privileges.[95] In the past, Saudi Arabia has had its share of insurgencies and military plots. They have all failed and been put down, at times, as in Mecca in 1979, with the help of foreign troops. The most important reason for the apparent political stability has been high oil revenues that have enabled the royal family to settle disputes and calm opposition by handing out money. As oil revenues stagnate and budgetary requirements increase, this facility is less available than in the past.

Its size and complexity have historically enabled the Saudi royal family to settle disputes and conflicts internally and to organize orderly successions. Today, there are reformist as well as conservative forces within the royal family.[96] The combination of more unstable and scarcer oil revenues, mounting popular discontent, a more vigorous religious opposition and a forthcoming generation change together with the need to reassess the relationship with the United States risks paralysing royal family politics. The royal family is better at giving generous promises than at turning them into reality.

The alternative to political stagnation with the risk of mounting Islamist opposition is to combine an impending generation change in the Saudi royal family with an opening up of Saudi society and gradual liberalization of political life. This would be compatible with economic requirements to diversify away from oil and with attracting foreign oil investment. This solution risks challenging the Islamist opposition, but would find backing among the liberal opposition and possibly stabilize the regime. It would also be compatible with US interests. It would also be possible to combine more liberal economics with a constitutional Islamist regime, as is the case in Iran.

A current misunderstanding in the West is that Islamists by necessity are violent terrorists. Usama bin Laden's extremist fundamentalism is but one of the dissenting Islamist currents of thought in Saudi Arabia, others being more peaceful and more democratic in the sense that they promote legitimate rights for the people.[97] Some Islamist preachers represent opposition to Westernization in the sense of cultural and ideological subordination; others profess the need for a more open dialogue between the rulers and the ruled, as well as the need for democratic reforms, the respect for basic human rights, and the need to uncover and fight corruption. There is also a Shia opposition voicing the same grievances, but it appears more open to the outside world. The common denominator is dissatisfaction with an opaque political system and an uneven distribution of wealth and income, as well as subjugation to US interests. These various factions do not necessarily threaten the Saudi state, but they are increasingly influential and likely to affect foreign policy, economic policy, military expenditure and perhaps oil policy.

To succeed in the transition to a more open society, Saudi Arabia needs peace and stability in the Middle East. Part of Saudi Arabia's predicament is a huge military budget that represents an increasing burden as the population grows and civilian needs rise. To alleviate this burden, Saudi Arabia needs political changes in the Middle East. For historical reasons, Saudi Arabia is caught in two triangles: Saudi Arabia, Iran and Iraq, versus Iraq, Israel and Syria. In the first case, Saudi Arabia is exposed to the double menace from Iran and Iraq. In the second case, Saudi Arabia is exposed to the instability resulting from the lack of settlement of the Palestinian issue. Turkey's reappearance in Middle East politics complicates Saudi Arabia's position with the risk that Syria will be pushed into an alliance with Iraq. Saudi Arabia needs an Iraq that is neither too weak nor too strong. A weak Iraq could represent a threat to regional stability caused by disintegration. A strong Iraq represents a military threat to the Gulf States. To offset this risk, Saudi Arabia has in recent years improved relations with Iran, especially under the more moderate Khatami regime.

The Saudi search for security and regional stability also implies taking some distance from traditional US positions, not only on Israel and Palestine, but also on Iran and Iraq. This is even more evident since September 2001. The fate of the two Middle East economic summits in 1997–98 is telling. The US-sponsored summit in Qatar was a failure. It aimed at isolating Iran and Iraq, but to integrate Israel in a zone of economic cooperation from Morocco to Oman. The United States had not taken Saudi interests and points of view into account. By contrast, the Teheran summit in January of 1998 was a success, largely because of strong Saudi backing. The outcome of the two summits was to isolate Israel and the United States, not Iran and Iraq. This was, until 2001, one of the most obvious signs of a changing relationship between Saudi Arabia and the United States. The United States also has an interest in Middle East peace, stability and disarmament.[98] The problem is that a general demilitarization of the Middle East would require the participation of both Iraq and Israel, neither of which is likely to identify with US interests.

The problems of the United States in relation to Israel, Palestine, Iran, Iraq and even Saudi Arabia open opportunities for a stronger European engagement. The European powers, however, have hardly any military capacity in the area. For Western Europe to substitute for the United States in the Gulf would require the removal of military, political and ideological regional threats to the Gulf regimes. That means that Iran and Iraq would have to appear as unequivocally peaceful and co-operative neighbours, maybe together with a settlement of the Israeli–Palestinian conflict. In any other circumstances, the United States is likely to remain an essential component in the Gulf oil producer strategies, even with a large European capital market, unless US–Gulf relations should deteriorate markedly.

For United States economic interests, the most perilous factor is political frustration in the Arab Middle East, as evidenced by the September 2001 attacks. US sympathy and support for Israel, combined with an ignorance of Arab interests and the isolation of Iran, Iraq and Libya, carry an economic and political risk, creating critics and adversaries of US interests, even in moderate countries. Terrorist groups are but the most radical manifestation of a profound malaise. For the Arab countries, the US hegemony in the area since the Gulf War is becoming embarrassing, particularly as long as there is no solution to the conflict between Israel and the Palestinians. The United States, instead of contributing to finding solutions, is seen as sharpening the problems.[99] US support for Israel is widely seen as encouraging Israeli intransigence. Escalating violence in Palestine since the end of the peace process is straining the ties between the United States and the key Gulf oil exporters.[100] Israel in the longer run could strengthen both the extreme fundamentalists in the Arab world and ultimately Saddam Hussein, possibly creating the basis for a dangerous coalition. In any case, it weakens the position of the United States in the Middle East, as well as the moderate Arab governments. A more moderate Iran could also be a competitor to US interests insofar as it would represent less of a political challenge to established Arab regimes.

Indirectly, the weakening of the United States in the Middle East could serve European interests. A stronger Europe could provide some of the countries of the region with an alternative to reliance on the United States, an opportunity to weaken the US hegemony and eventually an alliance with Europe.[101] For the United States, important interests are at stake. The weakening of the US hegemony does not necessarily imply the rise of a corresponding hegemony for Europe. Western Europe, or even the

European Union, will not be able to translate its prosperity into power to make a counterweight to the United States unless it accomplishes political union and assumes a greater responsibility for the world's problems.[102]

Even after September 2001, Saudi Arabia has reasons to remain attentive to US oil interests. Extremely low oil prices would in the longer run compromise oil production in the United States, with a risk of protective measures being taken.[103] Extremely high oil prices would enhance US marginal oil production, eventually stimulate the development of alternative energy sources and bring burdens on US consumers. Saudi Arabia and the other Gulf States have a political interest in the United States being at least indirectly dependent on their oil. The US's role in this seems to be to abstain from taxing oil consumption more heavily, together with the provision of military protection. Since the September 2001 attacks, the United States seems to be taking Arab interests more heavily into account, with a stronger concern for Saudi Arabia's economic and political balancing act.

For decades, rising US dependence on oil imports and at least indirectly on Middle Eastern oil exports has not been matched by a corresponding development of policy aimed at securing long-term relations. In some cases, as with the sanctions on Iran and Libya, there is a remarkable divergence between US economic interests and US policy. In the United States there is relatively limited insight into Middle Eastern affairs, and the insight is often heavily influenced by Israeli points of view. The United States therefore suffers from an insufficient understanding of Arab issues, or Iranian ones, compared to US economic interests in the Middle East. In many ways, this discrepancy has worsened. Israel appears to be a key factor. Apparently, the prevalent thinking in the United States seems to have been that Israel could be a US stronghold in the Middle East, helping to secure US oil interests. After the September 2001 events Israel through its policies toward the Palestinians appears to be more of a liability than an asset to US interests in the Middle East.

In 1948, the United States together with most other United Nations member countries sponsored the establishment of Israel, but there were serious concerns that this might harm US interests in the Arab Middle East. In 1956–57 the United States intervened to force France, Israel and the United Kingdom to pull out of Egypt after the occupation of Sinai and the Suez Canal. Whatever the motivation, by siding with British and French aggressors, at an early stage of its history, Israel defined itself as a foreign body in the Arab Middle East. At this time the United States was not importing oil. By 1967, the United States was an oil importer and hailed the Israeli victory in the Six-Day War. Following victory and the occupation of the West Bank and Gaza, Israel initiated the policy of establishing Jewish settlements in Palestinian territories, unopposed by the United States, which by then had become Israel's paymaster.

After the 1967 war, Israel and the United States missed a historical opportunity to establish a democratic state based on the rule of law in Palestine. That would have upset the corrupt and authoritarian Arab rulers then supported by the United States, but could have provided an example for the Arab populations and in the longer run contributed to the security of both Israel and Western oil supplies.

By 1973, dependency on oil imports was rising quickly and the United States was a target of the Arab oil embargo, explicitly motivated by the desire to discontinue the Israeli occupation of Palestinian land, and prey of the subsequent oil price rise, at a time when Israel was the subject of an Arab military attack. At that time, US–Saudi relations were at a low point. By 1979, the United States had sponsored the peace treaty between Egypt and Israel, to the dismay of Saudi Arabia, which for some time refused to offset the shortfall of Iranian crude by raising its own export volumes, hurting the United States through suddenly rising oil prices.

During the 1980s Iran was the common preoccupation of the United States, Israel and Saudi Arabia, until Iraq suddenly in 1990, by the attack on Kuwait, assumed the role of the common enemy. During the whole period from 1980 to 2001, US policy toward Saudi Arabia and Israel was facilitated by the sharing of foes, at first Iran, then Iraq. The opaque character of Saudi society makes it difficult to assess the popular acceptance or rejection of this sharing of foes with both the United States and Israel.

After September 2001, Israel risks emerging as a potential loser in the US reassessment of the need for friends and allies insofar as the United States gives priority to Saudi Arabia. The risk for Israel is to be marginalized and lose influence with the United States. Any US campaign against Arab or Islamist terrorists needs to keep Israel at a distance. Already before the September 2001 terrorist attacks, Israel's heavy-handed policies towards the Palestinians were seen as a serious problem for the United States in relation to the Arab Middle East. Israel's use of the terrorist attacks as a pretext to intensify repression and military actions in Palestine is directly harmful to US interests in the Middle East and shows poor political judgement. By acting in such a way, the Sharon government has managed to define itself as a nuisance to the United States. In the aftermath of the September 2001 attacks, open dispute with Israel could serve US interests in the Arab Middle East.

The co-operation of Saudi Arabia both has been and still is essential to US interests in the Middle East, whether they concern oil, money, military affairs or intelligence. To facilitate the delicate Saudi balancing act, the United States may have to distance itself more explicitly from Israeli policies and eventually put pressure on Israel to surrender most of the

Palestinian lands and make a compromise on East Jerusalem. Since September 2001, there are few signs in this direction. Even if this were to happen, it might still not be enough to convince the Saudi government to co-operate fully with the United States. The Saudi government can less and less afford to appear as an unconditional supporter of US policies in the Middle East without risking a serious domestic backlash[104]. The Saudi restrictions on the use of US air bases are telling in this respect. Heavy US pressure on Saudi Arabia might be counterproductive and accelerate Saudi demands for a US military withdrawal.

Iraq also is increasingly important in political terms to Saudi Arabia, as a neighbour with a nationalist, anti-Western profile. The events of 11 September 2001 may accelerate Iraq's return as a force to be taken into account. Saddam Hussein is once more a leader of international importance. Oppression in Palestine plays into his hands, forcing former foes to make friendly gestures and compromising moderate regimes that are on good terms with the United States. The United States nevertheless seems to lack an effective policy on Iraq.

Sanctions have not weakened, but strengthened Saddam Hussein's regime.[105] It has profited from the sanctions through payments from smugglers and black market traders and ensured elite loyalty through patronage. Although Iraq is being contained, the regime is being preserved. An international armed strike against Iraq seems unlikely and a unilateral US strike would be excessively risky. Sanctions are heavy and could not easily be made even stricter. Attempts to unseat Saddam Hussein through sanctions and exiles may turn out to be no more effective than US policy towards Fidel Castro, but Iraq is economically and strategically more important than Cuba.

Unless a more comprehensive settlement is reached in the Middle East, Saudi Arabia is likely to be torn between fears of a stronger Iraq, motivating closer links with the United States, and the perceived need to improve relations with Iraq, motivating more political distance from Washington. A way out of the dilemma for Saudi Arabia is closer links with Iran. So US–Saudi oil relations too have changed in the wake of September 2001. The need to keep some distance from the United States for the sake of domestic political balancing may induce Saudi Arabia to be a less compliant residual oil supplier, opting for higher oil prices, which would help Iran, but not the United States.

CHAPTER THREE

OIL SUPPLIES, OPEC,
OLIGOPOLY AND POLITICS

Concentration and market power

At any given moment the actual supply of oil is politically determined, dependent on leading OPEC governments. Outside OPEC, costs and prices essentially condition investment in oil and subsequent supplies, which are price elastic, so that higher prices cause rising volumes of oil to be supplied. In the OPEC countries, especially those of the Middle East, governments decide oil investment and supplies, essentially to secure revenues, but revenue targets can be met in several ways by different combinations of prices and volumes. There are also competing objectives.

Even if conventional oil is a fairly homogeneous commodity, it has different sources with dissimilar supply costs and a variety of uses with different opportunity costs. In theory, the marginal supply cost is that of idle capacity in the Gulf, perhaps $2 a barrel, and $4–5 delivered to North Sea or US ports. Because the low-cost suppliers usually have an interest in making an excess profit beyond normal return on investment, they tend to restrict output, keeping oil prices well above their supply costs. For this reason, in practice, there is no single marginal oil supply cost. Limitations on supplies of low-cost oil open the market for oil from high-cost areas such as Alaska and the North Sea. This has been the case since the early 1970s. Cost differences make oil suppliers unequally robust to price changes. With low costs and idle capacity the Gulf represents a major price risk for other oil suppliers.

Incentives to constrain supplies coincide with high barriers to entry in the oil industry. Obstacles to newcomers lie in geology, financing and technology, apart from landowner permission. Finding oil requires access to prospective acreage, risk capital, knowledge and luck. The outcome is often a limited number of firms operating in a given oil province. Depending upon their number and cohesion, they can collectively act to capture economic rent by controlling competition and withholding supplies.[1] This was the game of the oil industry throughout most of the twentieth century, at times assisted by local governments, as in the case of Texas.[2]

In theory, the supply of oil, as a finite resource, should be a function of the expected future price and the discount rate of the landowner.[3] Oil in the ground only has a value to the landowner insofar as it can increase in price at the same pace as the return from the investment of the revenues from its immediate extraction could have brought. The expected return on revenues is in principle an important parameter when deciding the rate of depletion. In practice oil supplies seem to be inexhaustible because of new discoveries and technological progress that also reduces cost.[4] Actual price ceilings, because of technological backstop, and the long lifetime of the ultimate reserves, make the present value of oil left in the ground not much above zero for the most resource-rich Gulf countries, even when applying low discount rates.

Competitive theory assumes that the different oil suppliers have complete information about geology, especially reserves and extraction costs, and that each individual supplier does not affect the price.[5] The assumption is also that the various suppliers share the objective of maximizing revenues, although their discount rates may differ. Accordingly, the least expensive oil will be depleted first, and oil prices will gradually rise as marginal cost increases. A different performance, with oil prices rising above marginal cost, means that the low-cost producers prefer to keep oil in the ground and not to produce as much as possible, expecting a higher price for the limited volumes extracted and eventually a higher return at a later point in time on oil not extracted but left in the ground. Low-cost producers remain the masters of the game, with capacity utilization being the clue. This is more pertinent to a monopoly or an oligopolistic market with high supplier concentration than to a classically competitive market with a fragmented supply side.

This result is in apparent conflict with conventional economic wisdom but is simply explained by the fact that the oil price cannot increase indefinitely, so that there is no long-term optimization for any oil supplier. For practical economic purposes it is senseless to discount at any rate revenues anticipated decades ahead at uncertain prices. Because interests and immediate concerns diverge, the short- and medium-term policies of the various oil suppliers are not identical, laying the ground for conflict and instability.

Outside OPEC, oil supplies are essentially determined by costs and prices. Higher oil prices lead to rising supplies, and the world oil market is basically competitive, but long lead times mean that price and supply changes are not synchronized.[6] Although in recent years costs and lead times have come down, oil extraction is still marked by long lead times and heavy capital investment. Oil supply costs should also depend on oil province dynamics. In most cases, as happens in new oil provinces, bringing oil to the market has high capital costs over an initial investment period and subsequently low operating costs for many years.[7] The variable cost of lifting a barrel of oil is generally low from fields that are already developed, but high capital costs and long lead times make important barriers to the development of new oil fields and especially new oil provinces lacking infrastructure. High oil prices stimulate investment in exploration and development, but several years lapse before oil comes on stream. In the meantime, the evident risk is that the market turns and oil prices fall, compromising the economics of the project. For this reason, many oil companies prefer to operate with conservative oil price assumptions, regardless of the immediate state of the market. This caution blurs the effect of higher oil prices on future supplies, as has been evident in 1999–2000 by the reluctance of the oil industry to commit capital even with high earnings.

Mature oil provinces are an exception to this rule, with high and rising lifting costs from already developed fields that suffer from a declining output. Low oil prices tend to discourage investment in maintenance and have an immediate negative effect on the output from mature oil provinces, but not from those that are less mature. Conversely, high oil prices tend to encourage investment in maintenance and to boost marginal oil supplies from mature oil provinces, but with little immediate positive effect on actual supplies from the less mature ones.

Cost and supply characteristics make the oil market a natural oligopoly, but an unbalanced one. By the beginning of the twenty-first century, the world's two most mature oil provinces, the United States and Russia, have the lowest average output per well and probably the highest average finding and lifting costs.[8] In both the United States and Russia, promising new oil prospects, such as in Alaska and Siberia, with below national average lifting costs, tend to suffer from remote locations and high transportation costs. Consequently, in the United States and Russia, actual oil output as well as investment in new oil fields is likely to be increasingly price sensitive. In 1999–2000 the Russian oil industry responded to higher prices and increased output, helped by privatization.

By contrast, the Gulf countries, especially Saudi Arabia, but also Iraq, still represent immature oil provinces in terms of promising exploration prospects, low capital costs, short lead times and low lifting costs. Here, neither oil output nor oil investment is likely to be price sensitive for the near future, at least within realistic price ranges. For Middle Eastern oil supplies, there is no relationship between volume and prices. Instead, output and investment are subject to government discretion as well as financial, political and strategic considerations. The flexibility is enhanced by the presence of spare capacity to extract oil in several countries. In these cases, capital expenditure on spare capacity can be seen as an investment in bargaining power, in relation to other Middle East oil exporters as well as outsiders.

By comparison, by the beginning of the twenty-first century the North Sea seems to be reaching maturity, as measured by exploration successes, capital costs, lead times and lifting costs. Although there is a difference between the United Kingdom and Norway in these respects, the general outlook is that actual North Sea oil output will not be price sensitive for some time yet, but that North Sea oil investment will be increasingly sensitive to the oil price. Iran possibly is in a corresponding or even more mature situation. Finally, Central Asia and the Caspian region appear as an immature oil province in terms of exploration prospects, capital costs, lead times and lifting costs, but so far these advantages seem to be offset by the costly and risky transportation to the world market.

Historically, the oil market has at critical times acted as if oil supplies were not price elastic. The spectre of scarce oil supplies shaped the market in the two oil crises of 1973–74 and 1979–80 and drove the price far above marginal cost. In the early 1980s, oil prices were $30–40 a barrel. The costs of extraction in most cases were less than $10 a barrel, including exploration, investment and operations. The oil rent was considerable and the oil-exporting countries harvested substantial windfall profits for some time.

So far, the oil crises have had their causes in politics, not in resource scarcity. The end of oil predicted many times during the twentieth century has not materialized. The world in the 1970s and early 1980s feared a looming resource scarcity, especially for energy, but the outlook around the turn of the millennium is that of resource abundance, permitting choices. Even if capital intensity makes energy markets react slowly to price changes, in the longer run they do react, often irreversibly because of the investment involved.[9] High oil prices between 1973 and 1986 brought about structural changes in the way the world markets demand and supply energy. The share of oil in the world's energy market peaked, and subsequently it has not rebounded in spite of falling real prices.

Declining oil replacement costs imply that the world is still far from the end in the exploitation of oil resources. Apparently, world oil reserves are far from being depleted, so that prospects are for oil supplies outside OPEC to remain price elastic. This is corroborated by technological development, enhanced geological knowledge, more flexible patterns of oil industry organization, and finally, by recent discovery rates for oil. For this trend to continue, the major prospective areas of the world need to open for exploration and development by a multitude of oil companies. This would decentralize supplies and diffuse the price risk, reducing the importance of the Middle East in the oil market.

Since the doomsday predictions of the Club of Rome in the early 1970s, more oil has been extracted and consumed than at that time was thought ultimately available, even at high prices. Present proven oil reserves are greater than at any time in the past, in absolute figures as in relation to annual consumption. Non-OPEC oil discoveries, reserves and supplies have been consistently underestimated.[10] OPEC reserves and supply potential are essentially unknown because of limited exploration since the early 1970s and the potential for technological progress. This logic applies even more strongly to other developing countries.[11] Because commercial oil companies do not need to control oil reserves in quantities representing decades of forward output, they are reluctant to invest more than necessary in exploration. Therefore, it may be futile to consider energy resources as finite, at least on a worldwide basis.

A contrary view is that oil is indeed a finite resource, but that the world oil market is distorted through power concentration and that prospects are for new price shocks because of steadily less price-elastic oil supplies, so that finding rates fall, costs escalate and output declines.[12] For oil prices, bargaining power, through the concentration of market share, is more important than marginal cost. The Middle East oil exporters could raise oil prices in the 1970s, as their market share rose, regardless of low costs, but they later chose to reduce oil prices as their market share eroded through outside competition at higher costs. The strategy has apparently been to capture economic rent through high oil prices, and whenever possible by a high market share, but also to take market share through low oil prices, at least temporarily, whenever seriously threatened by other major exporters. The consequence is that Middle East oil reserve estimates are inflated for political purposes, that costs are underestimated and that leading oil-exporting countries extract their oil at unsustainable rates. Oil supplies will concentrate on the Middle East, raising the price risk, before they diminish. This view holds essentially that OPEC keeps oil prices down, not up. If that really should be the case, the world would be facing an impending oil shortage, for geological, not political reasons.[13] Sharply rising oil prices would augment the oil exporters' revenues and provide incentives for oil exploration and development as well as for developing alternative fuels, but consumers would suffer.

A more balanced view is that imperfect competition, rigidities and inertia hamper the functioning of the oil market, so that the prospects are for persistently unstable oil prices. As finding rates and cost prospects for incremental oil supplies oscillate, so the Middle East oil exporters will at times meet volume challenges by raising output and lowering prices, but at other times will use their market power to capture economic rent. This simply implies that the large Middle East oil exporters, in the future as in the past, will be unable to find a consensus and a middle ground stabilizing the oil market.

The oil market is a natural oligopoly centred on the Gulf, giving the leading Middle Eastern oil exporters discretionary power in the oil market. Insofar as the Middle East oil exporters with the lowest cost do not maximize their share of the oil market, they keep oil prices above marginal cost, leaving room for other producers with higher costs and giving incentives to oil investment elsewhere. The advantage to the Middle Eastern oil producers is incremental economic rent, profits above the return on alternative uses of capital, in a market where demand has low price elasticity. Another advantage is political influence with the ability to raise or lower oil output and to change the oil price. The disadvantage is competition from other oil exporters whose actual output may not be price sensitive, with a constant risk of losing market share.

Since 1973, the core Middle Eastern oil exporters seem to be comfortable over time with neither a rising market share caused by relatively low oil prices, nor a declining market share caused by relatively high oil prices. When they increase output and lower oil prices, their total earnings often suffer at first, even if individual exporters may gain by higher volumes compensating for lower prices. When they cut output and raise oil prices, their total income may increase in the short term, but over time they risk losing both market share and income. The temptation to use spare capacity to gain market share arises anew. Because no middle ground has been found, the core Middle Eastern oil exporters at times manage to make OPEC operate as a cartel, successfully allocating quotas and market shares, but at other times they compete for market shares, disregarding any OPEC agreement. Since 1973, spare capacity has permitted a periodic stabilization of the oil market, adjusting supplies to demand fluctuations, but it has also been a cause of sudden price declines.

This leads to the oil market paradox. The cost structure of oil supplies heads back to the Middle East and in particular Saudi Arabia. The Middle East is the residual supplier and therefore the price maker, but with a market share well below the share of reserves. For this reason, there is a tendency for the relatively scarce high-cost oil in, for example, the United States, Russia, the North Sea and elsewhere to be depleted before the relatively more abundant low-cost oil of the Middle East.

The total supply of oil in the market at any time is arbitrary, determined more by Middle East politics and government considerations than by economic factors. Because there is no relationship between oil prices and volumes extracted in the Middle East, there is no marginal cost and no stable equilibrium in the oil market. Instead, there are strong cyclical tendencies, with economic and political factors interacting and with governments playing an important role, on and off stage. The Middle East oil industries are either fully nationalized or under close government control. As a consequence, for oil there is no market in the classical sense. The dominant actors are oligopolists, a small number of suppliers. Behind the scenes are governments, not only those of the Middle East, but also those of other leading oil-exporting countries and those of the major oil importers.[14]

Even if the shifting and often conflicting oil policy objectives have a background in economic conditions and predicaments, politics should be an important aspect of the analysis. Because the core Middle Eastern oil exporters can co-operate in stabilizing the oil market, they can also threaten each other by withdrawing co-operation, challenging salient oil interests of their immediate neighbours. Therefore, they can also challenge their neighbours' essential economic interests. As a result, they can also challenge their political stability. In short, the core Middle Eastern oil exporters can harm and hurt each other through their oil policies. In extreme cases, discord over oil policy can lead to military conflict. Iraq's attack on Kuwait in 1990 and the ensuing 1990–91 Gulf War, led by the United States, can be seen as largely motivated by oil. From this perspective, the oil policies of the core Middle Eastern oil exporters have at least two dimensions, one being economic interests, another being regional concerns. Wider international concerns in some cases make up a third dimension. In this way, the oil supplies from the core Middle Eastern oil exporters should be analysed in terms of both economic needs and politics.

For this reason, the interactions of external power interests with the Middle Eastern power balance are of great importance to the oil price. Experience has shown that conflicts between Saudi Arabia and Kuwait on the one hand, and Iran or Iraq on the other, tend to drive the oil price down. This is because when under threat, Saudi Arabia and Kuwait seek support from outside, essentially from the United States, and thus need to take into consideration the US's interests as a large oil importer.[15] The counterpart is that the settlement of such conflicts can stabilize the oil price at a higher level, because Saudi Arabia and Kuwait have less need to consider US oil interests. Therefore, a minimum of mutual trust between Iran, Iraq, Kuwait and Saudi Arabia seems a necessary pre-condition for OPEC to stabilize the oil market. This is, briefly, the politics of oil in the Middle East. For Saudi Arabia and Kuwait, oil policy also has an important dimension of foreign policy and security policy, whereas for Iran and Iraq the economic dimension is more predominant. These countries represent a risk both to each other and to the oil market.

Strategies of co-operation and conflict

In the oil market, as in any other market, the suppliers can gain from co-operation and lose from unlimited competition over market shares. Insofar as the major oil producers are rent seekers, not volume or market share maximizers, they may have more flexibility and less difficulty in finding co-operative solutions than suppliers in industries with less economic rent. Capacity utilization is the key. Insofar as withholding supplies relative to demand makes oil prices rise relatively more than the volume loss, it can be rewarding. The cost of keeping idle capacity can be modest insofar as variable costs are small in relation to capital costs, and the latter are depreciated. Idle capacity is not always necessarily costly in the oil industry. The other option is flooding the market, so that supplies increase relative to demand, making oil prices fall. Idle capacity represents a constant threat to oil market stability. For co-operation to work the interdependence must be evident and there must be some reciprocity, meaning a mutual reward as well as a mutual punishment.[16]

In the oil market, the low price elasticity of demand gives unusually strong incentives to co-operation, because small volume differences can make big price and income differences. From this perspective, the oil market is a co-operative game; collusion is possible to the benefit of all suppliers. Because one major supplier can influence the outcome for all oil suppliers, it is a non-zero-sum game. The critical participants are Iran, Iraq, Kuwait and Saudi Arabia.

The strong supply-side concentration with its oligopolistic features provides high risks for the major producers if they do not find co-operative solutions on market shares. Aiming at a larger market share can bring about retaliation as punishment for mutual cheating or defection, and a consequent price war. There are also strong incentives to cheat or to defect. Cheating has been a standard feature of every OPEC agreement. Defection has occurred from time to time. The absence of instant responses and symmetrical behaviour reinforces the temptation to make gains at the expense of others that continue co-operation and take the losses, getting the sucker's payoff or the fool's reward.[17] This is a permanent feature of the oil market and is descriptive of the problems of co-operation within OPEC and also between OPEC and some of the other major oil producers.

Insofar as the supply of oil appears finite, a small number of producers can have strong incentives to withhold supplies in order to capture economic rent.[18] Insofar as oil demand is comparatively inelastic, small changes in volumes supplied can have a huge price impact. In the oil market, maximizing economic rent can be quite different from maximizing income. Maximizing economic rent could imply reducing production in order to keep oil in the ground, push up the price and stretch the lifetime of an apparently finite resource.[19] The point has been proven by the oil crises of 1973–74 and 1979–80 as well as by OPEC co-operation in less dramatic circumstances.

The oil market can be seen as a game with some resemblance to the Prisoners' Dilemma, but it is a game at several levels and with different dimensions in economics, politics and time. The Prisoners' Dilemma is a game theory concept that shows the disadvantage of not reaching a binding agreement, in this case by the risk of stiffer individual sentences for each of two suspected criminals not knowing what the other will say. In a market-place, duopolists, two sellers that control supplies, each setting the price without knowing how the other will price, correspondingly face the risk of forgoing potential profits by not colluding or by not trusting each other. This is often the problem of oligopoly, few suppliers controlling the market. The dilemma is that it often pays to collude and act as a collective monopolist, but that it also pays for each of them to cheat and supply more than the share agreed upon, assuming that the others will respect the deal and defend prices. This approach has relevance to internal OPEC politics and to relations between OPEC and the leading non-OPEC suppliers.

Most of the non-Middle Eastern OPEC members, especially Nigeria and Venezuela, are on record as having cheated, evidently assuming that the Gulf core would stabilize oil prices. Among the Middle Eastern OPEC members, both Iraq and Kuwait have cheated on quotas. Iraq during the 1980s disregarded OPEC agreements, leaving the defence of oil prices to the richer Gulf countries. Kuwait likewise in the late 1980s disobeyed and produced above the agreed quota.

The supply politics of the oil market can be seen as a repeated game, as the strategic interaction between a small number of participants occurring in the same form many times. This enables the participants to learn about each other's strategies and therefore anticipate their adversaries' moves and prepare retaliatory measures as incentives or sanctions. The learning can over time change the game. The leading OPEC members have gained considerable experience in dealing with each other and with the leading non-OPEC oil suppliers, enabling them to better evaluate risks and opportunities. For example, during the 1990s, Iran and Saudi Arabia evidently learnt about each other's strategies, over time facilitating co-operation. To some extent, this boils down to a tacit mutual understanding of the risks and rewards of conflict and co-operation, with symmetrical behaviour. Since 1997, the Saudi signals to Iran have evidently been those of reciprocity and co-operation. For both, Iraq represents the major future oil market risk. Iraq has been out of OPEC formal decision making for many years and little is known about Iraqi intentions.

The success of participation in the oil market for the major producers can be analysed in terms of market shares and prices. Those suppliers that gain on both market shares and prices can be described as free riders, benefiting from the co-operation of others. Those suppliers that pursue a rising market share in a context of falling prices can be described as testing their competitive edge, eventually to gain positions for future bargaining. Those suppliers that suffer a loss of market share in a context of rising oil prices essentially gain from co-operation. Finally, those suppliers that lose market share in a context of falling prices can be described as reaping the fool's reward, for behaving as if the others did co-operate, when in fact they do not. These categories are pertinent to experiences in the oil market, especially for the oligopolistic suppliers that determine the outcome.

		Oil Prices	
		Rising	Falling
Market Share	Rising	*Enjoying a free ride*	*Testing the competitive edge*
	Falling	*Gaining from co-operation*	*Getting the fool's reward*

Table 2: Oil market experiences by prices and market shares

Within these categories, the position of free rider is the most enviable. Gaining market share while the others co-operate by withholding volumes to defend prices is a comfortable position, boosting economic rent. The suppliers that follow this strategy successfully appear as the oil market's winners. The next best category is that of participating in a successful co-operation, at least so long as the price gain more than outweighs the volume loss, meaning a rising economic rent. Testing the competitive edge by raising volumes as prices fall is not a prescription for capturing economic rent, but it can eventually represent a rational attempt at securing a position for future bargaining. Losing market share as prices fall is the least enviable position, but it can also represent an attempt at taking a conciliatory stance in order to incite the others to co-operate. Anyway, the suppliers falling into this category appear as the oil market's losers. Revenue needs make the Middle East oil exporters economically and politically vulnerable, at times inviting attacks through low oil prices.

Historically, Iraq has consistently tried to enjoy the benefits of being a free rider, aiming at a rising market share, leaving price stabilization to the rest of OPEC. Iran has often been in the position of reaping the fool's reward, losing market share in a context of falling oil prices. Kuwait's strategy has at times been to test the competitive edge, aiming at higher market share with falling prices. Saudi Arabia has a more mixed record, at times testing the competitive edge by aiming at a higher market share with lower oil prices, as in 1986 and again in 1997, at times reaping the fool's reward by losing market share with lower prices, as in 1983–85 and again in 1998, but mostly the aim has been to gain by co-operation to stabilize oil prices, with some renouncement of market share. This has been evident anew since 1999.

Engaging in a price war to gain oil market shares causes oil revenues to fall, as in 1997–98, but co-operating with neighbours and other OPEC countries to cut output and raise prices can yield higher oil revenues, as in 1999–2001. If fully utilizing present capacity carries a heavy economic risk, there are few compelling arguments to invest scarce capital resources in capacity expansion that may never be needed, except perhaps as a bargaining chip at OPEC meetings. Rising population and income requirements evidently strengthen short-term needs over long-term strategy.

Because oil supply decisions in OPEC countries are acts of state and the relationship among the leading oil suppliers is that of independent states, OPEC cartel politics should also be analysed from the perspective of international relations. There is some analogy between OPEC politics and the relations between the major powers during the Cold War, in the sense that the parties concerned make interdependent decisions and are able to inflict considerable harm on each other, but there is a basic difference. In the military arena of the Cold War, the nuclear deterrent could eventually be used once only, to great mutual damage. In the economic arena of OPEC politics, the deterrent of oversupply can be used, withdrawn and eventually used again. Oil supplier interdependence has a more dynamic character than the Cold War stalemate, but there is an evident risk of escalation.

The potential damage is not only economic but also military, as shown by Iraq's subsequent wars on Iran and Kuwait. There is evidently in OPEC politics the potential that a dispute over oil prices, market shares and revenues escalates into a total conflict, meaning war, with the aim of politically destroying the adversary and controlling its resources. The balance of power within OPEC, especially the Middle East OPEC core, not only depends on oil and money, but also on population, armament and outside alliances.

The relationship between salient OPEC countries is intrinsically conflictual because of divergent interests in relation to both oil prices and market shares. Normally, this conflictual relationship leads to continuous bargaining, a process in which concessions are offered and tacit or explicit threats are presented.[20] The ability to offer concessions depends on discretionary power and flexibility. The ability to threaten depends on a credible deterrent, whose ultimate success may be in its existence, not its use. The most successful oil price wars may be the ones that never take place, but eventually lead to serious negotiations to avoid mutual damage. To be effective, the deterrent must influence the other parties' decisions. To be rational, the deterrent must embody a reply to an eventual retaliation, which means offering a dynamic solution.

Normally, the conflictual interaction between OPEC countries is about setting oil prices and taking market shares, not about destroying each other. To avoid escalation and total conflict, the conflicting parties must leave each other room for manoeuvre and eventually a way out. Otherwise, the risk of mutual damage is great. In OPEC politics, this limits the power of the low-cost producers, because the differences in resource endowment and policy arsenals present an incentive for the higher-cost producers to escalate the conflict to a level where their position is stronger, meaning essentially more people and greater military strength. Again, as shown by the 1990–91 Gulf crisis, the low-cost producers have an intrinsic interest in avoiding such escalation and it is in their interest to compromise.

The higher-cost producers that have expectations of both oil prices and market shares based on political bargaining rather than marginal cost realize this. In plain words, Kuwait and especially Saudi Arabia are expected to take Iran's and Iraq's interests into account when making their oil policies, setting oil prices higher than they would have preferred based on their own interests and renouncing market share. This can be seen as an incentive for Iran and Iraq to behave peacefully toward richer and militarily weaker neighbours and not to escalate the conflict. Such an accommodation can also provide the basis for a mutual gain in the oil market. In the late 1990s, this seemed to work with Iran. Failure to reach such an accommodation would have forced both sides to call on sanctions, or at least to threaten to.

For Saudi Arabia and Kuwait, the obvious threat to make is that they will flood the market, causing economic damage to the higher-cost producers, if not also to themselves, with resulting mutual damage. So far, Iran and Iraq do not have any corresponding oil deterrent, in the absence of which they could be tempted to escalate the conflict. The option of shutting in oil capacity obviously also exists for Iran and Iraq, but the relatively high cost makes it doubtful whether the option will be used voluntarily. Iran's oil exports were shut down in 1979–80, but as the result of revolutionary turmoil, not because of a political decision. The ultimate reply to an escalating conflict is for the low-cost oil producers to seek foreign protection, as was the case with Kuwait and Saudi Arabia during the 1990s. The response for Iran and Iraq could eventually be to invite in foreign oil companies on generous terms to expand capacity. The outcome could be mutual damage.

For Iran and Iraq, to represent an actual or potential political and military threat to the low-cost producers is a bargaining asset in OPEC, which can provide additional revenues through price and quota agreements. If they pursue this asset too far they risk retaliation and eventually economic hardship through low oil prices. Correspondingly, Kuwait and Saudi Arabia represent a serious economic threat to Iran and Iraq, but if they pursue this asset too far, they risk political and even military retaliation, as in 1990. Promises constitute the counterpart to the threats. The low-cost producers can promise Iran and Iraq a certain level of oil revenues in return for political and military moderation. Correspondingly, Iran and Iraq may promise political and military moderation in return for oil revenues. Such promises are credible and effective as incentives only insofar as they have their counterpart in threats and sanctions.

In the oil market, as in other oligopolistic markets, bargaining power and the ultimate ability to influence price development are functions of flexibility and the ability to enforce threats and promises. Initiative is crucial. It is also a question of balancing proactive and reactive measures. For the low-cost producers, such as Kuwait and Saudi Arabia, keeping control of oil prices ultimately requires the ability to adjust volumes up or down, if not in co-operation with other OPEC countries then as unilateral measures of retaliation. Therefore, for the low-cost producers, investing in capacity represents a proactive measure with the intention of keeping level with other OPEC countries in the competition for market share and revenues. As such it constitutes a deterrent. This evidently also applies to capacity that normally will not be fully utilized. Using idle capacity to bring oil prices down and to regain market share represents a reactive measure, the enforcement of the threat. To retain bargaining power by representing a credible threat, the low-cost producers need idle capacity that eventually could be called upon at short notice, but its actual use should take place with great discretion. Investing in idle capacity is also an option for higher-cost producers, but for them it is a relatively more expensive proposition.

Any bargaining also includes pledges to reach compromises. Hence, for the low-cost producers, the ability to withhold supplies is crucial. Normally, this requires a financial surplus, as in the case of Kuwait, or the potential for budget cuts, as in the case of Saudi Arabia. From this perspective, a budget surplus, or the potential for budget cuts, in some OPEC countries represents a promise, an incentive for the others to reach a compromise on oil prices and quotas. Actually cutting volumes represents an enforcement of the promise. Nevertheless, withholding supplies can also happen by default, as was the case during the Iranian revolution.

The basis for bargaining over oil prices within OPEC can be seen as the relationship between withholding capacity and idle capacity, which determines the strength of those that want higher prices and those that want lower ones. Pledges to cut or raise volumes cannot be taken for granted. OPEC price and quota agreements must be enforceable, depending on the ultimate authority, that is, ability to affect the market balance. For example, if a coalition of OPEC countries that wants to raise oil prices is able to credibly muster a certain withholding capacity, any coalition of countries with opposite price interests should be able to muster at least an equally large idle capacity to demonstrate a credible deterrent. Correspondingly, if a coalition of OPEC countries that wants oil prices to fall is able to muster a certain idle capacity, a coalition of countries with opposite price interests should be able to muster at least an equal withholding capacity to neutralize the threat of the former.

This relationship between capacity to expand output and capacity to reduce it is crucial not only in the bargaining preceding the formal OPEC sessions, but also in the continuous adjustment of the supply side to the fluctuations of oil demand. In the oil market, power is not only a function of size, but also of flexibility. Influence comes with both idle capacity and budgetary freedom. Kuwait is so far the country that most enjoys this combination of assets. For the future oil price, Kuwait's relations with its immediate neighbours, Iran, Iraq and Saudi Arabia, may be crucial, in spite of Kuwait's small size in terms of both population and oil exports. Its assets make Kuwait a valuable ally to any coalition among oil suppliers. Kuwait is likely to exploit this advantage also to enhance security, remaining an unpredictable factor in the oil market.

The conflictual co-operation within OPEC invites brinkmanship. The smaller producers can more easily cheat on quotas, because their price impact is limited. The larger suppliers, whether low cost or high cost, risk retaliation because of the economic damage that their cheating inflicts upon the other parties. A salient case is Kuwait's oil policy in the late 1980s. After the termination of the war between Iran and Iraq in 1988, Kuwait saw the latter country as a threat to its security. Kuwaiti policy was to break OPEC agreements and to overproduce to bring down oil prices and to deprive Iraq of oil revenues to finance the military build-up.[21] This was an explicitly conflictual oil policy, chosen because Kuwait, rightly, did not trust the intentions of the Iraqi regime. In hindsight, by overproducing as a defensive measure against a potential aggressor, Kuwait contributed to the conflict escalation that led to the Iraqi invasion and to the Gulf War. By seeking to deprive Iraq of oil revenues, Kuwait also made Iraq's financial crisis worse and provoked the Iraqi regime to commit desperate acts.

The confrontation amounted to a mutual application of deterrents. Kuwait enforced the threat of overproducing to bring prices down. Then Iraq used its military threat with the intention of politically doing away with Kuwait, incorporating the country, its oil resources and other assets. Ultimately, foreign allies rescued Kuwait, but the basic elements of the conflict remain. This is also a story of how a limited conflict over oil prices can escalate into a total conflict, war. In hindsight, whatever Iraq's intentions might have been, Kuwait's pre-crisis oil policy left Iraq little room for manoeuvre.

Venezuela has on several occasions practised a conflictual oil policy in relation to OPEC. During the 1990s, Venezuela invested in capacity expansion, not to keep idle capacity, but to take market share. In the US market in particular, competition with Saudi Arabia intensified, which in 1997 was one of several factors to make Saudi Arabia opt for a higher output, driving oil prices down. Venezuela's strategy of conflict ultimately met a conflictual response, causing mutual damage. Like any stalemate in the oil market, it was a temporary situation, which in turn was replaced by an agreement and a mutual gain in the spring of 1999.

For the leading oil exporters, as oligopolistic suppliers, co-operation has the attraction of restraining the supply of oil and raising the price and revenues, and at the same time stretching out the lifetime of the reserves. This view is pertinent insofar as oil is seen as a scarce resource, so that present output compromises future output. From this perspective, the interest of the suppliers is to limit oil extraction and receive the maximum economic rent. This perspective was predominant in the 1970s and 1980s, when the paradigm prevailed that oil resources were limited and that there was a potential scarcity of oil and other forms of energy. This paradigm underpinned ideologically the co-operation of OPEC countries and strengthened OPEC as a cartel. Libya's decision in the early 1970s to curb oil output was motivated by concerns over the assumed limited resource base and the lifetime of oil extraction. Present extraction was seen as compromising future output, so that forsaking extraction today would be tomorrow's gain. Extraction at historical rates was seen as unsustainable. Libya's move set in motion a process that ultimately led to the first major oil price jump in 1973–74.

The spectre of scarcity gave incentives to extract oil according to reve- nue targets. In this model, as oil exports reach a certain value, which may be targeted in the budget and politically endorsed, the country in question responds to oil price increases by extracting less oil, not more. This is the backward-bending supply curve, meaning that oil supplies are negatively price elastic, at least in certain cases. The most recent case was Iraq in 1998, as the country was permitted by the United Nations to export oil by revenue targets.

The income needs of the rentier state

The important Middle Eastern oil exporters decide their oil policies in a complex context where income considerations mix with political concerns of internal stability and external threats and alliances. Disputes over oil price levels and oil market shares are but one dimension of a conflictual relationship that also includes territorial and ideological disputes as well as military threats among oil exporters. For OPEC, the historical problem has been to balance the long-term concerns of the oil exporters on the Arabian Peninsula, with a low population and a preference for low oil prices, with the short-term interests of the populous oil exporters, essentially Iran and Iraq, that need high oil prices. In recent years, high population growth has raised Saudi Arabia's income needs, making the country less resilient to lower oil prices and possibly strengthening short-term revenue interests over long-term oil price interests. Even if little is known about the Iraqi economy, there is a possibility that huge oil reserves and the potential for economic diversification will moderate dependence on oil revenues and eventually somewhat strengthen long-term oil price interests over short-term revenue interests.

Since no major Middle Eastern oil exporter so far has been able to industrialize and to live off the normal return on investment, they all depend on the economic rent accruing from oil. The dependence on economic rent means living off revenues without a corresponding investment. This may be politically expedient in the short term, but entails serious economic risks in the longer run, as was evident during 1998 when oil prices plummeted. The entire operation of the governments and the countries concerned depends upon economic rent from oil.[22] This fact distinguishes the major Middle East exporters from practically all other important oil exporters, especially those of the North Sea. Outside the Middle East, only Venezuela is in the same league. In economic terms, the dependency means that the major Middle East oil exporters essentially rely upon exports of a single commodity, oil, in some cases supplemented by exports of natural gas and petrochemicals.

The dependency on economic rent is a common predicament, as was most recently shown by the oil price collapse of 1998. The major Middle East oil exporters, also those Gulf producers with low lifting costs, experienced serious financial problems during 1998 because of low oil prices. The exception was Iraq, whose income increased as a result of rising oil export volumes, although from a low level. The problems were particularly awkward for Iran, but the more prosperous Gulf States also suffered. They all experienced deteriorating payments balances and budget deficits. The oil price collapse was a shared economic disaster with potentially ominous social and political repercussions. During the preceding years of relatively high oil prices, the major Middle East oil exporters, including the Gulf States, had been increasing public expenditure in response to demographic pressures and rising expectations. The common predicament in the late winter of 1999 provided the ground for a remarkably swift agreement on volume cuts and oil price stabilization at a much higher level, although external factors also played a role.

The experience of low oil prices from late 1997 until early 1999 showed that the major Middle East oil exporters share a threshold of economic pain when oil prices are low. The exact level of the threshold varies by countries and circumstances, as does the intensity of the pain, but there is undeniably a common interest in avoiding excessively low oil prices. From a comparative perspective, it is evident that countries such as Kuwait or the United Arab Emirates have much more robust economies than do, for example, Iran or Iraq, because of earnings from huge foreign assets. Relatively wealthy Saudi Arabia in 1998 suffered a negative economic growth of about 8 per cent, with a sudden deterioration of the current account balance. Low oil prices caused export revenues to fall by about 40 per cent, with a fiscal crisis brewing.[23]

In the Middle East, oil has caused a special, capital-intensive mode of development. With high oil revenues, capital accumulation could take place at a much higher rate in the public sector than in private business. The control of the accumulation process moved from private capitalists to public sector bureaucrats and autocratic rulers. Oil money strengthened the state and the bureaucracy in relation to private business, and created a distinctive political system based on the centralization of petroleum revenues with the state.[24] Ample oil revenues essentially mean that the state in these countries is a distributor of economic rent and favours instead of being a tax collector and redistributor. Private production, exports and investment got a reduced importance in the context of the state-run oil economy. The private sector lost political weight.

The political process is briefly that the rulers hand out selective privileges, financed by oil revenues, in return for loyalty and support from a largely parasitic private sector.[25] The access to large oil revenues channelled through the treasuries is a distinctive feature of the state in the oil-exporting Middle Eastern countries. The oil revenues make the state a distributor of economic rent from oil and therefore of privileges and transfers. This is radically different from the role of the state as a tax collector and a redistributor of money, which is the case in most other countries. This is the rentier state.[26] Most economic activities outside the petroleum sector depend on government permits, contracts, support and protection. This is usually coupled with an absence of taxes on property and income, except for the religious tax, *zakat*. Consequently, the Middle Eastern oil exporters have no market economy, but rather a protected concessionary and distributive economy, directed by the government. The contrast with the independent capitalist development of the Western world is striking. In the developed capitalist economies, organized economic interests use the state for their political purposes. In the Middle East oil-exporting countries, the state uses private business for its political purposes. This is a basic feature of the rentier state.

The result is the two-tiered economy. The public sector represents the developed part. It consists of the state apparatus, the national oil company, other key state enterprises and the leading financial institutions, owned or controlled by the state. It accounts for most of the value added. The private sector is less developed. It is dependent upon selective favours and transfers. Private businesses usually operate in the areas of imports, trade or services, but seldom in large-scale manufacturing. Agriculture is in most cases marked by a low productivity and is dependent upon public support. The merchant class, traders and craftsmen in the bazaar, needs differentiation. Some merchants have succeeded through public favours and concessions to gain considerable wealth. Imports and large-scale trading have marginalized others.

The absence of direct taxation has reduced the need for the state to prove its legitimacy to the population. When the state does not impose taxes on wealth and income, the need for liberal and democratic reforms diminishes. Instead, the state can buy legitimacy and support by granting selective economic privileges.[27] The bottom line of commitments to buy support makes up the critical minimum of oil revenues required. With oil revenues below the critical minimum the governments concerned are forced to make embarrassing choices about which one of the political clients to alienate by cutting transfers, at what magnitude and in what sequence. This has been the case repeatedly since the mid-1980s. Persistently low oil revenues make a powerful force for economic reform, disengaging the state and opening markets, with ultimately profound political consequences. This was the case in Iran and Saudi Arabia in 1998–99. When oil revenues stay below the critical minimum for a relatively long period, the taxation of income and property becomes a necessity, with strong arguments for representative government ensuing.

There are few reliable data on income distribution in the Middle East oil-exporting countries. A reasonable proposition may be that the surge of oil revenues in the 1970s and early 1980s at first laid the basis for a general prosperity, but that the measures of austerity imposed since the mid-1980s have tended to affect the poor more than the rich, but with profound differences between countries. In Iran, income distribution was highly unequal under the shah's reign, but has evidently become much more equal since the Islamist revolution. In Iraq, income distribution may have been relatively equal until the outbreak of the war with Iran in 1980 and has since deteriorated markedly. By contrast, the rulers of the Gulf States, including Kuwait and Saudi Arabia, have more consistently distributed the oil wealth to their populations in the form of social benefits, services, subsidies and jobs.[28] In these countries, income distribution is much more equal among citizens than among the working population, which includes a large number of foreign workers. The problem of the citizen population is not so much low incomes as unemployment and to some extent a questionable ability to work.[29]

The selective favours have their counterpart in equally selective measures of discrimination. The groups that do not benefit from the selective favours feel themselves to be second-class citizens. In the Gulf countries, contrary to Iran and Iraq, there are a large number of foreign workers with an inferior economic, political and social status. As an instrument of power, oil money is supplemented by use of the military.

The growth and power of the military are salient common features of most countries of the Middle East, whether oil exporting or not.[30] Military officers have repeatedly intervened to keep countries and political systems together, so that military rule has in many cases been the rule rather than the exception.[31] Iraq is a salient case. The social origins of the military, especially the junior officers, are to a large extent in the urban middle and lower middle classes. Gradually, the military establishment has become a conservative force in the Middle East. At the outset, military rule was socially radical, aiming at redistributing wealth and income, carrying out profound reforms and asserting national interests against the colonial legacy. It has over decades acquired its own vested interests, meaning budgetary appropriations, training and the most modern equipment, apart from personal fringe benefits and political influence.[32] In the oil-exporting countries the sudden influx of large oil revenues proved an irresistible temptation for the military establishment to demand more money. The military establishment represents a key part of the new class of technocrats, wielding power, but without the ability to earn revenues. Like the techno-crats of the public sector, the military establishment is essentially professional, recruited by merit.

Middle Eastern oil exporters have a preference for military spending not shared by oil exporters elsewhere. In 1998, Mexico spent less than 1 per cent of gross domestic product, GDP, on the military, Indonesia about 1 per cent, Malaysia, Norway and Venezuela about 2 per cent, Iran about 3 per cent, but Oman and Saudi Arabia about 13 per cent.[33]

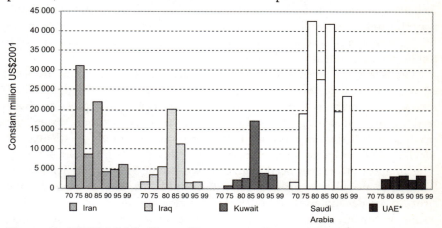

Figure 11: OPEC Middle East military expenditures 1970–1999
Source: The International Institute for Strategic Studies (IISS)

Not only regional conflicts but also foreign arms dealers, assisted by their governments, have convinced oil-exporting Middle Eastern rulers of their need to buy the most sophisticated and expensive military hardware. Local officers and friends and family members of the rulers also help in return for a commission. Military expenditure can indicate external threats, internal threats or the political weight of the military establishment and of those profiting from arms contracts. Figures on military spending are difficult to verify and the following data may be too conservative. Many governments are reluctant to reveal the scope of their military effort, but throughout the region a figure of between 12 and 15 per cent of GDP or between 30 and 40 per cent of oil revenues has been spent on military purposes since 1973.[34] Since the mid-1980s military spending has diverted funds from urgent civilian needs, such as health, education, infrastructure and food imports. High military expenditure helps the armed services compete for personnel and draw competence away from more productive civilian tasks.

High oil revenues in 1999 and 2000 have caused military spending to increase again.[35] Since the end of the Cold War, the Middle East has been the world's leading market for arms and its most militarized region. High military expenditure means conflict between civilian and military priorities, resulting from the persistently powerful political position of the armed forces and the consequent unproductive use of scarce resources. For external politics, the rearmament indicates the persistence of regional threats, tensions and conflict potential.

The military burden gives the oil-exporting countries flexibility in budgetary policies, provided that it is politically possible to cut money intended for the armed forces and that no serious threats appear on the horizon. Reducing military budgets would enhance oil policy flexibility. Cutting wasteful military spending is an alternative to raising oil revenues to meet the bottom line of revenues required to finance social services and the large public sector essential to employment.

The lack of representative political institutions exacerbates the problem of accommodating social and generational change and of redistributing income. Autocratic governments, with varying degrees of repression, have traditionally gained legitimacy by offering services without taxing the population.[36] Rising oil revenues at first financed rising public expenditure. Declining oil revenues have more recently caused cuts in public services. The political effect has been a gradual weakening of political legitimacy. The rapid population growth since the mid-1970s has exacerbated the problem of declining oil revenues. The sudden rise in oil revenues led to rising investment in health. The immediate result was falling mortality rates, but without birth rates declining significantly. Subsequently, investment in education benefited large youth cohorts, but they did not always find suitable jobs in a labour market depressed by declining oil revenues.

The leaps in oil revenues in the 1970s and early 1980s enabled the rulers of most Middle Eastern oil exporters to disengage their domestic economies from the world economy. Huge rentier revenues permitted the rulers to apparently square the circles of economic policy. Oil revenues permitted investment and consumption to increase simultaneously at high rates. Public expenditure could be raised as taxes were reduced. Oil revenues permitted selective and generous subsidies to both consumers and producers. Domestic prices were to a large extent decoupled from those of the world market. Heavy investment was made in both human and real capital, especially in ambitious infrastructure projects, but structural rigidities and market distortions were maintained.

The return on this investment is generally poor.[37] Since the early 1980s the countries of the Middle East have had low economic growth rates, except for the late 1990s, when oil revenues suddenly rose. The reasons are stagnant or declining productivity and the absence of structural reforms. The outcome is declining average living standards and increasing social inequalities. Poverty is advancing quickly and unemployment rates are among the world's highest. Equally seriously, the Middle East oil exporters do not seem to be able to manage any substantial diversification of their income base.[38] With a few honourable exceptions, the region sells almost only crude oil, oil products and natural gas to the outside world. For this reason the Middle East is missing commercial and industrial opportunities in a more open and economically interdependent world.

The economic monoculture in countries as different as Iraq, Iran and Saudi Arabia has caused remarkably parallel economic, social and political problems, but they are at different stages of maturity within a cycle of stages and events, which in substance, but not in form, have strikingly similar features. The basic common problem is the rentier economy, its exposure to oil market risk and consequent income discontinuities.[39] Because of differences in resource endowment in relation to population Iran was the worst hit by low oil prices in 1997–99, but Saudi Arabia was also badly affected. From a historical perspective, Iran is the most advanced case, Iraq probably the least, in a cycle of oil dependence that at first brings prosperity, then unmakes it.

The first stage is the establishment of the rentier state and the rise of the new class. The high oil revenues in the 1970s and early 1980s caused profound social change, uprooting the traditional society. During this period, the distributive rentier state was established, with an increasingly parasitic private sector. At this time, the merchant class was largely marginalized by the rising technocratic and military class. The rentier state also made substantial efforts in infrastructure, housing, health and education. At this stage, distribution of wealth and income was not an important political issue, except in Iran, where the rentier state was more established and inflationary pressures exacerbated the distribution issue. By contrast, in Iraq and Saudi Arabia, consensus in the 1970s was that the entire nation benefited from the oil boom.

The second stage is the consolidation of technocratic power at the expense of the merchant class and poorer parts of the population. In Iran this happened in the 1960s and early 1970s; in Kuwait, Iraq and Saudi Arabia ten years later. With stagnant or declining oil and gas revenues, the distribution of wealth and income suddenly became an important political issue.

The third stage is the new class refusing to give up privileges and power, in the face of rising opposition. In Iraq the new class has an important military component, in Saudi Arabia a royal part that cherishes privileges. In Iran confrontation took place in the late 1970s, in the other countries it has been less acute. The problem of accommodating social and generational change and of redistributing income is exacerbated by the absence of representative political institutions.

The fourth stage is the new class losing power. So far, this has happened only in Iran. In the other countries, the position of the new class, civilian and military, seems precarious unless compromises are made with the various forces of opposition.

Within this general cycle there are profound differences between countries, and outcome is not determined but conditioned by oil prices and political skills. Low oil prices put the rentier regimes under severe pressure, but also represent a challenge for reformers. This has been evident in Iran, Kuwait and Saudi Arabia since 1998. High oil prices dampen political pressure to change and can strengthen those conservative forces that fight economic and political reform. This has been evident in both Iran and Saudi Arabia.

When put under severe pressure, when resources are insufficient to satisfy the client groups and support is withering, rentier states can collapse or turn to external aggression. The fiscal crisis of the rentier state, caused by insufficient oil revenues, easily becomes a survival crisis for the regime.[40] Iran in the late 1970s is one salient case; Iraq in the late 1980s is another. The high petroleum revenues of the 1970s and early 1980s stabilized the rentier states. Subsequently low oil prices contributed to political destabilization. The Iranian regime collapsed under stress in 1978–79 because of falling oil revenues, a high priority given to the military and heavy industry and a grossly unequal income distribution. The Iraqi regime in 1989–90 suffered from falling real oil revenues. With a commitment to high military expenditure, it was unable to both import food and service the foreign debt. Even if the Iraqi debt to other Arab countries was unenforceable, the Iraqi government was in a precarious financial situation. This was one of the motives for choosing external aggression, attacking Kuwait, to eventually avoid a social and political upheaval with the prospects of a bloody end to the regime. A third way out, economic and political reform, at the time seemed out of the question.

Even when oil prices are high, as in 2000 and 2001, the need to create jobs is urgent in the Middle East. Youth unemployment is in many cases between 30 and 50 per cent. The need to replace foreign workers with locals, as in Saudi Arabia, raises difficult issues of labour productivity and income distribution. Iraq has traditionally been the exception, as a welfare state with relatively good social conditions. This is no longer the case, because of the Saddam Hussein regime, the war against Iran, the Gulf conflict and the subsequent embargo.

The highly centralized political leadership of the Middle Eastern oil-exporting countries is under increasing pressure to change. The consensus lacking about the rules of the game in politics and the absence of demo-cratic institutions build up pressures for political change, which could be of a revolutionary character insofar as there are no institutions able either to handle the pressures or to suppress them. Demographic pressure and frustrated expectations are irresistible. The power structures put in place by high oil revenues cannot survive long with low oil revenues without adapting. The coalition of the military and the technocrats risks losing power unless its base is enlarged. Iran is but one historical example of an apparently strong regime suddenly crumbling. The fate of the Soviet Union and the East European communist regimes shows that political monopolies carry high risk.

The leading Middle Eastern oil exporters have to ponder new options in their economic and oil policies. One option would be for each to keep oil exports fairly constant and together with other major Middle Eastern oil exporters gradually raise oil prices as demand picks up, or reduce volumes if demand should fall, aiming at gaining from co-operation. To avoid rivalry, market shares would remain constant. Civilian expenditure would grow at the expense of military spending. The political pre-condition is an understanding between the major Middle Eastern oil exporters, including Iraq, on oil prices and market shares and the absence of an Iraqi threat, which would permit Kuwait and Saudi Arabia to take US oil interests less into account.

The opposite option for each would be to yield to the temptation to test the competitive edge by unilaterally increasing oil output and exports, eventually with foreign investment, taking market shares from neighbours and if necessary cutting oil prices, aiming at volume gains to offset price losses. Politically, this would signify more antagonistic relations between Iran, Iraq and Saudi Arabia. This option might be most tempting to Iraq, on the condition that sanctions were lifted or ignored. If taken up by Saudi Arabia, the country would have an ensuing need for more arms purchases and US protection, raising military expenditure. Iran might emerge as the big loser, eventually leading to a further polarization of Iranian politics. Iraq might emerge as the regional challenger.

Its large population and corresponding income needs make Iran more vulnerable than Iraq or Saudi Arabia to lower oil prices. Iran's liabilities are considerable. In the Middle East, it is the oldest and most mature oil province. In recent years, output has declined and unit costs have risen, at least partly because the largest fields are being depleted. Among the major Middle East oil exporters, Iran was the most adversely hit by the 1998 oil price collapse. Oil exports account for about one-third of its budget revenues and 80–85 per cent of total export earnings. Expenditure includes subsidies on food and especially gasoline, which is sold below cost. Currently, about one-third of oil output is consumed domestically, and the proportion is rising.

Since 1980, annual population growth has been around 3 per cent, higher than economic growth, so that per capita income has declined by perhaps one-half. Food supplies are precarious for the bulk of the population. Iran's economic predicament is to a large extent due to the eight-year war against Iraq, but also to the attempt at imposing an administrative economy, leading to distorted prices, inefficiencies, low capacity utilization and lack of investment.[41]

Since 1980, Iran's productive capital stock and infrastructure have seriously deteriorated.[42] There is an urgent need for investment capital in all sectors of the economy, but foreign capital is reluctant to invest on a large scale because of legal problems and political risk. This means that oil will be the predominant source of foreign exchange for a long time. Iran has huge gas reserves, but no large-scale gas export project is likely to be realized for years. The bottom line is that Iran will need high oil prices and preferably a high OPEC quota. Any major decline in oil prices will have adverse economic effects, potentially leading to political instability.

Even if Iran is the most mature oil province of the Middle East, the country undoubtedly still has great potential. The lack of exploration for at least 20 years means that modern geological methods have not been applied to the Iranian subsoil. Should the country open up gradually to foreign oil investment, the state of existing oil fields is likely to improve, together with reasonably high success rates in oil exploration. Consequently, overall oil extraction capacity is likely to increase, although perhaps not to the level of the 1970s. Application of foreign oil management knowledge is likely to reduce costs, making the Iranian oil industry more competitive. The future of that industry is a question of politics, not geology.

The alternative would be to open the Iranian oil industry to foreign investors by offering better terms and operatorship, although this would require that the liberal reformers make decisive political victories. In this case, the outlook is for a gradually rising oil output, eventually with the volumes available for exports rising fairly quickly as the growth of domestic consumption subsides with the gradual withdrawal of fuel subsidies. This is a recipe for making Iran a more important actor in the world oil market, and also in OPEC. In this case, Iran would represent a greater economic challenge to Iraq and especially Saudi Arabia as well as the other Gulf States. With a more dynamic oil industry, Iran would reasonably demand a more important role and a larger quota. One option for Iran would then be to challenge Saudi Arabia's supremacy in OPEC by raising volumes and risking a price war, for which Iran would be ill prepared. The alternative would be to seek a co-operative solution by renouncing full capacity utilization, in the hope of stabilizing oil prices at a level that would yield a considerable economic rent.

Prospects of large natural gas exports improve the economic outlook for Iran as well as its political importance. Although Iranian natural gas consumption is growing rapidly, the country so far hardly exports gas. Iran is increasingly targeting emerging Asian markets, especially Pakistan and India, for gas exports. Insofar as Iran can have supplementary hard currency earnings from gas exports, the country has less reason to compromise oil export earnings by unilaterally raising volumes, even if the comparative cost position should improve somewhat. Iran has a record of not always fully respecting OPEC quotas, but also of seeking compromise solutions when oil prices and revenues fall.

Revenue needs mean that Iran needs OPEC to be successful in stabilizing oil prices at a high level. High costs and limited idle capacity mean that Iran has hardly any resources to defect from OPEC or an OPEC agreement, but the country certainly has the incentives and the means to cheat moderately. Transiting Caspian and Central Asian crude would enhance Iran's bargaining position within OPEC, particularly given Iran's ability to cause mischief, ultimately by withholding oil supplies. In the meantime, Iran has good reasons to co-operate more closely with the international oil industry, eventually granting advantageous terms.

The rapid rise of domestic consumption is Iran's most pressing oil policy problem. Unless drastic measures are taken soon, the outlook is that the volume of Iranian oil exports will diminish as domestic use increases and eventually oil output declines because of insufficient maintenance and investment. Prospects from this perspective are for a severe financial crisis with potentially serious repercussions, so that the Islamist regime might end in a way not dissimilar to the way in which the shah's regime ended in 1979. Measures called for are better conditions for foreign oil investment and considerably higher prices on oil products for Iranian consumers, but both actions may prove politically difficult. Iran's best option with OPEC is to aim at gaining from co-operation, with an evident risk of reaping the fool's reward. From this perspective, Iran needs peaceful relations with its Middle East neighbours.

Iraq is in a different league in spite of ten years of embargo and isolation. The country has potential for agricultural development and for
feeding its population, besides that for industrial development and large oil
resources. Iraq is potentially a rich country, provided it can get its politics
right. Since independence, it has developed an urban merchant class. Iraq in
the 1970s embarked on a capital-intensive economic strategy outside oil,
neglecting agriculture and food supplies.[43]

The country raised military expenditure in 1978 after Saddam Hussein
took power. The military effort increased in 1980 after Iraq attacked Iran,
and when higher oil prices were being earned. During the 1980s Iraq
increased its oil production substantially, to finance the war against Iran and
keep civilian life running with as little disturbance as possible. In the 1990s,
sanctions and isolation made the regime liberalize the economy, selling off
state industries, services and agricultural land.[44] President Hussein's immediate power base is probably a small number of family, clan and regional
affiliates, but also comprises a broader community of privileged persons.
Their loyalty is based on government positions and newly acquired private
property.

Privatization has enlarged and consolidated an Iraqi capitalist class. In
the rural areas, privatization of state farms has reconstituted the class of
large landowners originally put in place by the Turkish and the British and
swept away by the 1958 revolution. The outcome is a new social structure
with private capitalists in a prominent position and with a stake in political
stability and the survival of the regime, although desiring reforms when
conditions permit. Recruitment to the new propertied class will matter to
the viability of the new social structure. If it is restricted to the presidential
entourage or the Sunni Arab military and civilian technocrats, the chances
are that it may not survive the demise of the Saddam regime. If recruited on
a broader base, with Shia and Kurdish elements, the chances for survival
improve and it may bolster Iraq's integrity. An interesting rumour in the
summer of 2001 was that Saddam's son Udai had converted to the Shia
version of Islam, to improve his political standing among Iraq's Shia
majority against his rival younger brother Qossai.[45]

Before the Gulf War, Iraq had achieved a comparably high level of economic and social development.[46] Even if the income base was almost
entirely dependent on oil, Iraq ranked internationally among upper middle
countries such as Greece and Venezuela. The relative prosperity was
manifest through good nutrition standards, with a per capita daily intake of
about 3000 calories. The education system functioned well and illiteracy
had been almost obliterated.

The long-range objective of Iraqi economic policy in the 1960s and
1970s was to develop industry, to diversify and reduce dependence on oil.[47]
The objective was not reached, essentially because of the first oil price rise

that raised the share of oil in its overall output. For several years Iraq did, however, keep its oil production below capacity and output did not expand during the years immediately following the first oil price rise. Iraq also, until Saddam Hussein took power, tried to keep oil production and its revenues at a level that the country could absorb, preferably in investment projects with a reasonable return.[48]

After normalization of relations with the outside world, with or without Saddam Hussein, and assuming territorial integrity is intact, Iraq's assets will give options in economic policy. One option could be the easy petroleum way, to opt for extensive oil and gas development, regardless of consequences to the oil market. This would be a tempting option, given the combination of huge financial needs and an ample oil and gas resource base. An extensive petroleum development would not, however, create much employment, but large oil and gas revenues could eventually finance a huge public sector. The influx of large oil revenues might cause inflationary pressures as well as an overvalued exchange rate, compromising the competitiveness of agriculture and manufacturing.

An alternative economic strategy could be to opt for more moderate oil and gas development, coupled with investment in agriculture and manufacturing. This would provide more jobs and create a more diversified income base, with less risk of inflation, but it would not quickly provide the financial resources that Iraq needs. The choice of such a non-oil economic strategy would require an exceptional political moderation in a difficult situation, with the population's expectations running high.

A normalized Iraq seems likely to opt for an oil- and gas-based economic strategy, at least at the outset to respond to the most urgent financial needs. In the longer run, giving a gradually higher priority to agriculture and industry could mitigate the petroleum-based strategy, but Iraq may have a surprise potential also in the domestic economy. The hardship incurred by the war against Iran in the 1980s and the sanctions during the 1990s has spurred significant productivity gains.

With the world's second largest proven oil reserves and the potential for successful exploration, Iraq will enjoy a unique freedom of choice in oil policy once relations with the outside world have been normalized. Whatever option Iraq chooses, it will affect the world oil market and oil prices. After normalization, Iraq will attract the world's leading oil companies as investors. Provided political conditions are more palatable, Iraqi expertise is likely to return, strengthening the competence base of the national oil industry, with oil production expanding quickly, essentially financed by foreign investment. The issue is rather in what way quickly expanding Iraqi oil exports will influence the market and, essentially, what the eventual response will be from the other major Middle East oil exporters. With a huge resource base and low costs, Iraq is one of the few OPEC countries

with the potential ability for increasing oil revenues by expanding volumes
to offset declining oil prices. Iraq's preference may be to enjoy higher oil
revenues through a combination of higher volumes and comparably high
oil prices, eventually at the expense of other major Middle East oil exporters. Geopolitics, essentially the US presence in the Gulf and the military
balance, will decide the outcome. This observation stresses the potential for
oil market instability associated with Iraq.

Historically, Iraq has been a recurrent defector from OPEC agreements.
This was the case in the 1970s and 1980s until the Gulf conflict. It is likely
to be the case again, once sanctions are lifted. Iraq has the resources and
the incentives not to obey OPEC agreements, unless the country gets into a
dominant position where it can challenge that of Saudi Arabia in influence
as well as in volume. For the rest of OPEC, Iraq represents a risk: any
generous terms it might grant the international oil companies would
strengthen their bargaining position in relation to the oil-exporting countries and their national oil companies. Iraq has reasons to aim for a free
ridership in OPEC, going for a higher market share and leaving price
stabilization to its neighbours; alternatively it may decide to test the competitive edge. Ultimately, this is a recipe for conflictual relations with its
Middle East neighbours.

Even after a remarkable consolidation of its economy in the mid-1990s,
leading to a virtual elimination of the current account deficit by 1997, the
1998 oil price collapse once more demonstrated Saudi Arabia's economic
monoculture, the dependence on oil revenues and the sensitivity to oil price
changes.[49] With oil prices in real terms at the low levels of the early 1970s,
Saudi Arabia's economy suddenly faced one of its greatest challenges in
years, putting heavy pressure on the Saudi government to reach the OPEC
deal that in 1999 significantly raised oil prices and revenues. Oil revenues
still make up around 85 per cent of total Saudi export earnings, and 40 per
cent of the country's gross domestic product, indicating a persistent
vulnerability.

Government expenditure, and indirectly oil revenues, is the source of
practically all consumption in the country.[50] The economy did not develop
much during the 1990s. Military expenditure per capita is perhaps the
highest in the world. Financial imbalances have emerged. Income per capita
has been stagnant or even declining. Economic reforms aimed at bolstering
the private sector are needed to diversify income sources, but they also
imply political change.[51] Such changes appear forthcoming, although at a
slow pace. The pressure for change largely comes from the high population
growth and growing numbers of young people with few prospects of
satisfactory employment. Despite periodic efforts to diversify, Saudi
Arabia's economy is essentially oil based, although investments in petro-

chemicals have increased the relative importance of the downstream petroleum sector in recent years.

Paradoxically, Saudi Arabia faces the combination of a financial drain caused by millions of foreign workers and the prospect of unemployment among young Saudis. Saudi Arabia has a policy known as 'Saudization', the goal of which is to increase employment among its own citizens by replacing 60 per cent of the estimated 5–6 million foreign workers in the country. In order to do this, Saudi Arabia has stopped issuing work visas for certain jobs, has moved to increase training for Saudi nationals, and has set minimum requirements for the hiring of Saudi nationals by private companies. The successful replacement of foreign workers with Saudi nationals will require changing attitudes toward salaried employment by young Saudi males and a changing policy toward female employment. Such changes are possible, but are likely to take years in a conservative society whose traditions have been bolstered by huge oil revenues for at least a generation.

Government subsidies and losses by unprofitable state-owned enterprises are large burdens on Saudi Arabia's budget. They also represent a potential for cutting government expenditure, but with the risk of a high social and political cost unless alternative employment can be offered by the private sector. The economic squeeze raises the spectre of social and political reform in Saudi Arabia. The possibility of a gradual transition toward a more open society should not be excluded, as the country still has ample resources, and the ruling royal family has shown a remarkable dexterity in handling thorny issues and adapting to changing realities, helped by a competent civil service.

Because of ample resources and the potential for reducing government expenditure, Saudi Arabia faces real options in economic policy. As in the other major oil-exporting countries, the choice of economic strategy is dependent on politics. The easy way out for Saudi Arabia would be to opt for an oil-based economic strategy, aimed at raising output and exports, with the hope that the ensuing decline in oil prices would be offset by volume gains. Some young Saudi intellectuals advocate this option.[52] However, this route risks compromising the development of services and manufacturing that are more efficient generators of employment. An alternative economic strategy would be a more balanced development, gradually supplementing the state-run oil industry with a growing private sector based on services and manufacturing. A visionary solution could be to opt for high value-added industrial development based on the merchant class and the advances in education made over the past generation, but the risk is that a continued financial squeeze and declining living standards would exacerbate social and political tensions.

Saudi Arabia has a unique choice in petroleum policy. Saudi policy from the mid-1970s until the mid-1980s was to be the dominant oil producer and the residual oil supplier, stabilizing oil prices through minor adjustments in output. After 1980, with declining oil demand and the surge in oil output from other areas, beginning with the North Sea, this policy was increasingly costly by reason of the market share, export volumes and revenues forsaken. For some years, Saudi Arabia appeared to be reaping the fool's reward in OPEC.

Investment in additional capacity would make little sense for Saudi Arabia in a stagnant oil market, unless it were regarded as a strategic move to depress oil prices and take market share by squeezing out high-cost producers. This is within Saudi Arabia's possible reach, but it would contrast with its hitherto cautious oil policy. In 1986, Saudi Arabia did raise output and provoke a major oil price decline, but it did so only in close collaboration with Kuwait and after deliberations in OPEC. Then, Saudi Arabia could actually benefit, as the volume growth more than made up for the price decline. In 1997–98, it was a different story. Saudi Arabia together with Kuwait did expand output in the second half of 1997, as a prelude to Iraq's export growth, but the ensuing price decline was of such a magnitude that it more than cancelled any earnings gain caused by the volume growth. By 1999, Saudi Arabia was essential in forging the OPEC agreement on lower quotas and higher oil prices.

Any rapid expansion of Saudi capacity and output seems to be of limited benefit, unless oil demand should respond more quickly to lower prices than has been the case historically. For Saudi Arabia, any quick output expansion appears risky. The concern is not only the return on new projects, but also the impact of new investment projects on the economic rent from existing prospects, with capital investment fully depreciated and low lifting costs. The more reasonable oil strategy for Saudi Arabia seems to be a gradual capacity expansion, perhaps with some foreign participation, rather than flooding the market with cheap oil. To expand oil capacity without sacrificing other budget items, Saudi Arabia will reasonably need foreign investment, but capacity expansion is likely to be gradual, responding to the call of the market for Saudi crude. Opening the Saudi natural gas industry to foreign investors in 2001 represents an important initial step.

For Saudi Arabia, an alternative strategy could be to stop attracting foreign oil companies, to keep capacity stable and to seek closer ties with Iran and in the longer run Iraq. This seems unrealistic, but the issue of balancing US concerns with those of its Middle Eastern neighbours is likely to gain in importance. Saudi Arabia's most realistic option in OPEC is to continue the cautious policy of gaining by co-operation, unless challenged by quickly rising Iraqi oil export volumes. In that case, Saudi Arabia would have strong reasons to test the competitive edge by raising volumes even though this contributed to lower prices. If challenged by a strong Iraq and in the case of faltering US support, Saudi Arabia would risk reaping the fool's reward, losing market share as oil prices fell. Saudi Arabia's cautious oil policy and preference for co-operation leads to a need for peaceful relations with its Middle East neighbours.

Early in 2002, Saudi Arabia remains economically and politically dependent on oil prices in the range of $20 a barrel at least. Any lower price would increase budget and current deficits and enhance the need for economic and political reform. Lower oil prices would weaken economic growth and further aggravate youth unemployment. Consequently, the deteriorating domestic situation contributes to political tension, in addition to dismay over foreign policy and close ties to the United States. Even without any major upheaval there will be increasing pressure on the Saudi government to redistribute wealth, which could impede private and foreign investment. The prospects for Iran may be relatively somewhat better, with a gradual opening up for foreign investment, but any effective economic reform depends on the liberal forces winning over the conservatives. Iraq, by contrast, although on the basis of poor data, presents a somewhat more positive outlook, again in relative terms. Oil exports, legal and smuggled volumes, seem to contribute to relatively high economic growth rates, which in turn help to stabilize the regime.

OPEC politics

OPEC was founded in September 1960 by Iran, Iraq, Kuwait, Saudi Arabia and Venezuela. Later, Algeria, Ecuador, Gabon, Indonesia, Libya, Nigeria, Qatar and the United Arab Emirates also joined, but Ecuador and Gabon have since left the organization. Since 1990, Iraq has not taken part in OPEC negotiations over oil prices and quotas. OPEC countries at the end of 1999 had about 78 per cent of the world's proven reserves, but only about 41 per cent of output. The expected lifetime of OPEC reserves is close to 80 years at present output, almost double the world average of 41 years.

There is no single theory to explain how OPEC performs in controlling oil prices through supply adjustment. By withholding output, the low-cost producers can make oil prices rise far above marginal cost, and by using idle capacity they can make oil prices eventually fall towards the level of the marginal lifting cost, which is a fraction of the total cost. Both moves can make economic sense. By withholding output to raise prices, oil producers harvest income without investment, which is economic rent. By using idle capacity to lower prices, they deter competing investment. The opportunity depends on the market balance. The 1973–74 oil price increase, triggered by output withheld in the Middle East, was economically rational for the low-cost suppliers because it strongly augmented the economic rent, although it may have been excessive in view of their long-term interests. The 1986 oil price drop, triggered by the low-cost suppliers using idle capacity, essentially Kuwait and Saudi Arabia, was in their economic interest as they were the only oil suppliers for whom the volume gain more than offset the price decline, so that their oil revenues rose amid falling prices. Another gain was to deter competitive investment.

Low-cost suppliers have an interest in investing in capacity that is not always utilized. By keeping idle capacity, the low-cost suppliers can present a deterrent and eventually keep control of the oil market. They also have an interest in keeping some flexibility the other way, by eventually withholding output to stabilize or raise oil prices, if so desired. This generally implies keeping a financial surplus, so that oil policy can be adjusted without compromising the domestic economy. By keeping idle capacity and a financial surplus, the low-cost suppliers can act as the ultimate arbiters of the oil market. Kuwait is the classic case of an oil exporter that enjoys a financial surplus as well as idle capacity, providing the ability to withhold or raise output. Saudi Arabia has idle capacity, but a less advantageous financial situation, although there is ample room for budget cuts that could improve oil policy flexibility. To keep control of the oil market, the low-cost suppliers need to invest in extractive capacity that they normally will not use. This may seem extravagant, but the advantage is power in an imperfect market and the ability to make alliances and compromises with other suppliers. Investing in spare capacity is relatively inexpensive for the low-cost suppliers and provides market power.

The transfer of property rights in the 1970s from the major international oil companies to the oil-exporting countries enhanced their power to control the oil market.[53] For the low-cost oil suppliers, the 1979–80 oil price rise in hindsight appears to have been a mistake, resulting from a loss of control of the supply system and the oil market.[54] The subsequent gradual reduction of the real oil price and the major oil price collapse in 1986 can be seen as an adjustment to the long-term interests of the low-cost suppliers. During the early 1980s, the deterrent of idle capacity was used to enforce some discipline in OPEC, but in 1986 the threat of flooding the market became a reality, for a while. In the early 1980s, the low-cost suppliers, essentially Kuwait and Saudi Arabia, withheld supplies to defend the high oil price, but at the cost of losing market share and revenues. The policy turn-about in 1985–86 suddenly made the low-cost suppliers appear as winners, benefiting from their competitive edge. By renouncing on market share the low-cost suppliers gained market power through idle capacity. As co-operation no longer worked out for the low-cost producers, they raised output, making oil more competitive and increasing their market share. This pattern was somewhat repeated in 1997–98.

OPEC was originally established to defend the oil exporters' interests in relation to the international oil industry, not primarily as a cartel to set prices and quotas, although the regulation of output was envisaged from the outset.[55] During most of the 1960s OPEC was on the defensive on the oil price issue because large discoveries provided rising oil supplies at lower cost. OPEC discussions about pro-rationing to defend oil prices led to no agreement. At this time, most Middle Eastern and North African oil exporters wanted to attract foreign investors to raise their oil production, revenues and market shares. Instead, to protect revenues, the OPEC countries in the early 1960s considered changing petroleum taxation, essentially discontinuing the practice of crediting royalty payments against corporate income tax, raising the total government take by about 15 per cent. Even this modest move required lengthy negotiations between OPEC countries and with the oil companies and was not always fully implemented. During the 1960s, OPEC revenues essentially increased by means of growing volumes, meaning that OPEC member countries were competing for oil investment as much as they were co-operating. OPEC did achieve that royalties and taxes were to be calculated on the basis of posted prices instead of market prices, establishing a floor for the latter through the tax-paid cost below which market prices could not fall.[56]

Around 1970, conditions improved for OPEC. Because of quickly rising demand, the need for OPEC oil was growing at a fast pace. The closure of the Suez Canal during 1967–69, after the Six-Day War, had highlighted the importance of oil. The 1969 revolution in Libya, at the time the world's leading oil exporter, provided a government more determined to co-operate with OPEC against the international oil companies. About the same time, relations between Algeria and the French oil industry deteriorated.

Tight oil markets and stronger political cohesion favoured the OPEC countries, which in Tripoli and Teheran in 1970 and 1971 negotiated agreements with the international oil industry on price increases, higher taxes and the OPEC countries' progressive participation in their oil indus-tries. In 1972, the Geneva agreement gave OPEC countries compensation for the devaluation of the US dollar. By the early 1970s, OPEC's control was established. As early as 1972, Iraq nationalized the oil industry.

In 1973–74, under the impact of the first major oil crisis, OPEC unilat-erally took over the control of oil supplies and prices. In subsequent years, many OPEC countries, such as Abu Dhabi, Algeria, Kuwait, Qatar, Saudi Arabia and Venezuela, partly or wholly nationalized their oil industries. In the 1970s, OPEC sought agreement only on prices for marker crudes (a marker crude is a price reference quality of crude oil), leaving the stabiliza-tion of the markets to the member countries, not functioning as a cartel in the classical sense. The fall in oil demand meant that OPEC member countries had huge idle capacity, as the defence of the oil price had priority over volume. By 1977, Iran and Saudi Arabia agreed on a freeze of nominal oil prices to spur demand growth.

In the second oil price crisis of 1979–80, OPEC lost control of oil supplies and prices as the shortfall of Iranian oil caused prices to triple within 18 months. Only in early 1981 could OPEC resume control, but without Iran. From 1982 OPEC tried to act as a classical cartel, seeking agreement on both prices and market shares. The performance was different, however, because OPEC, unlike most other cartels, has no means to punish members that disobey or defect.[57]

Since 1981, OPEC's record in stabilizing the oil market has been mixed. Some member countries at times cheat on their quotas, but this seldom represents a major problem. In times of crisis for the exporters, meaning low oil prices, OPEC can show a remarkable resolve and within a short span of time agree on measures to raise prices and revenues. The 1999–2000 surge in oil prices is a good case. In more relaxed times, there is a tendency not to respect agreements strictly. At times, there is open dispute over market shares, leading to precipitous price declines, as in 1997–98.

In the oil market, as in other oligopolistic markets, bargaining power and the ultimate ability to influence price development are functions of flexibility and the ability to enforce threats and promises. The basis for bargaining over oil prices within OPEC can be seen as the relationship between withholding capacity and idle capacity, which determines the strength of those that want higher prices and those that want lower ones. OPEC's ability to set oil prices, and therefore the price stability of the world market, in the last instance hinges on Saudi Arabia, which usually has spare capacity and the ability to raise supplies and reduce prices, and has always at critical moments shown willingness and ability to reduce output to raise oil prices. Saudi Arabia's contribution was essential in defending high oil prices during 1982–85, in lowering oil prices in 1986 and subsequently raising them again, and finally in lowering oil prices in 1997 and raising them again in 1999. Saudi Arabia acts as a dominant firm in the world oil market, in reality deciding OPEC performance insofar as no other member country has a matching flexibility.

Most studies treat OPEC as a profit-maximizing cartel seeking collective monopoly profits by regulating supplies to set prices.[58] Other approaches assume that the oil market is basically competitive and that oil price discontinuities can best be explained by other factors than cartelization and occasional breakdowns. Some competitive approaches focus on the demand side, arguing that sudden changes in demand have caused oil price discontinuities.[59] Analysing the oil market with Saudi Arabia acting as a dominant firm because of large size and low costs gives statistically interesting results.[60] The dominant firm can influence the oil market by controlling its own output, but not that of competitors. For Saudi Arabia, this approach seems realistic, but not for OPEC collectively or even for the OPEC core (Saudi Arabia plus Kuwait, Qatar and the United Arab Emirates). Insofar as Saudi Arabia acts as the ultimate supplier, residual demand for Saudi oil is more price responsive than is overall demand for OPEC oil, especially as some OPEC countries seem to pursue oil policies subject to target revenues, meaning that volumes supplied are negatively price responsive, implying a backward-bending supply curve.[61] This approach focuses on the supply side of the oil market, whose instability since the early 1970s has provided discontinuities of greater amplitude than the demand side.

Because OPEC is an association of countries, cartel theory does not fit it easily.[62] A more fitting approach may be that of tacit collusion through risk aversion, as oil exporters resist incentives to raise output capacity out of fear of retaliation and a general pursuit of market share bringing oil prices far down.[63]

In political terms, OPEC can be described as an international interest group or a trade union of raw material producers.[64] In addition to its function as a price fixer, OPEC is also a forum for political discussions and a platform for common demands. All OPEC countries share the success of the organization. Their improved standing in the world is closely related to the performance of OPEC and this makes it important for them to maintain political cohesion and solidarity in spite of obvious differences in interests and points of view. There is as a result a stronger ideological cohesion in OPEC than in most, if not all, other cartels of raw materials exporters in recent history. This contributes to OPEC's survival chances and explains why minor price disputes pose no immediate threat to the cartel.

The main economic factors behind oil exports are the income requirements of the various OPEC countries, the size of their oil reserves, and the market conditions. The oligopolistic position enables the cartel, or its dominant members, to control the price of oil through decisions on the volume of exports. An oligopoly aims at maximizing income in the short term and maintaining its position over time. It is rational economic behaviour for oligopolists to set a price that gives an optimal income, which can be defined as the greatest possible income, compatible with continued demand in the market, and with the maintenance of a controlling position by suppliers. A price that is too high risks hurting demand, the position of the oligopoly, and future income. A price that is too low could imply an under-utilization of income-earning opportunities. OPEC has never managed to strike this balance and it is doubtful whether is possible in a dynamic oil market. In the early 1980s, oil prices were too high for long-term equilibrium, in the late 1990s too low, but the sobering fact is that there is no long-term equilibrium price.

In determining the volume of exports and bargaining for quotas, the individual cartel members have to take into account not only their own income requirements and long-term interests but also market conditions, especially the relationship between the amount they supply and the price this creates. The responsiveness of demand to changes in price is the crucial factor here. Consequently, OPEC's decision-making process might be described dynamically as follows. The OPEC members know their income needs, and they attempt to maximize their incomes to meet these needs. Given their oligopolistic position as price setters, they must strike a delicate balance, setting a price that maximizes their income without straining the consumers in such a way that future demand declines or their oligopolistic position is undermined by competition.

The main political factors weighed in considering the price and volume of oil exports from OPEC countries are the goals of economic policies, the long-term political interests related to oil, and foreign policy concerns. The oligopolistic position enables OPEC to use oil exports for leverage in foreign policy. Members seek both to maximize influence in the short term and to maintain their position over time. This calls for a certain amount of compromise because exerting strong influence in the short term can harm future positions.

OPEC's record, so far, is that of an imperfect cartel. Yet considering differences in resource endowment and interests, and wars between members, OPEC has managed remarkably well to survive and at least periodically to rule the world oil market.

One group of countries has large oil reserves and small populations and therefore easily runs financial surpluses. The linchpin is Saudi Arabia, which because of huge reserves and large production capacity plays a key role. In recent years, rising income needs have compromised Saudi Arabia's choice in oil policy. Kuwait is another example, although of less significance. Another group of countries has smaller oil reserves and large populations and generally spend whatever revenues they earn. Iran and Iraq are the most salient cases in the Middle East, but most other OPEC countries also fall into this category. The conflictual co-existence of two different member groups in OPEC explains why the world oil market has strong oligopolistic features prone to instability caused by differences in costs, financial needs and strategic preferences.

The 1998 oil price was driven by volume increases from Venezuela, Saudi Arabia, Kuwait and finally Iraq. The ensuing 1999 oil price stabilization took place without Iraq participating. In 1999, improved relations between Iran and Saudi Arabia, both fearful neighbours of Iraq, prepared the ground for an OPEC agreement on higher oil prices.

The dichotomy of the membership causing diverging economic interests is the essential obstacle to OPEC performing as a perfect cartel. While it has often managed to bargain its way to compromises enabling the oil price to remain stable through both rising and falling demand in the market, success has never lasted more than five or six years. After the first oil price shock of 1973–74, OPEC kept the oil price fairly stable until 1979, when it was outmanoeuvred by the Iranian crisis. After the market settled down in 1980–81, OPEC managed to keep the oil price fairly stable until 1985, by which time strong downward pressures had built up and demand for OPEC oil had become too small for the bargaining to lead to a viable compromise on market shares. Since 1986, OPEC's story has been less successful, yet not so bad, as prices have been kept not far from the $18 a barrel mark, with the exception of 1997–98. Without OPEC, in any case, oil prices would have had a considerable chance of falling again in 1975, although not to pre-1973 levels, and once more in 1983. Moreover, except for a few weeks during July 1986, the oil price was kept above its floor throughout the late 1980s. OPEC's major function has been to prolong periods of high oil prices by agreeing to cut volumes.

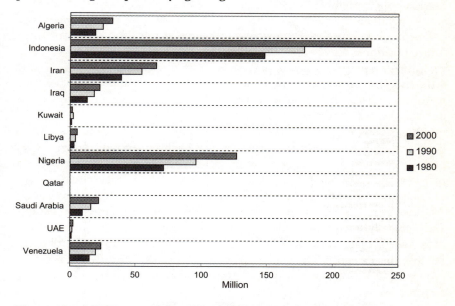

Figure 12a: OPEC population 1980–2000
Sources: The World Bank 2001; CIA The World Factbook 2001

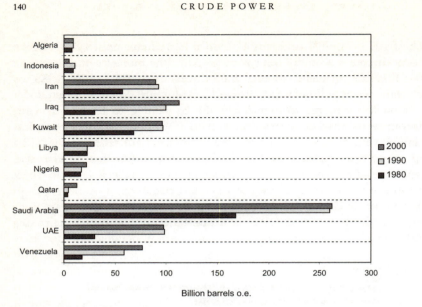

Figure 12b: OPEC oil reserves 1980–2000
Source: Energy Information Administration (EIA) 2001

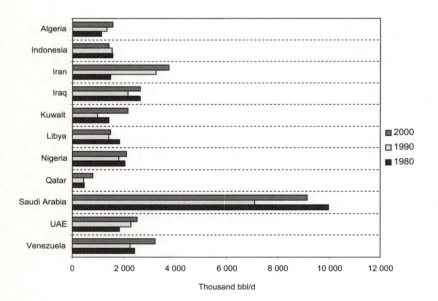

Figure 12c: OPEC oil production 1980–2000
Source: BP Amoco Statistical Review of World Energy 2001

The basic economic problem of the OPEC countries is a dependency on economic rent, so that even countries with low lifting costs experience serious financial problems whenever oil prices are low, as in 1998. As we have seen, the exception was Iraq, and the countries that suffered most were Iran and the more prosperous Gulf States.

The experience of 1998 provides incentives to avoid another round of low oil prices. The low oil prices of that year may perhaps prove to be an exception or at least indicate a floor for oil prices in the range of $10–12 a barrel for Middle Eastern marker crudes. Eventually, such a floor to oil prices would be set by politics, not by the marginal cost.

For all major OPEC exporters, unilaterally pursuing market share constitutes a risk of losing money, not increasing revenues, as economic rent is eroded when volumes rise. Correspondingly, a co-operative solution may imply gains for all parties involved, because economic rent increases with declining volumes. Within the confines of this common ground there is, however, a constant struggle for the division of market shares, in addition to more fundamental conflicts linked to differences in resource endowment and time horizons considered.

In the integration of oil policy and economic policy there has been a fundamental difference between the OPEC countries. This division is pertinent to the major Middle East oil exporters. There are two types of OPEC countries, those that produce at practically full capacity, regardless of the price, and those that do not, because they are concerned about the feedback effects of the oil price. The first group of countries are short-term or even immediate optimizers. Their long-term dynamic optimization boils down to immediate economic optimization, which is maximizing the output, whatever the price. The second group of countries are medium-term optimizers, because they know that the price today will affect both non-OPEC output and the level of economic activity tomorrow. In other words, they have to compromise between immediate revenues and tomorrow's revenues. These latter countries, such as Saudi Arabia, Kuwait and the United Arab Emirates, with large oil reserves and small populations, have had a reasonably limited need for revenues, as demonstrated by their financial surpluses, and have been operating with this kind of consideration.

By contrast, other countries, such as, for example, Iran and Iraq, together with Algeria, Nigeria and others, have always maximized output, or almost always. Venezuela is the only exception to this rule, at least periodically. Because of their large population, they have much higher revenue needs and correspondingly operate with high discount rates and a shorter economic horizon than the countries with large oil reserves, essentially those of the Arabian Peninsula. Because of this short time horizon, they are finally in the same basic situation as far as optimization is concerned. Their

ultimate reserve life is longer than their economic horizon and the value of
oil left in the ground is practically zero.

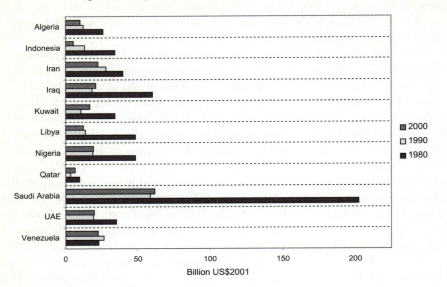

Figure 13a: OPEC oil export revenues 1980–2000
*Sources: Energy Information Administration (EIA) 2001; BP Amoco Statistical Review of World Energy
2001*

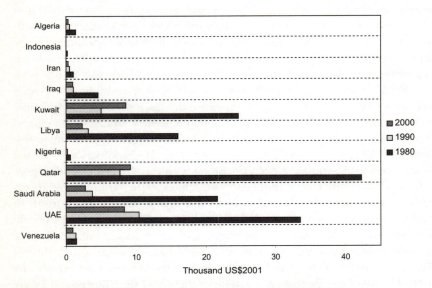

Figure 13b: OPEC oil export revenues per capita 1980–2000
*Sources: Energy Information Administration (EIA) 2001; BP Amoco Statistical Review of World Energy
2001; The World Bank 2001; CIA The World Factbook 2001*

For those countries that are able to compromise between the short and medium term, the future market largely depends upon oil staying competitive in price. Therefore, these countries not only need to maximize the immediate revenues, they also need a competitive price for oil in the future. They have incentives to increase output in order to force the price down, as was the case in 1986 and 1997, so long as, on the one hand, the immediate revenues are not much affected, and on the other hand, the revenues for 'tomorrow', two or three years later, are much enhanced.

There is a risk of a technical breakthrough, which can be triggered by any sudden price rise or by prices staying too high for too long. Against this background, Saudi Arabia, Kuwait and the Emirates have had and still have an inherent interest in continuously low oil prices to avert this backstop risk.

The best compromise between short-term, immediate revenues and medium-term ones mainly depends on the financial needs of the oil producer. If actual revenues are less than the level of expenditure desired, they will choose a lower price in order to stimulate demand and to depress non-OPEC production. Conversely, should the revenues be much more than desired, the countries in this situation might favour higher prices even if they led to dampened demand and stimulated production elsewhere. This theoretical economic framework has been influenced in practice by the political interaction of the three Arabian Peninsula producers with their neighbours. Moreover, internal factors in each of the countries should be taken into account. For example, Kuwait has a large financial portfolio and is most interested in the effects of oil price decisions on the world economy, with important parameters such as inflation rates, interest rates and growth rates.

These varying concerns for the future create fundamentally opposing price interests within OPEC and, more importantly, within the Middle East. Countries with high revenue needs want to deplete their oil not only quickly, but also at a high price. By contrast, countries with limited revenue needs not only agree on cutting the production rate, but they have also wanted, for the past few years and they still want for the next few years, the price of oil to stay low. As has been demonstrated on numerous occasions over the past 20 years, the latter countries have a considerable flexibility. They can reduce output so long as their revenue needs are fulfilled; yet they do not hesitate occasionally to 'flood' the market in order to bring the oil price down.

Correspondingly, the middle-term interests and short-term muscle of the three Arabian Peninsula countries pose an immediate threat to the economic interests of those with high discount rates and large revenue requirements. In this sense, the conflict between Iraq on the one hand, and Kuwait and Saudi Arabia on the other, is also a conflict of interest over oil prices and market shares in addition to older political and territorial grievances. This is no banal issue, as has been demonstrated in the summer of 1990. Iraq attacked Kuwait largely because of oil and money.

Venezuela's oil policy represents a special case. In economic terms, Venezuela's oil policy in recent years is hard to justify. The country has huge financial needs, partly in order to service the foreign debt, even though the country made substantial financial gains during the 1990–91 Gulf crisis. Therefore, the country could have been expected to limit itself to a symbolic participation in pro-rationing, like Algeria, and this has been the constant request of the national oil company and the country's business community. On the other hand, the political authorities have remained strongly attached to some symbols such as the nationalization of the oil industry, the foundation of OPEC, and North–South confrontation; this explains why the country has agreed to keep a high share of the burden of pro-rationing, limiting output by 25 per cent. After practically defecting from OPEC discipline in the late 1990s, competing with Saudi Arabia over the US market, since 1999 Venezuela is once again a loyal member, respecting OPEC quotas. Experience shows, however, that Venezuela is one of OPEC's weak links whose loyalty largely depends on domestic politics.

In recent years, OPEC appears to have learned from the ups and downs of the oil market since the early 1970s, in the sense that the OPEC countries have experienced their own interaction with the world economy and the risks involved in oil price discontinuities. Oil exporters may gain in short-term cash flow from an oil price shock, but the easy money dislocates their economies and subsequently they are subject to a traumatic income squeeze as oil demand falls as a result of the setback of the world economy triggered off by the initial oil price shock. This trauma now belongs to the common intellectual and political heritage of the oil exporters, including Iran and Iraq, but here it conflicts with priorities that are more urgent. The most important problem for OPEC in the mid-1980s was Saudi Arabia's need for revenues, which it ultimately settled by raising output. As a result of this experience there was until recently an apparent consensus among the OPEC countries that they might have more to gain from volume expansion than from price rises in the oil market. Consequently, the recommendation made by Saudi Arabia in the mid-1980s was that OPEC should opt for market share, not for high prices. This was backed by large oil reserves, especially in the Middle East. Iraq's incursion into Kuwait has upset this strategy of expanding the market for oil rather than raising the price, at least temporarily. The strategy pursued by OPEC between 1986 and 1990 was compatible with the interests of the oil-importing countries.

There was a further strategic wisdom in this choice. By keeping the oil price moderate, the technological backstop could be avoided or at least deferred. Development to replace oil in its primary market, the transportation sector, has been retarded. Any new oil price shock not only carries the risk of a nasty return through declining oil demand, which may be temporary, but also a risk of stimulating the development of alternative fuels. This means essentially non-OPEC oil, where production in North America is the most price sensitive, and natural gas, which when oil prices are high becomes a more interesting alternative. Coal and nuclear energy should perhaps be included as well. In the longer run, alternative fuels for automobiles and airplanes would be stimulated by higher oil prices.

For the key OPEC countries, the difficulty has been to translate this wisdom and apparent policy consensus into action, especially in a conflictual political environment. In order to take a larger share of an expanding world energy market, capacity would have to be enlarged. The problem in the late 1980s was funding investment in capacity expansion, most acutely for Iraq. Ten years later, the problem is still funding investment, but now also in Iran and Saudi Arabia, besides Iraq. It is also managing aggregate oil supplies to keep prices within an acceptable range and distributing market shares and revenues.

In the world oil market, the fundamentals are not only geology and economic entities, but also organization. OPEC certainly appears an exceptionally successful defender of the interests of a group of raw materials exporters that are also developing countries. In hindsight, OPEC has at times also been effective in stabilizing oil markets, and contributed to the stability of the world economy. Oil is probably the only commodity whose price has a macro-economic importance by influencing inflation rates and trade balances. From this perspective, the world economy benefits more from oil price stability, almost regardless of the level, than from erratic price movements. By means of negotiations and compromises between member countries' different interests, OPEC has for long periods enabled the oil price to remain fairly stable through both rising and falling demand in the market. Success has always been limited, however, to periods of no more than five or six years.

OPEC has experienced several ways of reaching agreement and avoiding internal conflict. Until the early 1980s OPEC only set the price of oil, leaving production and export levels to member countries. This procedure allowed some flexibility and its purpose was to free OPEC from many of the tensions that have plagued other exporter cartels. The price question was, however, divisive, as Saudi Arabia usually wanted lower oil prices than most other OPEC members. Since the mid-1980s, OPEC has switched to setting quotas, allocating market shares and the relative shares of oil revenues, without setting explicit price targets. This procedure apparently leaves oil pricing to the market, with the purpose of avoiding explicit disagreement. However, the issue of market shares is equally divisive, as demonstrated by competition between Saudi Arabia and Venezuela in

1997–98 over shares of the US market. OPEC appears unable to function as a perfect cartel, both setting prices and allocating market shares. OPEC successes alternate with failures. The challenges that provoke breakdown of OPEC cohesion and discipline usually originate in slumping demand for OPEC oil, caused partly by OPEC stimulation of non-OPEC competition through high oil prices.

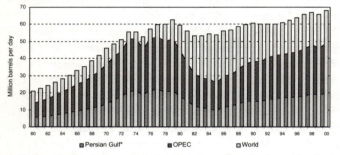

* *Persian Gulf nations are Bahrain, Iran, Iraq, Kuwait, Qatar, Saudi Arabia and United Arab Emirates.*

Figure 14: World, OPEC and Gulf oil supplies 1960–2000
Source: Energy Information Administration/Annual Energy Review 2001

Non-OPEC oil politics

By the time of the second oil price rise, in 1979–80, it was evident that high oil prices had stimulated investment in oil extraction outside OPEC to an extent that seriously undermined OPEC's market share.[65] Even if many countries outside OPEC produce oil, only a few are net oil exporters of world market significance. These countries are, in order of magnitude, Russia, Norway, the United Kingdom, Mexico, Oman and Canada. Their small number facilitates the eventual and occasional co-operation between OPEC and the leading non-OPEC exporters to stabilize the oil market. The diversity of interests between these countries, as between them and OPEC, makes co-operation ephemeral, adding to oil market instability.

Russia is by far the largest oil exporter outside OPEC, but much of Russian exports are in oil products, sold in neighbouring markets. In 2001, total Russian crude and oil products exports were about 4.7 million barrels a day, more than that of any OPEC country except Saudi Arabia. As a mature oil province Russia needs high oil prices to attract investment in exploration, development and infrastructure, but the major obstacle is the lack of political stability, proper legislation and an independent judiciary. There is no doubt that Russia has the geological potential to sustain and eventually expand oil output, provided it can attract foreign capital and expertise and so benefit from the general progress in petroleum technology and ensuing cost reduction. This would require Russia to get its politics and laws in order, so that crime and corruption would be less of a deterrent to foreign oil investors.[66] Russia would also benefit from oil prices staying above $16–17 a barrel at least. Failure on these counts is likely to compromise output levels and could sharpen Russia's interest in Caspian and Central Asian oil and gas, which would be less costly to develop and bring to the market than more remote Siberian reserves. After oil output declined by almost a quarter from 1992 to 1998, largely because of the lack of investment and maintenance, it has since been rising again and is expected to reach the 1992 level of 7.9 million barrels a day by 2002 or 2003. High oil prices have provided the Russian oil industry with earnings to finance upgrading and investment. Domestic oil consumption has also fallen, so that the decline in exports has been smaller. Over the next years, Russian oil demand is expected to rise, but at a much slower rate than oil extraction.

Norway has since 1970 become one of the world's leading oil producers and exporters, with net oil exports of 3.2 million barrels a day in 2001, above the level of all OPEC countries except Saudi Arabia. As an established oil province reaching maturity, Norway has an interest in stable oil prices, preferably in the range of $15–20 a barrel, to sustain exploration and development in more remote and deep-water offshore areas. Norway's major problem is insufficient competition resulting from a generation of resource nationalism during which a handful of domestic companies enjoyed preferential treatment. Policy changes affecting licensing, taxation and industrial structures are likely to provide incentives for exploration and development, with the prospect of output and export levels staying high for decades. Norway's biggest risk is a lasting oil price decline, with prices in the range of $10–15 a barrel for several years, which could compromise activity. Nevertheless, Norway has been one of the main drivers and beneficiaries of progress in petroleum technology, for which price instability has been a major incentive.

The United Kingdom is the third largest net oil exporter outside OPEC with net oil exports of about 1.6 million barrels a day in 2000, expected to decline by 85,000 barrels a day in 2001. As a mature oil province, its major challenge is to sustain exploration, development and output as prospects become smaller and more unfavourable. For this purpose, high oil prices are helpful, but the task is as much one of technology and organization facing worsening geological adversity. The United Kingdom has also been a major driver and beneficiary of progress in petroleum technology.

Mexico is the fourth largest net oil exporter outside OPEC, with net oil exports of about 1.5 million barrels a day in 2000. As an oil province, Mexico is of mixed maturity, with heavily explored and developed areas as well as promising, hardly touched areas, particularly offshore. The major problem for the Mexican oil industry is not prices, but inefficient industrial organization resulting from state monopoly. Privatization and competition would most likely boost activity and output.

Oman is the fifth largest net oil exporter outside OPEC, with net oil exports of about 0.9 million barrels a day in 2000. The country has fairly limited oil reserves, but substantial reserves of natural gas, giving it an interest in fairly high oil prices to boost gas exports.

Canada is the sixth largest oil exporter outside OPEC, with net oil exports of about 0.7 million barrels a day in 2001. As an oil province, the country varies from mature areas in Alberta to immature areas off the Atlantic Provinces, and to virgin territories in the Arctic North. To sustain exploration, development and output Canada needs stable oil prices, preferably at least $20 a barrel, and a simpler regulatory framework, which is complicated by Canada's confederal political structure.[67]

Altogether in 2001, these six countries accounted for net oil exports of about 12.7 million barrels a day. Consequently, together the leading non-OPEC oil exporters represent a considerable weight in the world oil market. The most important ones, Russia, Norway, the United Kingdom and Mexico, also have a potential influence alone, insofar as other oil exporters, within or outside OPEC, would not neutralize their actions.

All non-OPEC oil exporters of some importance face difficult trade-offs in their relations with OPEC. They have an interest in stable and preferably high oil prices, but they also have wider economic, trade policy and foreign policy interests. Some of the non-OPEC exporters are rich, industrialized countries; others are poorer developing countries. The essential common denominator among these countries, and between them and the OPEC members, is that they are net exporters of oil and have economic interests in relation to petroleum, but of varying importance in relation to other economic interests. Their strategies in relation to OPEC vary from co-operation to free ridership.

Historically, Russia in the guise of the former Soviet Union has been one of the main beneficiaries of OPEC cohesion, essentially as a free rider. Soviet oil and gas exports increased sharply in value in the early 1970s as oil prices shot up. Indeed, with high prices the Soviet Union became heavily dependent on oil and gas for hard currency earnings. High prices also improved the profitability of the Soviet oil and gas industry, permitting investment to sustain output. Most probably, high prices in the early 1980s deferred the anticipated decline of Soviet oil supplies by several years, from the late 1970s to the late 1980s. In hindsight, the Soviet empire was held together not only by military means, but also by abundant and at times cheap Soviet energy. The 1986 oil price decline severely hit Soviet hard currency earnings and was one of many factors undermining the empire. Post-Soviet Russia likewise remains dependent on oil and gas revenues. The 1998 oil price decline was an important factor behind the Russian financial collapse in the late summer of that year. Correspondingly, in 1999–2001, high oil prices have helped Russia's economic recovery.

In spite of the dependence on oil and gas exports, Russia, or the Soviet Union, is not really on record as having co-operated with OPEC to stabilize oil prices. Russia's oil exports are to a large extent in the form of refined products, which complicates co-operation to stabilize markets. From time to time, Russia has been in consultation with leading OPEC countries, but in the end, Russia has always chosen to pursue crude oil market share, leaving price stabilization to others. In late 2001 the Russian government agreed with OPEC to cut output for three months, but the decision was publicly opposed by the Russian oil industry.[68] With rising oil output and a doubtful commitment to co-operation, Russia is emerging as a major challenge to OPEC and oil market stability.[69]

Norway has had a more ambiguous policy towards OPEC. The 1973–74 oil price rise not only made the North Sea oil province significantly more profitable, it also caused concerns in Norway about too much oil money and economic overheating. Norway announced a commonality of interests with OPEC and deferred new oil licensing. The go-slow policy was abandoned in the late 1970s, as oil revenues were insufficient. The 1979–80 oil price rise helped Norway out of an economic squeeze. Subsequently, heavy investment made Norwegian oil output rise quickly, taking market share from OPEC and contributing to a downward pressure on oil prices. The 1986 oil price decline caused economic worries and Norway then announced co-operation with OPEC, through which oil output in the following years would increase less than technically feasible. This lasted until the 1990 Gulf crisis. Norway once more declared its intention to co-operate with OPEC in 1998–99 to help oil prices recover. This time, the moral support was important, but a number of investment projects were deferred, so that output did not actually increase as previously anticipated. The economic issue was that the oil prices of around $10 a barrel apparently put Norway on the threshold of financial pain, suffering a current account deficit for some months, although huge reserves cushioned the impact.[70] In political terms, the willingness to co-operate with OPEC without joining the cartel could be seen as a desire to stay between consumer and producer interests, enhancing Norway's international position. Norway's collaboration with OPEC has been more symbolic than real, indicating a position as a free rider disguised as co-operation. In late 2001, Norway declared its intention to co-operate with OPEC by cutting oil output by 150,000–200,000 barrels a day.

The United Kingdom has consistently abstained from any co-operation with OPEC, even if high oil prices in the late 1970s and early 1980s were essential in making the UK part of the North Sea an attractive oil province. As the UK has a large industrial and service base, oil means less to its economy. In political terms, the signal is that the UK has its interest with the oil consumers, especially the United States, not with OPEC or the other oil exporters.

Mexico, by contrast, has on several occasions willingly co-operated with OPEC to stabilize oil prices. In 1986 and 1999 Mexico actually cut output, facilitated by the nationalization that gave the government full control of the oil industry. Indeed, the record of nationalization and oil policy nationalism facilitated the move politically within Mexico. Also co-operation with OPEC was a way for Mexico to signal some political distance from the United States.

Oman has also co-operated with OPEC to stabilize oil prices in recent years, for example in 1999–2000. Politically, it makes sense for an Arab Middle Eastern country to take part in such a deal, initiated by neighbouring Saudi Arabia. Oman's impact is not negligible, as the country's net oil exports are not much less than those of Qatar, and far above those of Indonesia, both OPEC members.

Canada has at times shown sympathy for OPEC, but actual co-operation has been hampered by the conflict between federal and provincial interests.[71]

Mexico, Norway and Oman, as already stated, are the only other oil exporters that have shown political willingness to co-operate with OPEC. For all three, it can make economic sense to lower oil export volumes to support an OPEC effort to stabilize or raise oil prices, provided the volumes withheld are not taken by others. All three countries are largely dependent on oil revenues. From the buyers' viewpoint, Mexican or Norwegian oil is especially attractive because of the security of supply resulting from geographical location and political stability. This gives both countries a good bargaining position, but it also makes them likely subjects of pressure from major trade partners and allies to increase the level of production. Therefore, on the issue of production policy there is a conflict of interest between consumers on the one hand and Mexico and Norway on the other. This conflict was last open around 1980, but could become more acute again should Middle Eastern oil supplies appear precarious.

Other non-OPEC exporters are Angola, Argentina, Denmark, Malaysia and several others. They are each of fairly limited importance in the oil market and their interests are diverse.

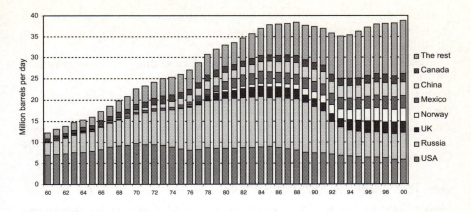

* *Ecuador (withdrew from OPEC in 1992) and Gabon (withdrew in 1994) are included for all years.*
***1960–1991: Former USSR., 1992–2000: Russia.*

Figure 15: Non-OPEC* oil supplies 1960–2000
Source: Energy Information Administration/Annual Energy Review 2001

CHAPTER FOUR

THE POLITICAL ECONOMY
OF OIL PRICES

The prescription of economic theory

According to economic theory, oil prices should at any moment converge toward the lowest marginal cost, meaning the cost of the cheapest additional barrel.[1] Because of the need to factor in oil scarcity, this should be seen from a long-term perspective, preferably taking into account the supply cost of alternative motor fuels, for example hydrogen. Therefore, from a dynamic perspective, oil prices should rise gradually to account for increasing marginal cost as the less expensive prospects are depleted and the industry needs to develop steadily more costly reserves.[2] Oil reserves are not only a quantitative concept: they differ in quality, which is determined by accessibility, prospect size and costs. From this perspective, oil prices should ultimately rise to the cost level of substitutes as depletion reaches low-quality prospects, with corrections for technical improvements that reduce costs and new discoveries that enhance the resource base.

The economically rational behaviour is to exploit high-quality and low-cost reserves before the low-quality and high-cost ones, so that marginal costs gradually increase as low-quality prospects substitute for depleted high-quality ones. The conditions are that all acreage, high-quality and low-quality prospects, and information are freely and equally accessible, so that investors can choose at will, that there is effective competition among oil investors, and that the oil market is competitive with no barriers to entry and that no single supplier can influence the state of the oil market.

Owners of oil assets in principle choose the depletion rate of the reserves by weighing price assumptions, anticipated returns in the financial markets and cost expectations. The basic rule is that reserves left in the ground can only give a return to the owner by appreciating in value at a rate above the return in financial markets, where proceeds are invested.[3] Therefore in situations where oil prices are assumed to rise at a rate below the rate of return in financial markets, it is rational to extract oil reserves at the quickest possible pace, to transfer assets from oil-in-the-ground to the capital market. Conversely, in situations where oil prices are expected to rise at a rate above the return in financial markets, it is rational to leave oil in the ground and defer extraction. This simple picture should be modified by cost assumptions. Insofar as costs are expected to decline because of technical progress, future extraction will be relatively less costly than at present, representing a quality improvement and a value increase of the oil in the ground, modifying the decision whether to extract or not.

The outcome in any case is that in principle, an extractive activity, such as the oil and gas industry, is a historical process, because resources are ultimately depleted. At any time, extraction limits are dependent upon the historical depletion record, volumes already extracted and the proportion and quality of reserves left in the ground. Present levels again set the limits for future extraction volumes. From this perspective, the extraction is a dynamic process. Ultimately, volumes decline and costs rise.[4] In a fully competitive market, the average return on investment in oil would in the longer run adjust to returns in the capital market, corrected for risk, so that investors would be indifferent to the balance of their assets in oil or financial instruments. Still, investor preferences would differ. Some would have a greater propensity than others to deplete oil reserves quickly.

In this setting, marginal costs would gradually rise, accompanied by oil prices. If the industry were fully competitive, the cost and ensuing price increase would be fairly linear, stabilizing at the cost level of substitutes, corrected for the impact of technological development. In this process, investors with assets producing at less than marginal cost would reap windfall profits, an economic rent as return on investment above normal, again corrected for risk. Moreover, inventive and efficient producers would also reap windfall profits by lowering costs before others. Conversely, investors with assets producing at marginal cost would be punished when oil prices declined as a result of technical progress.

The major practical consequence of this theory is that oil supplies would be price elastic, corrected for lead times, provided that markets were competitive. With rising prices, more oil would be available in the market, again corrected for lead times. Conversely, stagnant prices would gradually lead to declining oil supplies caused by depletion of reserves, unless corrected for by the impact of technical progress. From this perspective, oil supplies should represent no problem provided markets are competitive. Ultimately, oil prices will reach a level that encourages investment in substitutes.

The historical experience of the various oil provinces corroborates this point of view. So far, all known oil provinces seem to go through a development of distinct phases. At first, unit costs decline as new, large fields are found and infrastructure is put in place. Then, unit costs stabilize when the largest fields have been found and developed. Cost development usually reverses when half the oil in place in an oil province has been depleted.[5] Finally, unit costs rise as ever-smaller fields are developed. At present, the

United States is the world's most mature oil province. A large number of small fields provide a comparatively high share of production at a high cost. In Russia, oil production has moved into more remote areas with higher costs as the major historical fields have been depleted. In the North Sea, development and production are moving into fields that are more marginal. In the Middle East, Iran is the oldest and most mature oil province. In recent years, output has declined and unit costs have risen, at least partly because the largest fields are being depleted. Even in Saudi Arabia, unit costs are probably higher for new fields than for old ones.

The theory of oil prices following marginal cost is contradicted by salient micro-economic features of the petroleum industry and by the political framework. These considerations in principle apply equally to oil companies and to oil-exporting countries, especially those in the Middle East.

The essential economic feature of oil supplies is that fixed costs usually outweigh variable costs.[6] This general rule applies to crude oil extraction at the wellhead, to oil refining and to oil and natural gas transmission, as well as to oil product and natural gas distribution. The typical cost structure of an oil project is a limited amount of expenditure for exploration, a larger amount for capital investment, and hence a small amount for each unit extracted. This translates into a cost schedule with the bulk of costs being carried in the early years of the project, during the exploration and investment phases, while during the operations phase costs are low, although they tend to rise over time as depletion proceeds and prospect quality deteriorates. The schedule simplistically means that exploration and investment are sunk costs as operations and revenues commence, whether these costs have been depreciated or not.

During the operational phase, unit marginal costs are much lower than total project unit costs. Supplies from fields in operation are as a result robust, providing prices stay above marginal variable cost, but low prices evidently compromise investment in new capacity with higher total costs. The prices needed to justify investment in new capacity will give surplus profits, economic rent, to current operations insofar as they are depreciated. Once the sunk cost has been depreciated, the project is less exposed to price risks. When landowner-governments try to recapture the economic rent by special taxes, oil supplies get further insulated from price movements. The same reasoning applies to oil refining as well as to pipeline transportation and distribution of oil and in particular natural gas. An oil refinery is highly capital intensive, but variable costs are usually low.

Owners of producing but depreciated oil assets have a considerable choice of options for weathering a market glut with low oil prices: they can continue low-cost output or wait it out, taking the risk that future prices and profits will be higher. Conversely, facing a tight oil market and high prices, owners of producing and depreciated assets have the choice between raising output, if technically possible, to profit from the moment, or withholding supplies, to extend the life-time of their oil reserves, producing by revenue targets rather than volume targets or by a desire to maximize immediate profit in situations where volume cuts are more than made up for by price rises.[7] This is a backward-bending supply curve, established by the economic logic of the petroleum industry. It may, however, be more pertinent to oil-exporting countries than to private oil companies.

The practical consequence is that at any given moment the relationship between oil prices and costs is distorted and that oil supplies are not price elastic, except perhaps over a long time horizon. Falling oil prices do not necessarily cause current oil supplies to contract, at least not on a world-wide level within ranges experienced since 1970. Conversely, rising oil prices do not inevitably lead to rising oil supplies either. Apparently, in the world oil market at the aggregate level, prices and volumes are mutually independent entities, at least in the short term.

Multiple factors contribute to explain this remarkable state of affairs that seems to run contrary to the very sense of economic theory. The conditions required for a competitive oil market do not exist worldwide. Even with the opening of new areas for the petroleum industry during the 1990s, all acreage is not accessible, especially not in the Middle East, the world's most prospective oil province with the largest concentration of high-quality prospects. Information is often limited and restricted. Conse-quently, investors cannot choose at will, but often have to settle for lower-grade prospects. Even if the oil market has become more open since 1970, there are still important barriers to entry in terms of geological and techni-cal insight and financial strength. Finally, the low short-run price elasticity of oil demand means that several important suppliers can influence the state of the market and oil prices. This enhances the oil market risk for all major actors, whether governments or oil companies.

Since the supply of oil is concentrated, a small number of producers can have strong incentives to withhold supplies in order to capture economic rent.[8] Insofar as oil demand is comparatively inelastic, small changes in volumes supplied may have a huge price impact. In the oil industry, maximizing economic rent can be quite different from maximizing income. Maximizing economic rent could imply reducing production in order to keep oil in the ground, push up the price and stretch the lifetime of a finite resource.[9] This point was proven by the oil crises of 1973–74 and 1979–80.

As we have seen, the incentives to constrain the supply coincide with the high barriers to entry in the oil industry. Obstacles to newcomers are in geology, financing and technology. Finding oil requires access to prospec-tive acreage, risk capital, knowledge and luck. The outcome is often a limited number of firms operating in a given oil province. Depending upon their number and cohesion, they can collectively act as a monopoly, as a tight oligopoly or as a loose oligopoly. Hence, in most oil provinces and oil markets, many oil companies seem to capture economic rent.

Progress in knowledge, technology and organization lead to a continuous cost decline and corresponding quality upgrade of both older prospects and newer finds. Therefore, over time, in spite of the depletion of the resource base, in practice volumes do not decline much and costs do not rise, at least for long periods. Improved knowledge results in finding more oil and in getting more oil out of existing fields. Technical advances keep costs down in spite of the industry moving into marginal fields and remote areas.

The continuous discovery of new oil fields and even new oil provinces corroborates this point of view. Continuous progress in knowledge, organization and technology points in the same direction. It leads to the upgrading of reserves for existing oil fields and provinces at low cost.[10] The recent record points in this direction. Over the past decades, the inventory of proven reserves has risen in relation to annual extraction. Supplies have become more diversified with new oil provinces coming on stream. Costs have fallen and real prices have declined substantially since their peak in 1980.

The concept of economic rent

The concept of economic rent is essential to understanding oil pricing.[11] The intrinsic value of oil in the ground means that crude oil prices are generally above the simple supply factor costs such as exploration, field development and lifting. Oil in the ground represents resource capital for the landowner.[12] Oil has a value because of inherent properties and multiple uses. It is a substance provided by nature whose uses give it a market value above the sum of factor costs, including a normal return on investment.

The oil industry has an extraordinary profit potential because it concerns the extraction of a rare and finite resource whose energy content and wide range of applications give it an intrinsic value, even before it is extracted from the ground. The uneven geographical distribution of oil resources is more important than any ultimately finite resource base. The whole world uses oil, but oil is found only in a few places, and in uneven levels of concentration.

The extractive conditions and market price generally determine the economic rent accruing from oil. The extractive conditions are the size, the location and the geology of the field. Oil extraction generally has important economies of scale, so that unit costs decline considerably with field size and extraction per production well. Other factors such as access to infrastructure and the specific geology also determine the degree of adversity and costs. Oil extraction is not a uniform economic activity. It ranges from exploiting oil fields where the value of the oil extracted substantially exceeds all relevant costs to exploiting fields where the value of the oil extracted barely covers costs.[13] Some oil fields, principally large ones, are highly valuable because of their potential for economic rent. Other fields, principally small ones, are much less valuable because of their limited potential for economic rent. The wide range of prospective economic rent provides the oil industry with both high risk and an exceptional potential for profits.

Economic rent is a not a measure but a concept, which is difficult to define and quantify. This problem is corroborated by the imperfect competition in the oil industry. The challenge is usually to distinguish economic rent, the intrinsic value of oil in the ground, from monopoly or oligopoly profit. There are no generally accepted accounting principles in the petroleum industry that permit a precise determination of economic rent. The definition of economic rent is elusive, relying on economic theory rather than on objective principles established through practice and observations.

One analytical approach is indicated by the classical economic definition, which sees economic rent as income not requiring any effort or real costs.[14] It amounts to a 'free gift of nature', accruing from passive ownership or luck in disposing of a rare or scarce resource, not an active involvement by effort and investment, and whose ultimate supply is not influenced by human effort.[15] By this definition economic rent essentially accrues from the naturally finite supply of a resource and its income potential, not from market imperfections.[16] From this perspective, economic rent represents a durable income as payment above factor cost items, although the level tends to vary over time because of changes in the market. This is the basis for the Middle Eastern oil revenues.

Another approach is indicated by the historically more recent neoclassical definition of economic rent as the excess income over opportunity cost.[17] The rent from this perspective is income exceeding the minimum payment needed to attract the same product from an alternative source or from an alternative use. Economic rent is a factor payment above cost. This is a seller's gain in the factor market. The usual definition of cost includes a fair return on capital, so that the factor payment above cost implies a return on capital above the level needed to attract new investors to the industry. Such an excess payment may imply a resource scarcity or an imperfect market with barriers to entry or both. The problem with this definition is that there is no single level of return required. Jack Hirshleifer's definition is that 'Economic rent is income exceeding the minimum payment needed to attract the same product from an alternative source or from an alternative use'.[18] This is essentially the basis for oil revenues for more costly non-OPEC producers, who run the risk of being undercut by Middle East low-cost producers.

Pricing oil usually reflects the desire of the seller to keep some of its intrinsic value. The success in capturing part of the rent depends on the degree of competition in the market. It is a universally accepted principle that companies that have been granted the exclusive right to extract natural resources from a given area should pay as compensation a charge to the landowner.[19] The licences that give exclusive rights to oil extraction also represent barriers to entry, obstacles to newcomers and distortions of competition that will tend to protect the economic rent.[20] In the oil industry, the excess cash flow will tend to be a more permanent feature than in industries with fewer barriers to entry.

Market imperfections may have their origins in a concentration of bargaining power in a monopoly, a single seller, a dominant firm with a high market share, or an oligopoly, a small group of sellers. From this perspective, the concept of economic rent as excess payment is largely linked to market imperfections. This perspective applied to oil has been elaborated by Maurice A. Adelman. His view is simply that 'Economic rent is caused by imperfect competition'.[21] Adelman essentially reduces or even denies the importance of economic rent arising from the intrinsic value of the properties of oil in the ground, and instead explains payment above factor cost by market imperfections alone.

Such market imperfections are complex and cover a range of situations, but they are all expressed in the balance of supply and demand.[22] For example, a monopoly or oligopoly acting in collusion will have both the incentives and means to restrict supplies to raise prices, eventually increasing the economic rent. Furthermore, such imperfections are usually occasional or temporary. This approach does not really accept economic rent as a durable element of an economic system. In the longer run, market prices and supply costs will tend to converge. Applied to oil, this perspective is that oil prices will tend to approach the lowest cost of marginal exploration and development. For this reason, this approach accepts much less the notion of a durable or structurally differentiated return in investment. Market forces will cause returns to even out over time. For example, even if the ultimate supply of land is limited, its actual supply to the market is not fixed.[23] From this perspective, the challenge to the government is eventually to provide tax incentives and regulations so that competition and increasing factor supply reduce economic rents to more normal levels of return on investment.

A possible compromise is that some market imperfections are occasional distortions caused by exceptional events and will be corrected over time, others are not. The critical factor is market entry. Examples of an occasional distortion are when a storm knocks out a power line or actions of war destroy tankers. A recent case is the temporary scarcity of fuel oil in the US Northeast in the winter of 1996, caused by a sudden spell of cold weather. This caused an occasional excess profit, not an economic rent. Since deregulation, the US natural gas market has probably become the world's most volatile energy market. Demand and prices seem to be driven by the weather, which is unpredictable. Temporarily high prices because of cold winter weather cause occasional windfall profits for the gas producers, not a durable economic rent.

Kenneth W. Dam has a more elaborate definition of economic rent relating to oil, recognizing the quality differentiation of oil reserves:

> The resource rent accruing from oil, that is the payment above normal factor cost, varies strongly by fields and even oil producing regions. The general rule, although simplified, is that the economic rent essentially is a function of field size. Hence, some oil fields, principally large ones, are highly valuable because of their potential for economic rent. Other fields, principally small ones, are much less valuable because of their limited potential for economic rent. Indeed, most oil fields have costs that almost reach prospective revenues. The wide range of prospective economic rent provides the oil industry with both an exceptionally high risk and an equally exceptional potential for profits.[24]

The definition of economic rent relating to oil chosen here is the excess of the sum of all payments for crude oil and products, through the chain from the wellhead to the user, over the normal return on capital adjusted for risk. One problem is that the risk-adjusted return required varies according to prospects and investors, and throughout the chain. It is usually much higher upstream, in exploration, development and production, than downstream in transportation, refining and distribution. Economic rent is therefore a concept rather than a measure. In practical terms, because it is price sensitive, it will also include occasional profits.

The degree of control exercised by a dominant firm or small group of firms, an oligopoly, and the potential entry for newcomers are pertinent to the distribution of economic rent from oil. A few dominant firms have strong incentives to adopt joint strategies in pricing and product development and in establishing high barriers to entry to secure high profits and a high share of the economic rent. After initial competition, they observe each other and often seem to respect an unwritten code of common benefit. They are seldom rivals to each other. Smaller rivals can be ignored, as they seldom have the resources to challenge the dominant firms. They have to adapt and submit to the strategies of the larger ones. They may operate as independent units and aim at enhanced efficiency and profits within a small share of the market. The social cost is excess profits over a long time and little incentive for innovation.

A single dominant firm has by usage at least 50 per cent of a market or twice the share of the second firm.[25] In any industry, a dominant firm will be able to set the conditions and to a large extent impose its strategic interests on other firms. It can capture economic rent by arbitrary and discriminatory pricing to the extent it commands critical positions in an industry. To the extent that it controls bottlenecks, it can capture quasi-rents from other firms. Such a dominant firm will be in a strong position to capture economic rent. The control of infrastructure is often critical in this respect. This was the case with Standard Oil in the United States.[26]

A tight oligopoly is by usage a market where the four leading firms have at least 50 per cent between them. The limited number and high market share facilitate co-ordination, and with high rewards. The joint high market share enables an effective control and high barriers for newcomers, resulting in high profits well above normal factor cost. Other firms have to adapt to the strategies of the leading four firms, seeking economic rent rather than market share. The leading firms have both the incentives and means to seek economic rent together. This is the situation in many of the world's markets for oil products and in some important oil provinces, such as the Norwegian and UK continental shelves of the North Sea. The practical outcome is a certain transfer of the economic rent to the investors as oligopoly rent.

In the oil industry, long lead times for the development of new fields and the scarcity of some input factors limit the supply impact of high prices. Experience and knowledge are critical factors in short supply and represent more important barriers to entry than funding. An oil company with a successful risk record essentially represents a unique symbiosis of geological, engineering and financial insight. The scarcity of experience and knowledge qualifies it for quasi-rents. It is the combination of unique experience and technology that seems to be the crucial factor for oil companies to earn returns above average.[27]

Oil windfall profits

In addition to the structurally determined economic rent accruing from oil exploration, oil producers also benefit from occasional windfall profits caused by disruptions of oil supplies to the world market. Over the past 40 years, such disruptions have taken place sporadically. The first major disruption of oil supplies from the Middle East to the European market took place in 1956 after the British–French–Israeli attack on Egypt and the subsequent closure of the Suez Canal. The result was a price rise for oil in the entire Atlantic market, benefiting even oil producers in the Americas far removed from the theatre of conflict. The second major disruption took place in 1967, in conjunction with the Six-Day War between Egypt and Israel. The Suez Canal was closed at this period too, causing a disruption of oil supplies to Europe, an oil price rise in the Atlantic market and occasional windfall profits to other oil producers.

The third major disruption in 1973 was followed by a more important and more durable oil price increase. The war between Egypt and Israel in 1973 in many ways triggered an oil price adjustment that seemed long overdue to correct the long-term balance between supply and demand. Contrary to the two earlier disruptions, the 1973–74 crisis had a lasting effect. Oil companies did not only reap an occasional windfall profit during the crisis, but were rewarded afterwards with a much larger economic rent. Oil prices went up, but their production costs in established areas stayed even. Oil suddenly became much more valuable for both landowners and operators. This provided oil-exporting governments with challenging tax issues. The next crises in 1979 and 1980, triggered by the revolution in Iran and Iraq's attack on Iran, also had more lasting effects. Huge windfall profits were made. The industry benefited from a subsequently even higher economic rent. For the North Sea oil industry, the combination of high oil prices and a rising US dollar exchange rate in the early 1980s provided an additional increase of the economic rent. Likewise, the 1990–91 Gulf crisis, by causing suddenly rising prices, provided oil exporters and oil companies with substantial windfall profits. In 2000, bottlenecks in US refining, transportation and storage of crude oil and products caused local scarcities and price rises unrelated to the state of the world oil market.

Controlling oil supplies and trading

In any market, the corporate structures, meaning the numbers and concentration of sellers and buyers and the degree of integration, determine the degree of competition and bargaining power, and consequently, price formation and the distribution of profits. The properties of the oil market with a large element of economic rent make the corporate structures even more important for performance. Indeed, historical evidence is that market organization and corporate structures are pivotal issues for the supply of oil. Barriers to entry are crucial in this respect.

Traditionally, the oil industry has been dominated by a small number of large, vertically integrated oil companies. Mainly, their historical supply base has been the Middle East and North Africa. For example, BP has its historical origin in Iran, but also had leading positions in Iraq, Kuwait and the United Arab Emirates. Exxon-Mobil and Chevron-Texaco were dominant in Saudi Arabia until the 1970s. TotalFinaElf had its origins in Iraq and Algeria.

Control of transportation and trading has been essential, often conditioned by access to capital. Total supplies are less a sum of an infinite number of individual spontaneous decisions concerning output by price takers than the outcome of deliberate considerations about the overall state of the markets by a small number of price makers. This further explains why oil supply patterns at times are remarkably robust in relation to price changes and why oil prices do not always respond to changes in supply or demand.

Standard Oil achieved its legendary dominance by its control of oil refining and transportation in the United States from around 1880 rather than by owning production. Economic rent accrued to the middleman, Standard Oil, because oil producers in the US Northeast had no other company to sell to and consumers no other company to buy from. Standard Oil acted as a monopsony, a single buyer to multiple producers, and as a monopoly, single seller to multiple consumers. The scale of refining and transportation operations ensured it had lower costs than any competitor, permitting selective pricing to kill off competition.[28] Standard Oil also stabilized the US oil market, ensuring a rapid expansion of refining and transportation infrastructure. The Standard Oil dominance was only reduced after the US Northeast got alternative low-cost oil supplies following large new finds in Texas. Standard Oil was finally broken up by a court decision in 1911. In Europe, competition from Russian oil prevented Standard Oil from getting a monopoly.

In the meantime, integration appeared to be a sensible solution to the oil industry. The Royal Dutch company, producing oil in Indonesia, had problems servicing markets in Europe and elsewhere. At the same time, Shell Transport had developed tankers to transport oil at low cost over long distances. By 1906 the two companies were co-operating closely, and by 1911 they merged into Royal Dutch Shell. This was the world's first vertically integrated oil company. Control of supplies, transportation and markets facilitated co-ordination, a better utilization of the capital stock, and higher profits. This was soon to become the model for the international oil industry. Vertical integration also facilitated the co-ordination between companies, to protect market shares and profits.

In 1928 the Achnacarry agreement took place. This is the popular name for the Pool Association of 17 September 1928 to set up an oil cartel.[29] The agreement covered the whole world except the United States and the Soviet Union, with the aim of freezing market shares and co-operating in the use of facilities such as refineries to avoid duplication of investment. The initiators were seven large international oil companies (BP, Chevron, Esso, Gulf, Mobil, Shell and Texaco), which within months were joined by the French CFP-Total and a number of US oil companies with significant international operations. The background was a price war that emerged as the major oil companies gained control of Middle Eastern oil and developed a consequent desire to avoid mutual loss. The agreement institutionalized the major oil companies' control of international oil trading for decades. The worldwide contract was soon duplicated by many similar agreements at the national level.[30] Until the early 1960s, with some exceptions, a de facto cartel of international integrated oil companies controlled oil supplies to the major markets outside the USA. The objective was to stabilize markets, shares and prices. The effort was successful for decades.

In the 1960s, the cartel market power was eroded because of the combination of quickly growing demand and the rise of competing supplies from the Soviet Union as well as a number of Middle Eastern and North African countries eager to expand their oil exports and earnings. Lower shipping costs were important in opening the market to newcomers.

Until the early 1970s national oil companies had little international significance. Yet in 2001, they supplied close to three-quarters of the oil sold in the world market. As outlets for crude oil, the national oil companies are essential in securing the market power of the leading OPEC countries. Saudi Arabia's Aramco, Kuwait's KPC, Iran's NIOC and Venezuela's PdVSA are the trading instruments through which the supply decisions are translated into actual earnings.

The rationale for a direct state participation in the oil industry has been to secure crucial national interests, supposedly more efficiently than market forces and private initiative alone. The national interests to be defended have been defined as partly economic, such as to secure a reasonable part of the economic rent related to oil for the exporters. This was particularly important in the 1970s and early 1980s. The national interests related to oil have also been defined as partly political, such as to secure oil supplies for the importers. This was the predominant rationale before the era of abundant and cheap oil in the 1960s. Political motives have been important for the oil exporters also, such as to secure national control of oil extraction and oil exports. In these countries, the desire to acquire insight into the oil industry has also been an important motivation for establishing a national oil company. Considerations extraneous to the market have been decisive in the establishment of such companies. The result has been to engage state capital, to risk the taxpayers' money in oil exploration, extraction, transportation, refining and marketing.

In most OPEC countries, and in all major Middle Eastern oil-exporting countries, large national oil companies dominate the oil industry. They usually represent a considerable potential for rationalization and cost cutting. They play, however, an essential role in translating government volume-supply decisions into oil market realities of prices and terms. Saudi's Aramco is in this respect the world's most important oil company, followed by Kuwait's KPC, Iran's NIOC, Venezuela's PdVSA and Norway's Statoil. For this reason, a complete privatization of the oil industry of the leading oil exporters would require new instruments for translating oil policies into oil market realities, or for the exporter governments to renounce ambitions of market control, with possibly negative effects on the capture of economic rent.

The outcome is a dichotomy of the world's oil industry. Upstream, in their traditionally dominant position, the large multinational oil companies have to a large extent been replaced by state-owned companies. Since their number is much larger, the result is paradoxically a more competitive crude oil market. Downstream, the competition is stronger between larger numbers of highly different companies. The main trend is that the required return on investment and operational efficiency is stronger downstream than upstream and stronger for private than for state-owned companies. The preliminary conclusion is that in a world petroleum market with intensifying competition, there are strong efficiency gains in specialization. Even the large multinational oil companies that historically had the ambition to do everything related to oil everywhere increasingly specialize to cut costs. Also, specialized and cost-effective companies are less exposed to price risks. Finally, specialization means reduced competition and higher chances of above average rewards, of capturing a larger share of the economic rent.

The oil trade has changed profoundly since 1970. Historically, the major way of supplying markets was through integrated trading, meaning that oil was the subject of transactions between the producing, the refining and the distribution subsidiaries of the same group, and sometimes also the shipping subsidiaries. These internal transactions were enhanced by swaps of crude oil and products between major oil companies. The trading system was essentially closed, and costs and intermediary prices were not transparent. In hindsight, this was the way the international oil industry could capture a large part of the economic rent accruing from oil, at the expense of the oil-exporting countries. Until about 1970, integrated trading represented perhaps 85–90 per cent of international oil trade. The wave of oil nationalizations in the 1970s and early 1980s, and the consequent loss of large parts of the supply base for the major oil companies reduced the volume and significance of integrated trading. At the turn of the millennium, integrated trading is still practised, but it represents a much smaller part of world oil trade, besides being more transparent and usually priced according to spot or futures markets.

The traditional supplement was spot trading, which is a network of worldwide informal contacts that sell and purchase cargoes of crude oil and oil products.[31] Reference is usually made to significant refining and storage facilities, such as New York, Rotterdam or Singapore, or to major oil fields, such as North Sea Brent. In the past, the spot market concerned a small volume and was considered the last resort for oil companies wanting to balance demand and supply. Therefore, spot market prices would fluctuate considerably because of marginal volume changes and not always reflect prices in integrated trading, which until 1970 was the essential world oil market. Spot trading took off under the impact of the oil supply crises of

1973–74 and 1979–80, as buyers cut off from their traditional supplies would seek alternative sources. The surge of spot trading improved oil market transparency and therefore helped the oil-exporting countries capture a larger part of the economic rent. Today, spot market participants are oil companies, traders and brokers. The number of traders, who contrary to brokers take risk by buying and selling crude oil and products, swelled in the 1970s, but has since been much reduced because of bankruptcies. The spot market remains an outlet for excess deliveries and a source of supplies.

Forward and futures trading developed in the 1980s and 1990s as instruments to provide information and share risks.[32] By enhancing transparency, they also facilitate OPEC's potential control of the oil market. A forward deal means locking prices and margins at the moment of agreement. It transfers risk from the seller to the buyer, who often will have no interest in the physical volume. Such deals take into consideration timing, such as the time required for a cargo to reach its destination. Forward deals usually involve two parties and have many forms. Futures contracts, by contrast, are standardized, specifying quality and volume as well as location and the obligation incurred, cash settlement or physical delivery. The two major exchanges are Nymex in New York and the International Petroleum Exchange, IPE, in London. During the 1990s, futures trading became the significant mechanism for setting oil prices. The volumes traded and the large number of contracts, in London and New York each several hundred thousand deals daily, ensure transparency and efficiency.[33]

Expectations about oil supplies are the driving force for price assumptions and inventory behaviour. Anticipations of undersupply stimulate the build-up of inventories, adding to gross demand in the oil market, whereas prospects of oversupply stimulate inventory drawdown, reducing gross demand. For this reason, inventory behaviour tends to amplify the cyclical oil market trends. The problem with inventory behaviour is imperfect information, especially about inventory volumes and supply risks. With the exception of the United States and a few other countries, inventory data are notoriously deficient, increasing the risk for oil companies in building up and drawing down inventories. Moreover, inventory behaviour is partly motivated by market psychology, where appearances, moods and fears may be as decisive as facts. Only such references can explain the panicky behaviour of the oil market, for example during the oil crises of 1973–74 and 1979–80. During the oil market turbulence of 1997–2000, inventory data and expectations of OPEC behaviour were essential in driving oil prices.

Spot prices respond directly to physical trading volumes, where inventory changes are essential. Saudi Arabia and the United States are the major actors in this respect. Saudi Arabia normally keeps large oil volumes in tankers at sea, so that the actual volume of Saudi oil sold in the market can fluctuate and differ considerably from a normally stable wellhead output within agreed OPEC quotas. The United States has the ability to influence the oil market by augmenting or reducing the Strategic Petroleum Reserve, SPR. In the autumn of 2000, for example, the US government decided to sell oil from the SPR to moderate spot oil prices. Futures prices reflect anticipations of the supply and demand balance, including inventory behaviour and OPEC supplies.

Oil industry restructuring and rent division

The OPEC countries sell oil to the international oil industry, largely the major oil companies. The wave of restructuring in the international oil industry that commenced in the late 1990s has evident repercussions for trading with the oil exporters, especially the OPEC countries. So far, the international oil companies have had vertical integration as an important comparative advantage in relation to the oil exporters' national oil companies, excepting those of Kuwait and Venezuela which have extensive downstream operations. Although return on investment in refining and distribution has been judged unsatisfactory by most major oil companies, downstream outlets at least provide a market security and a risk diversification that the non-integrated national companies lack. Large downstream operations have made Kuwait's and Venezuela's oil earnings more diversified and less exposed to the risk of crude oil price changes than is the case for most other OPEC countries. This can provide some explanation for the at times less than perfect adherence by these two member countries to OPEC quotas.

Worldwide, the oil industry is subject to continuous restructuring as a result of changes in technology, organization and financing. Determinants of the oil industry structure are, briefly, barriers to entry, economies of scale and technology availability, as well as market and trading control. The historical structure can be described as stability by oligopoly and cartel, with the major multinational oil companies in a predominant position. Outside the United States there were strong barriers to entry. The oil industry had important economies of scale. Technology was largely the restricted domain of the major multinational oil companies, who tightly controlled oil markets and trading. Huge intermediary profits provided a cushion, and the company earnings largely financed investment.

Between 1970 and 2000 external shocks changed the oil industry structure. OPEC, oil price rises and nationalization undermined the predominant position of the large oil companies. Barriers to entry fell because of lower costs, permitting the emergence and growth of smaller oil companies. High oil prices reduced the importance of economies of scale upstream, but not downstream. Technology became widely available in the market. Oil markets and trade opened up and became more transparent as nationalization in OPEC countries and elsewhere made integrated trading less important. Between 1970 and 1980 the basic operating conditions for the oil industry changed profoundly. In the early 1980s, the US oil industry was subject to a wave of largely hostile take-overs, reducing the number of oil companies.

Multiple forces have driven the recent oil industry transformation, and the precise rationale differs from case to case, as circumstances vary. The merger and acquisitions wave of the late 1990s, under the impact of low oil prices, was largely based on negotiated fusions. The general problem for the oil industry outside OPEC was the need for a higher return on capital employed and an insufficient growth potential. Financial markets focus increasingly on value added for investors, but the 1990s were disappointing for most oil companies because of low volume growth, declining reserves, rising costs and a slower pace of technological change.

Concerns about investor value added made the financial markets take an active part in oil industry restructuring in the late 1990s.[34] Volume growth and efficiency gains were to be made by mergers and acquisitions, as with synergy through complementarity. The need to replace reserves as current assets were depleted was of growing concern for many companies. Lack of exploration success could find compensation in mergers and acquisitions.

The stagnant oil market of the 1990s combined with efficiency gains caused a crowding-out effect in the industry. For some companies to grow and show a performance acceptable to investors, others had to shrink or disappear. Facing the low oil prices of 1997–99, some companies were eagerly looking for partners with which to merge to provide growth. If they failed to do so, investors could realize value added by selling the company.[35] The more successful oil companies could take over the less successful, whether the process was named a merger or an acquisition. The process also portrays some unwillingness in established oil companies to take upstream risk by fresh exploration in view of oil price uncertainty, or to break into new markets. Even efficient oil companies highly valued by the market, such as Mobil and Petrofina, preferred merging with a stronger partner rather than risking a continued independent life with a limited growth potential.

Nowadays there is a fairly clear relationship between size and market value in the oil industry, but that was not the case around 1990 and will not necessarily be the case ten years hence. The change is largely due to a small number of big mergers. BP and Amoco were each around 1990 two large, not very profitable oil companies. At first BP cut costs vigorously and then absorbed Amoco, whose staff was largely discarded. The outcome is a large and profitable oil company. The merger of Exxon and Mobil was followed up by massive cost reduction, so that the new company is both larger and more profitable than the previous ones. The merger of Total and Petrofina likewise led to a streamlining of operations and massive cost cutting, but integrating Elf may prove more difficult. The shedding of assets by the largest oil companies by necessity provides opportunities for the others.

To sustain efficiency, the large oil companies are likely to become increasingly selective in upstream engagements, but more generally seek market power downstream, so that there seems to be a growing space for smaller and medium-sized upstream oil companies. Differences in resources, strategies and costs make for an increasing potential for trading upstream assets. Through the purchase of assets, mergers and acquisitions there is a growing potential for new, medium-sized international oil companies, mostly in the United States but not only there. Insofar as smaller oil companies have cost advantages over larger ones, they may be attractive investment objects.

Stricter environmental regulations put a further squeeze on downstream operations. Further restrictions on emissions from refineries and fuels will require heavy investment that the large oil companies may easily finance, but whose burden will increase inversely with size, so that the stage seems set for a continued consolidation of the downstream oligopoly, but the upstream may look quite different. Natural gas may give a new lease of life to smaller and medium-sized oil companies, especially if they benefit from the opening-up of markets.

On balance, the international oil and natural gas industry seems to be heading for greater diversity, driven by liberalization, integration and specialization. Strong forces drive the industry toward a more oligopolistic structure downstream. The major oil companies are moving heavily into the gas and power industry, for example in the United States. Few electricity companies or gas transporters or distributors would have the resources to out-compete the major oil companies in natural gas and eventually electricity trading. Moreover, most electricity companies have little competence in natural gas trading. For the major oil companies moving into general energy markets, there is a prospect of at least an oligopoly rent. By such a move they will also show growth and investor value added. The counterpart is that the more the major oil companies engage in downstream operations, whether in oil, natural gas or electricity, the more their crude or natural gas deficit is likely to grow. They are likely to remain large net buyers of oil and natural gas, but selective in their upstream engagements. This could be a blessing for the smaller and medium-sized companies that are squeezed out of downstream operations or have never been there. The rising oil and natural gas deficit of the major energy companies also represents a strategic challenge to OPEC.

Consumers will foot the bill unless governments develop more aggressive and more independent regulatory and anti-trust agencies. The benefit of size is not secured. The traditional advantage of large oil, natural gas or electricity companies has been their ability to buy input goods and services at low cost, to streamline operations to cut cost and to wield considerable market power. They have also to a large extent controlled expertise and technology. Their disadvantage has been conservatism, inertia and high overhead costs. Smaller firms, by contrast, are more innovative, more agile and have lower overhead costs, but they have less clout in the markets, as buyers or sellers. In the new world of more integrated energy markets, large energy companies may draw advantages from servicing customers with integrated services, if that is what customers want.

More consumer-driven markets are likely to be more specialized, fragmented and dynamic. Smaller markets are often best served by smaller, specialized companies. Except for some marginal cases, the issue is no longer access to or availability of expertise and technology, but the application. In power generation, the development of the combined cycle natural gas turbine has lowered barriers to entry and significantly reduced economies of scale, threatening the large, established power companies. Any parallel development in the supply of motor fuel would threaten the large, established oil companies in their downstream positions.

The wave of mergers makes the international oil industry more oligopolistic. The outcome will be fewer, larger and stronger companies, enhancing the potential for both co-operation and conflict, and for market instability. This is likely to reduce competition in refining and distribution and raise return on investment in this segment of the industry. This amounts to transferring part of the economic rent from upstream to downstream operations, from extraction to refining and marketing. The effect will also be to transfer profits from oil-exporting to oil-importing countries. Such a measure is likely to meet the approval of the oil-importing governments. For this end, the international oil industry has good incentives, insofar as taxes are lower on downstream than on upstream operations. Moreover consolidating downstream operations, through mergers, streamlining and divestment, is likely to enhance the competitive edge of the international oil companies over the oil-exporting national oil companies.

The international oil companies enjoy greater strategy discretion than do their counterparts, the exporters' national oil companies. Being already integrated, the task for the international majors is to improve downstream profits and expand upstream operations, in order to achieve a better balance between refinery needs and equity crude output. This represents a new challenge to the exporters' national oil companies, whose task is to acquire downstream positions at a time when only the least profitable assets will be for sale, as well as to improve upstream efficiency and profits. The stage seems set for competition between the international majors and the exporters' national oil companies over markets as well as upstream positions.[36] The former have capital, knowledge and market outlets as their main assets, the latter have resources. At stake is the balance of economic rent in upstream and downstream operations, as well as the future shape of the international oil industry.

With slow market growth and uncertain oil prices, the mergers and acquisitions are likely to continue. As in the past, circumstances and motives are likely to diverge. The pursuit of volume growth will propel reserve acquisitions as well as the take-over of competitors.[37] The pursuit of shareholder value through efficiency and return on capital employed will lead to the slimming and discarding of operations seen as less valuable. The large oil companies have grown because they are efficient, they are not profitable just because of size.

In the modern oil industry, with lower barriers to entry because of available technology, falling costs and easier access to capital, size does not imply efficiency or high profits.[38] Size is no longer a guarantee of superior share price performance. In upstream operations, cost and risk control are essential. There is no relationship between size and profitability in exploration and production, where competent risk management is the key to success. Since 1990 there has been a remarkable convergence of costs and a rapid diffusion of technology. The cost and technology leadership of large oil companies is no longer evident. The comparative advantage of large oil companies is rather in regional downstream concentration. This changing performance pattern of the oil industry has important repercussions for the oil-exporting countries.

Between the wave of oil nationalization in the 1970s and the merger wave of the late 1990s, there was a certain division of labour between the exporters' national oil companies and the international majors. With some exceptions, the former had a crude surplus, whereas the latter generally had a crude deficit. This complementarity has provided the ground for co-existence, but the division of economic rent has mostly been favourable to upstream operations. Continuing this tacit understanding would in the short term provide a mutual reward through self-imposed constraints, but would in the longer run reduce earnings and stifle the development of the international majors.

If the international majors are more successful in substantial upstream expansion than the exporters' national oil companies are in gaining downstream positions, they will compete on increasingly unequal terms. Integration and better balancing reduce overall risk exposure for the international majors, providing them with both incentives and the means to transfer economic rent downstream, in a step that the exporters' national oil companies cannot follow easily, because competition will intensify more upstream than downstream.

If the international majors do not succeed in a substantial upstream expansion, but the exporters' national oil companies succeed in gaining downstream positions, they will again compete on increasingly unequal terms, but with upstream profits dominant, as competition will be less upstream than downstream. Integration and better balancing will reduce overall risk exposure for the exporters' national oil companies, providing them with both incentives and the means to transfer economic rent upstream, in a step that the international majors cannot follow easily because access upstream remains restricted.

If the international majors succeed in expanding upstream and the exporters' national oil companies succeed in acquiring downstream positions, the outcome will at first be intensifying competition at all levels, with economic rent diminishing. This amounts to a mutual punishment. The less efficient oil exporters and companies risk being driven out of the oil business. Subsequently, the surviving entities will have strong incentives to co-operate, to increase economic rent by limiting competition.

The ultimate solution might be a new wave of cross-border integration, with mergers and acquisitions between the exporters' national oil companies and the international majors. Insofar as co-operation would bring benefit, this could amount to a mutual reward in the international oil business.

Oil market stability is even more precarious when the interdependence of the oil-importing countries and the major international oil industry is taken into account. Co-operation with the oil-importing countries is difficult because of their attempts to capture economic rent through consumer taxes or protective measures. The division of economic rent will also have an impact on the potential for co-operation between the oil-exporting countries and the major international oil companies. If the oil-exporting countries retain a large share of the economic rent from oil, they will also have a strong bargaining position in relation to the international oil industry. The potential for high upstream profits gives incentives for the major oil companies to co-operate with the oil-exporting countries to stabilize the market. If the oil-exporting countries lose a large share of the economic rent from oil, potential upstream profits will be less, with weaker incentives for the major oil companies to co-operate. If the trend toward vertical integration persists, oil prices will be increasingly affected by decisions in vertically integrated companies, with an ensuing risk of transferring part of the economic rent downstream.[39]

Risk by market mismatch

The oil industry value chain has distinct stages: exploration, field development, extraction, transportation, refining and marketing of petroleum products. Surplus capacity, scarcity and profits move along the chain, and never stabilize.[40] Different risk estimates for these various activities lead to different risk premiums, which together make up the average risk premium in the oil industry. Vertical integration from exploration to marketing was historically the normal form of organization in the oil industry. Risks and losses in one activity can be offset by gains in other activities. The overall economics of an operation ultimately matter to integrated oil companies. The usual practice in the oil industry, as in banks engaged in oil financing, is also to consider the risks of the various activities separately. For most oil-exporting countries, including most OPEC countries, upstream concentration enhances risk exposure.

The exploration for oil (and natural gas) is the most risky part of the industry. Because of geological uncertainties, there is a risk of drilling a large number of dry holes before hitting commercial quantities of petroleum, though this risk may be reduced through a portfolio effect (diversification) for a firm that undertakes exploration in various unrelated geographical areas. This is the strength of the large multinational oil companies. This risk reduction is much smaller if all exploration is undertaken in the same general geographical region. An oil company with a high concentration of its exploration projects in one country is more exposed to risk than a company with its exploration more diversified throughout the world. This is a drawback for the national oil companies of the OPEC countries. Exploration in any OPEC country is attractive to a major oil company with activities elsewhere because of the diversification effect. Practically, this means that a diversified international oil company is likely to borrow for investment purposes in a given OPEC country at better rates than the undiversified national oil company of the country concerned, and for this reason can capture a somewhat larger share of the economic rent.

Because of the high risk, exploratory drilling is normally financed by internally generated funds only. This reliance upon internal financing in the exploration phase constitutes a certain barrier to entry in the oil industry, based on a threshold of financial strength. In the exceptional circumstance of external financing being involved, the risk premium is generally much higher than the industry average.

The development is much less risky than exploration, as it only takes place after the existence of commercial quantities of petroleum has been proved. There is a persistent resource risk, linked to the characteristics of the field, such as recoverable reserves and depletion rates, as well as the technical operating conditions of the field at subsequent stages of exploitation. The resource risk is generally inverse to the estimated size of the field, with a comparatively small risk for large fields and a larger risk for smaller fields. The risk premium for developing smaller fields is higher than for developing large oil fields. There are also possibilities of cost escalation, of delays and of price decline, potentially compromising the economics of the operation. These risks too may be reduced by diversification.

The risk of cost escalation is particularly great in offshore conditions or in remote areas. The innovative character of the field development and limited experience in offshore construction at first led to considerable cost escalation in most of the early North Sea fields, as well as to prolonged delays, involving further interest costs and price risks. For this reason, the state of technology and project experience of the industry in general, as well as of the particular company, are important factors in assessing the cost and time risks. In the late 1970s and early 1980s North Sea oil development appeared particularly risky because of the unexpected cost escalation and delays.

The risk of a price decline during construction work, before the commencement of extraction and revenues, depends upon the state of the oil market. There are apparent cyclical trends in the development of the oil market, but they are at best uneven and uncertain. By the same argument, the probability of price loss is comparatively great after a major oil price increase or a prolonged period of high oil prices, but these cyclical trends in the oil market are difficult to forecast. As has been evident in 1999–2001, the major oil companies are reluctant to invest high earnings in renewing the resource base and expanding the supply potential out of fear that during the lead time between investment decisions and the cash flow, crude oil prices will fall and more of the economic rent will move downstream. Corresponding concerns limit capacity expansion in the OPEC countries.

Lenders charge a risk premium in financing a specific field development. The risk premium depends upon the exact field and the company involved. The general practice of the oil industry, with the exception of the major international companies, has been to rely upon a high degree of external financing for field development in order to reduce risk. This trend has become more pronounced with the oil industry moving into less accessible areas, such as the North Sea, which has brought on a need for risk diversification. The increasing reliance upon external financing has been especially important for small oil companies.

The major international oil companies have, on the other hand, tended to finance field development through loans to subsidiaries. These loans reflect the assumed conditions and risk evaluation of the financial markets for this kind of a project. In this case the resource risk, linked to the particular characteristics of the field in question, is especially important in determining lending conditions. In any oil province, there is a combined cost risk and price risk, together with a resource risk for the smaller oil fields considered for development. The financial markets in general demand a risk premium for lending to field development.

At the oil-extraction stage of operations, the risk is generally much smaller. The reason is that the risk in this case is linked to unexpected reservoir behaviour, unforeseen technical problems and unexpected price developments during the course of field depletion. The general practice of the oil industry is to finance extraction costs from current revenues, but there are several examples of oil companies contracting loans to finance operations. In these cases, the risk premium is generally below the industry average, again with due consideration for the field in question.

If the oil companies adjusted perfectly to the capital markets, they would transfer their borrowing according to the shifting differences in real interest rates between the various capital markets. In this way they would benefit systematically from the lowest possible real interest rate. Experience shows that this is not always the practice. Many oil companies prefer to stay with their established banking connections and to continue to raise capital in their local financial markets, even if that may temporarily mean a higher interest rate, to maintain a client relationship with established and preferred sources of capital. This is particularly the case with national oil companies, which because of the higher unsystematic risk tend to stay with established sources of finance.

The oil market currency risk

Oil prices, at least in the short term, do not seem to adjust for changing relative exchange rates: this is because of market rigidities, imperfect competition and low price elasticities for both oil demand and oil supply, at least in the short term. The low short-term price elasticity of demand means that the value of oil traded in relation to other goods and services is more immediately affected than volumes. In the oil market the price risk is supplemented by a considerable currency risk for all agents who do not make transactions in their own currency. In practice, this is today the case for agents outside the United States or countries with currencies tied to the US dollar. For those agents, the oil price risk and the currency risk represent mutually independent risk parameters.

Today, all international crude oil transactions are made in US dollars. For oil traded across borders, the dollar is the only accepted unit of account, standard of contracts and medium of exchange. Moreover, it is the preferred store of value for countries that export oil. Oil prices are formed in spot, term and future transactions with several geographical locations as references, but they are all in dollars. Spot oil bargains in Singapore, futures deals in London and term arrangements in New York have one common denominator, the US dollar.

Since oil price movements and exchange rates do not always offset each other, the oil-exporting countries also experience a currency risk, enhancing the oil price risk to their terms of trade. The exact risk depends on the structure of the foreign trade, essentially the origin of their imports. The dollar depreciation against European currencies in 1972 gave OPEC reasons to renegotiate oil prices upward, because most member countries had most of their trade with Europe. Today, Western hemisphere oil exporters, such as Argentina, Canada, Colombia, Mexico and Venezuela, are little exposed to a currency risk in relation to oil because most of their foreign trade is with the United States. Other oil exporters are more exposed to a currency risk enhancing the oil price risk, because their foreign trade is geographically more diversified. The North Sea oil exporters are highly exposed to a currency risk because for both Norway and the United Kingdom, Euroland is the major trade partner. For both these countries, oil prices and exchange rates influence the terms of trade to a considerable degree. This risk is particularly high for Norway, as is highlighted by the weakness of the Norwegian currency during 1998 when oil prices were low.

Currency movements will in principle not affect the value of oil in relation to other imported goods, for example bananas or tin. By contrast, currency movements do affect the value of oil against goods and services that are not traded internationally. Even against goods and services that are traded internationally, price adjustment to currency movements is often a slow and imperfect process because of protection and imperfect competition. The same commodity can have different relative values in different markets, even if the long-term trend is in the direction of equalization. Imported goods decline in relative price when a country's currency appreciates and they rise in relative price with a depreciating currency. That, of course, also applies to oil.

The international issue is that experience shows oil prices in nominal dollars do not immediately adjust to currency movements. If the oil market had been characterized by perfect competition, movements in the dollar exchange rate against major currencies would have had a counterpart in changes in the nominal dollar price of oil, to retain the market equilibrium and guard the stability of the supply and demand balance. Such a perfect competition and instantaneous adjustment would have an expression in a close negative relationship between the nominal dollar oil price and the dollar exchange rate of the currencies of important oil-exporting and oil-importing countries. In principle, a high dollar exchange rate would accompany a low dollar oil price and vice versa. In this case, currency movements and oil price changes would tend to even out. The choice of currency for pricing oil would be without importance for its value in the various markets.

Experience since the first oil price rise in 1973 indicates that the adjustment between oil prices and exchange rates is imperfect and slow, but with major differences between periods and countries. The oil price and the dollar exchange rate represent overall mutually independent risk parameters for agents outside the USA, but with varying intensity and direction. The historical pattern, seen from Western Europe, is that in some cases, movements of the dollar exchange rate enhance oil price movements, but that in other cases the dollar exchange rate tends to mitigate oil price changes. The lack of a clear pattern shows that oil prices and currency exchange rates have overall different driving forces. Sometimes they coincide, sometimes they diverge.

For example, after the first oil price jump in 1974–75, and again in 1977–78, the decline in the US dollar exchange rate in relation to European currencies was not compensated for by a higher dollar oil price. Nominal oil prices fell in Western Europe, so that the purchasing power of a barrel of oil sold in the European market declined. The oil price rise in 1979–80 hit both the United States and Western Europe, but the rising dollar exchange rate in relation to most European currencies during the years 1980–81 and 1982–85 caused an additional oil price upsurge for most of Europe. It was only partially and belatedly followed by a dollar oil price decline. The purchasing power of a barrel of oil rose relatively more in Europe than in the United States. In 1986, by contrast, the Europeans experienced both a dollar oil price and a dollar exchange rate decline, causing a larger nominal oil price drop in European currencies than in the US dollar. By 1998, currency appreciation had contributed to oil having relatively less value in the German market than in the United States or in Norway, compared to the 1986 reference point.

Pricing and invoicing in dollars mean that the price risk in the oil market in reality is less for US buyers than for those in Europe. US oil importers save on the currency-hedging costs that burden their European counterparts. A recent example is that US oil buyers could avoid the further oil price rise during the years 1981–85, over the one of 1979–80, which hit Europe because of the dollar appreciation. On the contrary, US oil buyers were able to benefit from lower oil prices by as early as 1983. Because oil is the price leader in the energy markets, US businesses could benefit from relatively lower energy costs several years before their European or competitors. This might have been one of several factors that caused an economic upturn in the United States some years ahead of in Europe. Close political ties with the Gulf oil exporters induce the exporters to place their financial surpluses in the United States rather than Europe. Moreover, with the dollar the United States commands the internationally most accepted medium of exchange and store of value. At any eventual new oil price increase, the United States would be in a more favourable position by being able to transfer the deficits abroad and run a large trade and payments deficit because of the dollar's position as the world currency. This is a practical advantage of seigniorage, the right to issue money. For this reason, the choice of currency for pricing and trading oil is not only a technical issue of economic adjustment, but also an issue of distributing power and risk.

The impact of taxation

The definition of economic rent chosen here is price sensitive as it includes all payments by end-users, including duties and taxes. It is a universally accepted principle that companies that have been granted the exclusive right to extract natural resources from a given area should pay as compensation a charge to the landowner.[41] This is irrespective of whether the landowner is a government, as in most cases, or private interests. The efforts to levy special taxes on petroleum extraction are generally motivated by the desire of the landowner to recapture at least a part of the intrinsic value of oil in the ground.

Because oil in the ground represents resource capital for the landowner, lifting the oil means depleting the owner's resource capital, for which the landowner usually demands compensation in the form of levies, special taxes or profit sharing. These charges are basically different from ordinary taxes on income, turnover or capital. The general taxes on income, sales or wealth in principle apply in a compulsory way to all citizens and businesses in a society. By contrast, charges on the extraction of oil or other mineral resources are paid to the landowner, usually the government, by individuals or corporations that have voluntarily and successfully applied for the exclusive right to extract natural resources from a given area.[42]

The licences that give exclusive rights to the extraction of oil also represent barriers to entry. These barriers to entry represent obstacles to newcomers and distortions of competition that will tend to protect the economic rent.[43] In the oil industry excess cash flow will thus tend to be a more permanent feature than in industries with fewer barriers to entry. Insofar as the government is both the owner of the oil resources and confers exclusive rights of extraction, it also has a reasonable claim to some, if not all, of the ensuing economic rent.[44] The division of economic rent is a matter of bargaining between the landowner and the companies that enjoy the right to extract resources, depending on who needs whom the most, the landowner the capital and the services of the companies, or the companies the access to the land and the resources. This is relevant to the relationship between oil-exporting countries and the international oil industry.

The market value of crude oil causes an excess cash flow, the economic rent that is the target of the governments through special petroleum tax measures. Economic rent represents excess profits above the return on capital needed for investment to go on, so that in principle, changes in the size of the economic rent do not influence the willingness to invest in the particular industry, as long as return on capital is satisfactory, compared with the second-best investment option adjusted for risk. This is but one reason why changes in crude oil prices have comparatively limited effect on supply patterns. Landowner taxation represents another cushion between crude oil price changes and oil supply economics, especially insofar as taxes are levied on a net basis. For a company investing in oil extraction, the key economic concept is tax-paid cost, which is the sum of capital costs, operating costs and taxes.[45]

The tax-paid cost and the market price for oil determine the rate of return for the private investor. Insofar as targets are established for the return to the private investor, the tax-paid cost is a dynamic concept. Normally, when oil prices rise, so does the tax-paid cost. Oil investors gain from oil price rises, but they seldom recapture the entire gain from the price rise. Correspondingly, when oil prices decline, the tax-paid cost usually falls. This is due to the rent taxation adjusting to oil price changes. Oil investors typically lose from oil price declines, but many rent tax systems significantly soften the impact. When the government through taxes takes a large part of the economic rent, it also takes a corresponding part of the price risk.

The government-landowner is concerned with the concept of total government take, revenues through sales proceeds, fees, royalties, rent taxes and corporate taxes, with due regard to the rate of return desired for the private oil investors. Just like the tax-paid cost, total government take is a dynamic concept, moving with oil prices, both in its absolute size and in its relative share. Insofar as the government-landowner has specific targets for the private oil investors' return, the total government take has to adjust to oil price changes by adjusting tax rates. To provide a normal rate of return or an agreed share of the economic rent, total government take has to be much more sensitive to oil price changes than is the return for private oil investors.

From a historical perspective, the bargaining position of host governments strengthened gradually after the first major oil concessions were handed out in Iran at the beginning of the twentieth century. The outcome was gradually stiffer terms for the companies on the size and duration of concessions, as well as on total government take. This included fairly continuous renegotiations of historical terms. Likewise, fiscal conditions were getting tougher. At the time of the first oil concessions, oil-exporting governments had a weak bargaining position in relation to the international oil industry. The example had been set by Iraq, which in 1925 imposed a payment of four gold shillings per tonne produced. Saudi Arabia introduced a similar fee in 1933. In two new concessions handed out in the 1930s, the

Iraqi government had the right to 20 per cent of the oil produced at the wellhead. The government had the choice between taking the crude or money calculated according to the market price for oil.

Only after 1945 did royalties based on a percentage of production become a usual feature in oil-exporting countries. Venezuela initiated the 50/50 division of net oil revenues in 1948. It was facilitated by a US tax credit that enabled the avoidance of double taxation. Middle Eastern oil exporters such as Iraq, Kuwait and Saudi Arabia soon followed the example. In Iran, it was complicated by the absence of a similar tax credit in the UK. This was an important factor in causing the 1950–53 crisis between Iran and the UK.

By the late 1950s, the generally accepted international practice was for oil-exporting governments to impose a gross production fee, a royalty, usually varying between 8 and 20 per cent of the oil sales value. The value was generally based on a posted price, a government determined export price set to overcome the hurdles of an opaque international oil market where real prices to a large extent remained company secrets. The royalty did not enjoy a tax credit against US corporate income tax. In the host countries, the royalty was considered a cost to oil companies and could be deducted from the income tax base.

Until the mid-1960s, the general rule was a 50/50 split between host governments and oil companies of the net income from oil after royalties. In the 1960s, rising oil demand strengthened the bargaining position of the oil exporters. The host governments managed to raise their share to 60 or even 75 per cent of the net income from oil production. This was particularly the case for new exploration concessions.[46] Host governments also managed to renegotiate the terms on existing concessions in return for new acreage.

In 1960, the OPEC countries changed their petroleum taxation, putting the emphasis on excise taxes rather than on income tax. Excise taxes set a floor to oil prices in the marketplace, representing a cost element below which prices could not fall. Oil company earnings made up the buffer between the tax-paid cost and the market price, and they were eroded in the 1960s.[47] Income distribution between host governments and oil companies emerged as a matter of bargaining strength, changing over time according to circumstances. In the 1960s and especially in the latter part of the decade, the bargaining position of host governments in relation to oil companies was strengthening significantly. The consequent trend was a steadily higher total government take on oil. Historical concessions were not sheltered from higher taxes. As the economic rent increased through higher prices, the government-landowners inside and outside OPEC made efforts to recapture a greater part of it through new fiscal measures. Oil companies could not expect that concessionary and fiscal terms would be unchangeable anywhere in the world.

The quadrupling of oil prices in 1973–74 made evident the shortcomings of the established tax system, based on royalties and ordinary corporate income tax, when it came to capturing the ensuing large economic rent. Royalties, a limited gross tax, only capture a minor part of the rent. Corporate income tax targets companies in their entire array of activities, not specific activities and projects. Unless supplemented by special provisions, it is a general and blunt fiscal instrument, permitting and encouraging the diversification and cross-subsidization of activities and projects, with losses in some activities being offset by gains in others. Before tax is paid, large profits in some activities can be neutralized by losses elsewhere, making corporate income tax an ineffective tool to capture economic rent from oil extraction.

Fiscal considerations after the 1973–74 oil price rise encouraged a number of OPEC countries and non-OPEC oil exporters to take over their oil industries in whole or in part in order to capture gross earnings. Some countries, such as Norway and the United Kingdom also introduced special petroleum taxes aimed at capturing a larger share of the economic rent accruing from oil.

The 1970s thinking on oil taxation represented a U-turn on conventional taxation philosophy by considering the division of rent and the rate of return desirable for private investors in a given industry. The intention of the new taxation was to capture for the government-landowner the excess profits. There was no precedence in tax history for such a selective measure, designed exclusively to capture economic rent from petroleum activities.

In theory, a petroleum tax should capture all economic rent, leaving the private investor just with the risk-adjusted return to make the investment worthwhile.[48] The ideal petroleum tax should be progressive, rising with the rent, but also providing incentives for efficiency to the investors. In practice this is difficult, largely because costs are diffuse and unknown. There are basically two systems of petroleum rent taxation. One is bonus bidding, aimed at capturing economic rent before activities commence. The other is a resource rent tax, aimed at capturing economic rent as activities proceed. In theory, the two systems are not mutually exclusive as they can complement each other to capture economic rent with due regard to economic efficiency, but in practice government-landowners tend to opt for one or the other.

Consumer countries' duties and taxes are analytically problematic. Insofar as duties and taxes paid to consumer governments depress world market oil prices, they capture economic rent at the expense of the oil exporters, not least OPEC. Within the consumer countries, it is a transfer of money, not a rent capture, insofar as the citizens benefit through public services or other tax reductions.

In consumer countries, pricing oil is a socially and economically complex issue, especially in developing countries. Indeed, a large number of developing countries, which together have a large part of the world's population, have consistently low oil prices, at times below opportunity cost. Some oil-importing developing countries apparently consider their populations too poor to bear world market energy prices, however defined, while many oil-exporting developing countries, for example in the Middle East, seem to consider themselves too rich to let their populations pay world market energy prices. This is particularly pertinent to the pricing of oil products, for which there are transparent world market prices. Therefore, some poor oil-importing governments tend to use some of their scarce financial resources to subsidize oil consumption, while oil-exporting governments whose income has declined tend to renounce revenues by pricing oil for domestic use below world market prices. In both cases, a rent is passed on to consumers.

The welfare arguments in favour of passing an energy rent on to consumers point to the fact that incremental energy use, especially the use of oil products, is an indispensable part of the process of economic development. The argument is that charging high prices for energy would have a high social cost and that the benefits of low energy or oil product prices outweigh the costs. Moreover, energy expenditure represents a higher burden on low-income household budgets than on high-income ones. Consequently, oil product price increases tend to hit the poorer segments of the population more than the well-off.

The counter-argument is that pricing oil products below cost is not sustainable because it gives the wrong incentives to economic development, which will tend to be more wasteful in regard to energy, or oil product use, than necessary. Moreover, the government budget could more efficiently allocate scarce financial resources represented by the energy rent passed on to consumers. This is relevant to, for example, Iran.

Because oil demand, especially in the transportation sector, is fairly insensitive to price changes, there is little relationship between the amounts received in oil product taxes by consumer governments and any loss of economic rent by producer countries. Even if taxes should modestly depress demand, OPEC has the ability to cut output and maintain prices or even to raise them, as has happened. In 1992, the spectre of higher oil taxes in Europe caused OPEC to refrain from raising output.[49] The argument was that if oil demand were to be reduced by higher consumer prices, the oil exporters should benefit rather than the importer governments.

Since 1999, OPEC has substantially increased its economic rent accruing from oil, even if oil product taxes in the European Union are higher than ever. To sum up, from 1998 to 2001, oil exporters, oil consumer governments and the oil industry have all received increased earnings from oil. Indeed, the relationship between consumer end prices for refined products and crude oil prices is almost as small as it is between the latter and the costs of production.

Most countries tax oil products, usually through a general sales tax, or value-added tax, and a special excise tax or duty. Whereas a sales tax is proportional and will ensure that end-user oil product prices move in tune with crude oil prices, an excise tax or duty has the opposite effect. Being levied as a specific amount in a volume unit basis, it will insulate end-user prices from crude oil prices, to the benefit of the consumer government, which in this way will capture part of the economic rent, often a major part.

Excise taxes and duties levied by consumer governments vary by product and country. Europe generally has the highest excise levels on oil products. On average, in 2001, about two-thirds of the end-user price of oil products in the European Union was tax, with oil exporters and refiners and distributors sharing the rest fairly equally.

As early as 1945, governments in Europe and Japan began taxing oil products to raise much-needed revenues for empty state coffers and to discourage consumption and imports, safeguarding the trade balance. This is an important historical reason why oil products, especially motor fuel, have lower end-user prices in the United States than in Europe or Japan. At this time, the United States was still a net oil exporter with a trade surplus.

From the outset there was a remarkable contradiction in the European and Japanese motivation to tax oil products. Insofar as the objective was to raise money for the treasuries, the implicit assumption was that oil demand is not very price elastic, so that taxes do not severely reduce demand, making motor fuel, for example, a convenient source of income for the state. Insofar as the objective was to discourage consumption and imports, the implicit assumption was that oil demand is price elastic, so that taxes do reduce demand, making them an efficient tool to safeguard the trade balance. This policy contradiction persists in Europe and Japan, unexplained. As far as is known, no finance ministry has ever endeavoured to clarify this contradiction, or to elaborate on the social cost of high oil product prices.

In hindsight, it seems that the first argument should prevail. Motor fuel, which so far meets little or no competition, is indeed a convenient source of income for European and Japanese treasuries. Here, the major part of what the consumer pays at the pump is tax, either as a sales tax or as an excise tax. Therefore, the major cost factor to motorists is their own government, not the oil producers or the oil industry. Consequently, when European or Japanese motorists fill their tanks, they essentially pay tax.

Even in the United States, the government adds significantly to the cost of motor fuel through taxes.

Remarkably, motor fuel taxation in Europe and Japan and many other countries over time is not symmetric, meaning that the government intention evidently is to tax, not to discourage use or safeguard trade balances. When crude oil prices rise, as they did in the 1970s and again in 1990, consumer governments usually respond by raising fuel taxes further. The explicit intention is to discourage consumption, regardless of the social cost. When crude oil prices fall again, as they did in 1986, 1991 and 1998, the response is not to lower fuel taxes to pass the benefit on to consumers, enhancing the social benefit, but in many cases to raise fuel taxes further, ensuring that consumers do not benefit from lower energy prices, so that the consumer government can capture an even greater share of the total economic rent accruing from oil. This is, briefly, the mechanism that transfers an ever-rising part of the total economic rent from oil producers to consumer governments. Only in the summer of 2000 did European consumers start protesting at high fuel prices, intelligently directing criticism at their own governments rather than at the oil exporters.

The spectre of environmental taxes

The use of oil products is generally associated with environmentally harmful emissions of sulphur, nitrogen and especially carbon dioxide, CO_2. Although government restrictions have led to increasingly cleaner fuels, especially motor fuels, the regulation and in particular taxation of oil products are high on the political agenda. The 1997 Kyoto agreement perhaps represents a breakthrough for restrictions on oil use through environmentally motivated taxation and the trading of emission permits.[50]

Measures considered to curb emissions are green taxes, energy taxes, carbon taxes and the trading of emission permits. Green taxes aim at transferring the tax burden from labour to resource use and pollution.[51] In theory, this transfer should give a double dividend by raising demand for labour and employment and at the same time reducing finite resource use and harmful emissions. The argument behind taxing CO_2 emissions is that the revenues incurred could be used to reduce taxation of labour.[52] Ideally, the gains by reduced taxation of labour could eventually justify high taxes on harmful emissions.[53] The overall purpose is to make businesses internalize in their accounts the costs of waste, emissions and using resources that today are externalities and do not have market prices. There is ample evidence that taxes on waste and emissions of, for example, sulphur in many cases have had positive effects.

In principle, it may be reasonable to tax pollution instead of labour, but in practice there are serious problems. According to economic theory, labour and energy are mutual substitutes, but the actual use of energy depends on the level of economic activity. In practice, this means that rising energy prices can lead to either a more labour-intensive pattern of production and strengthen employment, or to a reduced level of economic activity and reduced employment. The outcome depends on circumstances and implementation. Economic theory does not give any decisive clue as to whether a reduced tax on labour will raise employment. The outcome again depends on circumstances and implementation. With lower taxation, some people might prefer to work fewer hours, so that to some extent the supply of labour is a negative function of net real wages. Moreover, there is an evident risk that green taxes will slow or even reverse the historical process of gradually replacing human labour by machinery that uses energy, although more and more efficiently. Insofar as energy demand is closely dependent on the level of economic activity, higher energy costs act as a tax on business and reduce the level of economic activity and therefore also demand for labour. Consequently, there is a risk that green taxes cause economic damage and a social cost. For example, green taxes can make transportation more costly, causing market expansion, the division of labour, specialization and productivity gains to slow down. A final consideration is that higher energy prices tend to be socially harmful because for households, the proportion of the budget spent on energy tends to diminish with rising incomes, although actual energy use tends to increase.

Although many options are available, energy taxes can simplistically be seen as excise taxes levied on the end-user regardless of the form of energy and its origin. The purpose can be seen as the curbing of energy demand in general, not only emissions. Consequently, they are more harmful to the more efficient and clean forms of energy. Their effect in, for example, power generation is therefore to punish the more efficient natural gas relatively more than the less efficient and polluting coal. Basically, the same economic and social arguments can be raised against general energy taxes as against green taxation, but more forcefully so, insofar as energy tax hikes have not been accompanied by reduced taxation on labour.

Carbon taxes are in a different league. Reducing CO_2 emissions will have a cost and constitute an economic burden whether it happens through direct restrictions, or indirectly through taxes or other mechanisms. National carbon taxes will raise end-user prices on fossil fuels. Ideally, to be cost effective they should depend on the carbon content of the different fuels. Therefore, they should be highest on coal, lower on oil and lowest on natural gas. Politically, this would require neutralizing the influence of coal producers. In the energy market, such differentiated carbon taxation would favour natural gas, essentially at the expense of coal, and possibly cause an accelerated transition from coal to natural gas in power generation. Insofar as carbon taxes lead to a general energy price increase, they invite the same critical arguments as energy taxes mentioned above.

It is generally accepted that trading emission quotas is the most cost-effective method.[54] The cost of abating CO_2 emissions depends on one's initial position and the potential for substitution. Taxes on CO_2 emissions hit indiscriminately and tend to be socially regressive. By contrast, trading emission permits provides incentives for abatement to take place where it is the least expensive. In principle, the market can allocate the emission reduction in a more efficient way than a general tax. The trade with sulphur dioxide emission rights in the United States is a relevant and successful example.

In any case, energy taxes or emissions permit trading would represent a prime price risk to the major Middle Eastern oil exporters and to OPEC oil-pricing strategy. Any taxation of oil consumption represents a transfer of economic rent from oil producers to oil consumer governments. Any trade in emission permits represents an additional cost to the consumer, also transferring economic rent by depressing world market prices. This reasoning assumes that consumer end prices on oil products are already at their maximum, at the level that the market can take without demand falling and consumers switching to alternatives. In practice, this is hardly, if ever, the case. Indeed, the consumers' value added from using energy tends to increase with economic growth and technical progress. In principle this means that with rising real incomes, consumers are presumably willing to pay ever more for energy. In practice, real energy prices tend not to catch up with economic growth or technical progress, at least not in an even way, so that over time, energy costs tend to represent a diminishing share of the budgets of consumers, whether they are businesses or households. The main exception is energy-intensive heavy industry.

The combination of an increasing value added from using energy and a decreasing budget burden evidently represents a potential for raising energy prices at the producer level or energy taxes in consumer countries, or both. In practice this means that the potential for making the consumer pay more for energy is rarely, if ever, exhausted, unless the end price rises are abrupt. Analytically, this means that the concept of total economic rent should be seen from a dynamic, not a static perspective. There is a potential for expanding the total economic rent by making consumers pay ever more, especially if the price increases are administered gradually. Both oil exporters and oil-importing countries could increase their revenues from oil for a long time yet. Historical examples are the oil price rises of the 1970s that were followed up by tax increases on oil products in Europe and Japan. The consumers were forced to pay more, and both oil exporters and consumer governments made more money out of oil. The abrupt character of increases in both crude oil prices and oil product taxes together caused economic damage and had a high social cost.

A major problem in implementing additional taxes on oil consumption is the risk of OPEC retaliation combined with the impossibility of stabilizing crude oil prices in the longer run. New taxes on oil products could invite OPEC to raise crude oil prices to compensate for the rising share of economic rent captured by the oil consumer governments, reasoning that the oil price rise would not cause a corresponding volume loss so that there would be a net revenue gain. The alternative could be to flood the market with cheap oil to make up in volumes for a perceived loss in world market crude oil prices. The risk is that either option would overshoot and enhance instability.

CHAPTER FIVE

THE PERSISTENT POLITICAL RISKS

Iraq as a conflict factor

The Gulf War of 1990–91 was essentially over oil, not only for the West, but also for Iraq. In the future, as in the past, conflicts between Middle East neighbours over oil prices and market shares risk escalating, ultimately into armed aggression, because the survival of regimes is at stake. Unless conditions for dialogue and compromise improve markedly, the Middle East and the oil market will remain as prone to conflict and instability as ever, particularly as loosening sanctions give back to Iraq the sort of flexibility and power they had before the Gulf crisis. Middle East conflict patterns have not changed substantially and are likely to affect oil supplies and prices in the future as they have done in the past.

Normally, the conflictual interaction between OPEC countries is about setting oil prices and taking market shares, not about destroying each other, but in recent history there have been two important exceptions: Iraq's wars against Iran and Kuwait. To avoid escalation and total conflict, the conflicting parties must leave each other room for manoeuvre and eventually a way out. Otherwise, the risk of mutual damage is great. In OPEC politics, this concern limits the power of the low-cost producers, because the differences in resource endowment and policy arsenals present an incentive for the higher-cost producers to escalate the conflict into a level where their position is stronger, meaning essentially more people and greater military strength.

Ten years after the Gulf War, Iraq is re-emerging as a force in Middle East politics and in the oil market. It has regained political initiative, and the United States, with the United Nations, is essentially being forced to consider reactive measures. As the United States has not managed to unseat Saddam Hussein, it is left with the uncomfortable choice of accepting the Iraqi regime or overthrowing it by force, meaning invasion and occupation, with a high political risk that makes this option scarcely realistic. The odds are therefore that the United States will tacitly have to accept the presence of the Iraqi regime and watch sanctions being eroded. For the United States, Iraq represents an immense hazard. US oil companies are running a risk by staying out as Asian, European and Russian oil companies move into Iraq. In the Middle East, the United States is in danger of facing on hostile terms an economically progressing and politically more influential Iraq, ultimately representing an oil market threat.

Iraq's regional position is strengthening as relations improve and trade expands with its Middle East neighbours. The UN-imposed sanctions are gradually loosening, being increasingly disrespected. Large trade surpluses since 1998 have caused a comfortable financial position, in spite of a huge foreign debt, largely to the Gulf countries, as a result of the war against Iran in the 1980s. In the domestic economy Iraq has made important reforms. In the oil industry, Iraqi engineers and technicians have shown remarkable skills in maintaining, restoring and expanding capacity. The international oil industry shows an increasing interest in Iraqi oil. The question is not so much whether Iraq will ever again be powerful, as when and under what circumstances. The outcome depends as much on the outside world as on Iraq. The Iraqi regime seems well entrenched, with little or no serious opposition, although it does not control the northern, Kurdish part of the country. Should Iraqi politics change profoundly, through the replacement of the president or a transformation of the regime, the outside world, especially the Middle East neighbours, would have to deal with a country in dire need of oil revenues, but with a regime with which they would want to establish peaceful and friendly relations. The more realistic alternative is perhaps that the Iraqi regime will not change profoundly, with or without Saddam Hussein, in which case a more hostile country will demand a larger share of OPEC oil revenues. The point is that regardless of the political outcome in Iraq, OPEC and Iraq's Middle East neighbours will increasingly have to take Iraqi interests into account when setting oil prices and quotas.

Between them, Iraq, Iran, Kuwait, Saudi Arabia and the United Arab Emirates have more than 60 per cent of the world's proven oil reserves. In the future, as in the past, their interaction will determine the evolution of the oil market as well as their internal economic and political development. Even if Saudi Arabia in the longer run has ultimate market power to unilaterally set oil prices, the others, especially Iraq, have the potential to cause trouble. OPEC oil-pricing strategy and the division of market shares are reasons for discord, compromising oil market stability. In the future, as in the past, the major Middle Eastern oil exporters will be able to inflict considerable damage on each other. In 1998, Iraq participated in lowering oil prices and in 1999 did not participate in the effort to raise oil prices. In 2001, uncertainty over Iraqi potential and intentions is a major destabilizing factor in the oil market, helped by a trade surplus. By abruptly reducing or halting oil exports, Iraq can cause oil prices to rise, or force oil-exporting neighbours to raise their volumes, insofar as they have spare capacity. Inversely, by abruptly raising volumes Iraq can cause oil prices to fall, or force oil-exporting neighbours to lower their volumes. In both cases the other oil exporters risk losing revenues. With huge reserves and low costs Iraq could eventually make up the revenue loss from lower prices by larger volumes.

Even if the overriding objective for all Middle East oil exporters were the maximization of revenues, time horizons and the means at their disposal diverge fundamentally. In the late 1980s Kuwait had the closest to a coherent long-term strategy, Saudi Arabia seemed to muddle through pragmatically by seeking compromises, and Iraq had urgent short-term requirements. Their diverging oil strategies led to an acute conflict of interest and direct confrontation. Iraq tried to contest Saudi Arabia's hegemonic position in the oil market, eventually using military means[1]. Kuwait before the conflict chose to actively dissociate itself from Saudi policy. Saudi Arabia was and is the country with by far the largest oil reserves. Its ability and willingness to expand capacity were and will be crucial to oil price development. Kuwait was and is the oil exporter with the least dependence on oil revenues, while Iraq was and will be again crucially dependent upon them. The three countries' oil price interests are not the same, and the relationships were and will be complex.

Iraq's flexibility and performance since 1998 may be but a precursor of the instability to be expected as Iraq gains in oil potential without being politically integrated in the Middle East. As long as Iraq has conflictual relations with neighbouring Middle East oil-exporting countries, it has reasons to cause trouble by not revealing its intentions and by suddenly changing oil policy and volumes extracted. The point is not only to make money from oil, but also to use oil policy as a means of being noticed in the Middle East and in the oil market, and to gain in political bargaining power.

Iraq represents a threat to oil market stability, which requires that Saudi Arabia alone or preferably in co-operation with the other Middle Eastern OPEC member countries, assumes the role of a swing producer, adjusting ultimate supplies to demand fluctuations. This again requires a certain minimum of mutual understanding and trust, as well as respect for common rules of conduct, so that the important participants can each pursue the best possible strategy knowing the other participants' strategies and being able to anticipate their conduct. Transparent interaction reduces the potential for surprises and risk. Iraq is obviously the obstacle.

One risk is that Iraq will disregard any calls for co-operation in OPEC to stabilize oil prices and will unilaterally raise volumes. The intention could be to provoke Saudi Arabia to pay more attention to the Iraqi challenge than to co-operation with Iran, causing at least a temporary breakdown in OPEC discipline and another oil price collapse. Another risk is that Iraq simply demands a higher oil market share, trying to force the richer Gulf States, and ultimately also Iran, to cut volumes, in which case oil prices might rise, at least temporarily. Whatever happens, the long-term peaceful integration of Iraq into Middle East and OPEC politics will require another round of oil market instability, followed by bargaining and compromise, barring military conflicts.

The common economic interest in raising and subsequently defending the new, high oil price was predominant among the Middle Eastern oil exporters in the 1970s, overcoming political tensions among the leading oil exporters. Countries as different as Algeria, Iran, Iraq, Kuwait, Libya and Saudi Arabia managed to agree on a common oil price policy and to implement it. OPEC was able to serve as the forum for setting a rational oil price policy to the common benefit of all the participants, in spite of occasional cheating on quotas and prices, but the important Middle Eastern oil exporters did not threaten each other's security.

Since the Iranian revolution confidence and agreement have been lacking. Iraq's invasion of Iran in 1980 signified the end of effective oil price co-operation among the Middle Eastern producers and within OPEC. Iraq's invasion of Kuwait in 1990 reiterated the message. In both cases, the immediate effect was an oil price rise, but the long-term effect was oil price instability.

Throughout much of the 1990s, a slack oil market caused rivalry over market shares, but more profound political tensions and conflicts have been equally important. Any oil market agreement is impossible when two of the leading suppliers, Iran and Iraq, are perceived as threats to the other's territorial integrity and political system, and both are perceived as equally serious threats to two other leading suppliers, Kuwait and Saudi Arabia. In such a political context, denying revenues to the enemy neighbours becomes as important, if not more important, than securing revenues for oneself, particularly if accumulated assets provide a cushion. For Kuwait, denying Iraq revenues through disrespecting OPEC quotas and pushing prices down was apparently an important oil policy objective, regardless of the impact on its own oil revenues, but Kuwait also had ample investment income.[2] At a less intensive scale, similar considerations apparently played a role for Saudi Arabia in its actions against Iran at times when relations were tense. The common experience of economic pain and distrust of Iraq paved the ground for spectacularly improved relations between Iran and Saudi Arabia, an understanding on oil prices and the OPEC agreement of March 1999.

Iraq in the late 1980s had an interest in higher oil prices than either Kuwait or Saudi Arabia, but Kuwait's position was volatile. Saudi Arabia apparently had a greater interest in stable oil prices than either Iraq or Kuwait, but Iraq preferred stable prices to volatility with a downward risk, so that there was a potential for shifting coalitions and alliances. This added to the potential instability of the oil market, and capacity utilization became more questionable. Depending on the circumstances, Saudi Arabia and

Kuwait could oppose Iraq in a desire to raise the oil price, or Iraq and Kuwait could join forces to drive the oil price up, in spite of Saudi policy, or, as a third alternative, Kuwait could oppose Iraq and Saudi Arabia in a desire to bring the oil price down. On some occasions, Kuwait would oppose Iraq and Saudi Arabia simultaneously by raising volumes above quotas, then reneging on OPEC agreements.[3] By doing so in the late 1980s, Kuwait took a miscalculated risk in provoking Iraq.

As Iraq's immediate neighbour and victim of aggression, Kuwait deserves special attention because of the risk that conflictual relations may endure. Kuwait in the late 1980s had a record of desiring unstable and generally low oil prices, essentially because of considerations for the world economy and the effect on investment revenues. Its main instrument was to raise output and force prices down. For this purpose, Kuwait needed spare capacity and foreign financial assets. The United Arab Emirates is to some extent in a similar position, although with less political coherence and clout. For both countries, the fundamental oil interests have not changed since the 1980s.

Saudi Arabia has a long record of giving priority to oil price stability, for a number of economic and political reasons. Its main instrument was and is its resource base, the ability to expand oil output and eventually assume the role of a residual producer. For this purpose, Saudi Arabia needs revenues, in order to invest in additional capacity and to have a flexible production schedule.

Iraq, by contrast, in the 1980s, had a record of giving priority to revenues, through a larger market share and through higher prices. Its main instrument was and is a demographic and military power base enabling the country to disregard other Middle Eastern oil exporters and eventually to intimidate them into complying with Iraqi interests. For this purpose, Iraq needed revenues, in order to ensure domestic stability and to continue its military build-up. This is likely to be the case again in the future.

In the late 1980s, the conflict between Kuwait, Saudi Arabia and Iraq concerned the level of oil prices and their stability, as well as shares of markets and revenues. Kuwait apparently in the late 1980s had little interest in oil price stability, unless it should be at a fairly low level, being the persistent cheater on quotas. Saudi Arabia apparently at this time desired stable oil prices at a level ensuring a modest growth of demand that could easily be met by rising supplies, and at this level a fair market share for itself. Iraq, finally, had an obvious interest in high, but not necessarily stable oil prices. The same pattern of interests and cleavages reappears in the first decade of the twenty-first century.

In pursuing their interests and eventually maximizing revenues, the three countries had and still have strikingly different means at their disposal. For Kuwait, maximizing revenues means an embarrassment of choices between oil revenues and investment revenues. The country has a highly favourable reserve-to-production ratio and oil in the ground for perhaps 300 years at present extraction rates. It also has the ability to step up output considerably at short notice and at low cost. Kuwait is not dependent on its oil revenues because of equally important investment revenues and a financial surplus that often matches the oil revenues. As a result of this favourable situation, Kuwait can reason in terms of overall portfolio management.

The country needs to manage the portfolio of foreign assets as well as oil assets in the ground. Because oil assets are finite, even in Kuwait, and financial assets in principle are infinite, Kuwait could have an interest in transferring wealth from oil into financial assets, and in hedging the latter more than the former. By doing so, Kuwait would transform itself from an oil producer into a rentier, respecting intergenerational equity by diversifying assets away from oil. Such considerations require a long-term perspective, eventually explaining why Kuwait in the late 1980s consistently played the role of a maverick in OPEC and in the oil market.

Given the diversification of its assets, the interaction between the oil market and the world economy is more important for Kuwait than for any other OPEC country, except Abu Dhabi and Qatar. Insofar as priority is given to hedging the foreign investment, Kuwait has an interest in low oil prices. The country can benefit from both the ups and downs of the oil market. When the oil price plunges, Kuwait gains on the value of foreign assets and investment earnings. When the oil price shoots up, Kuwait gains in financial liquidity and can seize new opportunities in foreign markets. An extreme Kuwaiti strategy could be to maximize the oil price shocks upwards and downwards, by reducing oil output in a strong market and raising it in a weak market. This to some extent was the case in the 1980s and could still be Kuwait's interest in the future.

Saudi Arabia is in a different situation, because of modest foreign reserves and large revenue needs. For Saudi Arabia, there is little choice when it comes to the question of whether or not to maximize revenues. The country essentially has oil revenues only, hardly any investment revenues. It also has a highly favourable reserve-to-production ratio and oil in the ground for perhaps 100 years at present extraction rates, not counting the potential for discoveries. It has the ability to step up output, but a major expansion could only be achieved at considerable capital cost. Saudi Arabia too can reason in terms of portfolio management, but the portfolio essentially consists of oil in the ground. The country needs to manage its petroleum portfolio in a way that combines long-term market stability and demand for Saudi oil with short-term revenue considerations.

For Saudi Arabia, respecting intergenerational equity is a question of managing the oil assets and the oil market, not of diversifying away from oil This situation gives Saudi Arabia a dual interest in oil prices and explains

THE PERSISTENT POLITICAL RISKS

why it consistently takes the role of a stabilizer and moderator in OPEC and in the world oil market. Combining the long-term and short-term considerations is difficult enough in a stable market; in an unstable market it is impossible, so that Saudi Arabia in any practical situation has to choose between long-term market and short-term income concerns. Rising population numbers and ensuing revenue requirements give steadily more weight to short-term income concerns, as has been evident from the choice of an OPEC oil price range of $22–28 a barrel, well above average 1990s oil prices. With rising youth unemployment, the need for economic reform becomes more urgent, as does the country's need for stable oil revenues.

The interaction between the oil market and the world economy is important for Saudi Arabia because of its interest in oil price stability. Unlike Kuwait, Saudi Arabia is in no position to transfer wealth on a large scale from finite assets at home into infinite ones abroad. Because of contradictory oil price interests, Saudi Arabia benefits from neither the ups nor the downs of the oil market. For Saudi Arabia, when oil prices shoot up, a short-term financial gain is a long-term strategic loss, as may have been the case in 1999–2001. When oil prices plunge, the long-term strategic gain has a heavy short-term financial cost, as was evident in 1998. The reasonable Saudi strategy is to support the price in a weak market, by withholding output, and to moderate the price in a strong market, by raising output, as has been demonstrated numerous times since the early 1970s. The Saudi position of being a residual producer invites criticism from all corners, to which the country is sensitive, but the policy is essentially chosen by self-interest, not by generosity.

Iraq was until 1990 and is again in yet a different situation, because of a large population, a huge foreign debt and hefty revenue needs. For Iraq, maximizing revenues implies only a choice between higher oil exports, higher oil prices, or both. The country essentially has oil revenues only, no investment revenues, but a potential for agricultural and industrial development.

Unlike Saudi Arabia, Iraq is in a position to transfer wealth on a large scale from finite assets at home into more infinite industrial assets, also at home. For Iraq, respecting intergenerational equity is a matter of domestic economic development, financed by oil revenues. It also has a favourable reserve-to-production ratio and oil in the ground for perhaps 100 years at the extraction rate of the late 1980s, not counting future discoveries. It has the ability to step up output, but this requires considerable capital investment. Iraq too can reason in terms of portfolio management, but the portfolio today essentially consists of oil in the ground. There is a reasonable possibility of creating other assets that might even earn export revenues. The country needs to manage its petroleum portfolio in a way that synchronizes as far as possible the depletion of the finite petroleum assets with the creation of other, more durable assets, with investment in productive sectors. Instead, Iraq has so far to a large extent used oil revenues for military purposes. It is in practice the only OPEC country that could and still can represent a military threat to others, as has been amply demonstrated in recent decades.

The interaction between the oil market and the world economy is of less importance to Iraq. It had until 1990 and has again an interest in both high oil prices and a large market share. To some extent, Iraq's oil market strategy is not unlike that of Kuwait, but for less sophisticated motives. In a weak market, Iraq could seek to gain a larger market share by unilaterally raising output, leaving others to defend the price. Eventually, the country could have the means to coerce neighbours into complying with Iraqi oil market interests. In a strong market it could contribute to defending a high price as long as there were more to gain from high prices than from large volumes. Nevertheless, large unused Iraqi capacity would represent a threat to oil market stability.

The spectre of Iraqi volume growth raises the issue of eventual retaliation. Iraq taking market share and depressing oil prices could invite at least Kuwait and Saudi Arabia to respond by raising output to force Iraq to compromise. An Iraqi output expansion putting downward pressure on oil prices could invite Iran, Venezuela and other OPEC members to cheat on quotas. Iraq as a non-participant represents a menace to any OPEC agreement. As the Gulf conflict becomes more distant and sanctions are eroded, this menace is likely to intensify.

Inviting Iraq to join an OPEC agreement is difficult, but necessary for stability. After the 1990–91 Gulf conflict, Kuwait and Saudi Arabia took shares of Iraq's former OPEC quota. Any restoration of Iraq's quota would reasonably be at the expense of Kuwait and Saudi Arabia, which would have to forsake volumes and revenues. The two countries might be reluctant to transfer funds to a potentially hostile neighbour. This again raises the political issue of the future Iraqi regime.

A hostile Iraq, under the present regime or a similar successor, would evidently be seen as a threat by Kuwait and Saudi Arabia and complicate any OPEC agreement. By contrast, a peaceful Iraq, under a more democratic regime, would be seen as a potential partner in co-operation, facilitating an OPEC price and quota agreement. With a peaceful Iraq, Kuwait and Saudi Arabia would have less reason to maintain huge military expenses, enhancing budgetary discretion. Oil market stability largely seems to depend on Iraqi politics and the country's interaction with neighbours. The lack of economic and political integration and insufficient institutional development of the Arab world, or the whole Middle East, become problems also for the oil importers.[4]

Because UN sanctions, driven by the United States and the United Kingdom, have not succeeded in bringing down the Saddam Hussein regime or in preventing Iraq from gaining political ground in the Middle East, it is up to Iraq's neighbours to manage affairs. Integrating Iraq peacefully into the Middle East economy and politics is a challenge, particularly to Kuwait and Saudi Arabia, which dispose of incentives and sanctions. But, put quite simply, the less populous and less well-armed neighbours have an interest in a disarmed Iraq that does not rearm and that accepts inspections for this purpose, and which preferably takes part in and respects OPEC agreements. Incentives are a floor oil price, which Kuwait and Saudi Arabia could guarantee for a defined period, and a negotiated share for Iraqi oil, giving Iraq guaranteed minimum revenues. The most important incentive would be to waive Iraq's debt, whose repayment in any case cannot be enforced, on the condition that Iraq did not rearm and accepted inspections by neighbouring states for this purpose. The follow-up could be the institution of comprehensive Middle Eastern economic co-operation, aimed at free trade and free movement of capital across borders. A larger market would help the oil-rich countries to diversify their economies and transform their oil assets into productive assets. Financially rich states such as Kuwait would get the opportunity to serve as regional bankers, and through closer economic relations with neighbours enhance their security.

The reasoning is simply that a prosperous Iraq, unburdened by huge debts, would be a more comfortable neighbour than a poor Iraq with an enormous debt burden. A magnanimous and public offer to this effect would reasonably destabilize any government that would not seriously consider it. Kuwait is in a critical position, with a looming Iraqi menace, and an Iraqi debt that will probably never be repaid. Any claim for compensation or reparations for damages to Kuwait risk being politically counterproductive, strengthening Iraqi resolve and distrust of the outside world. The question is whether Kuwait, by waiving the debt, could buy security. Historical references are France's claim for German reparations after the First World War, with politically disastrous consequences, and the United States' assistance to Germany after the Second World War, with politically beneficial effects.

An Iraqi regime committed to economic development and peaceful relations with neighbours, and which could be assisted in gaining higher revenues through a combination of moderate prices and larger volumes, would be a major gain both for oil market stability and for the Middle East. The solution could involve foreign aid to Iraq to invest in capacity expansion, or preferably, that Iraq opens up for foreign investment in the oil industry on conditions that are acceptable to foreign investors. In the longer run, this could mean not only that Iraq becomes a more important oil exporter, but that Iraqi oil interests would be more compatible with those of Kuwait, Saudi Arabia and the United Arab Emirates. This is a scenario for reducing tensions between the major Middle Eastern oil exporters and a prescription for oil market stability. This would represent a certain co-optation of Iraq and a new situation in the Middle East, in OPEC, and in the world oil market.

In the longer run, such an outcome would also represent a lessening of the threat to the long-term economic interests of the countries of the Arabian Peninsula. With Iraq covering its income requirements by means of rising volumes at moderate prices, the most acute political tensions between Iraq and its southern neighbours would be reduced. Saudi Arabia, with Kuwait and the Emirates, would have less reason to expand oil production in order to bring oil prices down; they would lose in bargaining power, but gain in security with a consequent need to spend less money on arms. Even a different Iraqi regime would need oil revenues badly and a financial squeeze would not only help bring down the present regime, but could also compromise future political stabilization, which is not a prescription for oil market stability.

Unsteady Iran

Iran is in a different situation. The country's assets are an increasingly educated population, considerable oil reserves and a geographical position on the Gulf. Its liabilities are a food deficit and urgent income needs. Historically, Iran has played an important role in international oil politics. This is likely to be the case also in the future, even if Iranian oil exports since the 1979 revolution have been much lower than they were in the 1970s. The Iranian domestic political situation seems to be stabilizing, with the regime becoming more moderate in spite of fierce conservative opposition.[5] This has led to Iran gradually renewing relations with outside powers and opening up for international trade. Iran's reintegration into the international community also means that Iranian interests and problems will have a greater significance for Middle Eastern politics.

Iran's liabilities are considerable. Since 1980, annual population growth has been around 3 per cent, higher than economic growth, so that per capita income has declined by perhaps one-half. Although food and energy are rationed, supplies are precarious for the bulk of the population. Iran's economic crisis is largely due to the eight-year war against Iraq, but also to the country's isolation and economic mismanagement, leading to low capacity utilization and lack of investment.

Since 1980, Iran's productive capital and infrastructure have seriously deteriorated. There is an urgent need for investment capital in all sectors of the economy. Foreign capital, however, is reluctant to invest in Iran on a large scale. Oil, at least during the next decade, will be the predominant source of foreign exchange and investment capital. Iran has huge gas reserves, but no large-scale gas export project to Europe is likely to be realized in the near future. Iran has smaller oil reserves than Iraq or Kuwait and the oil fields are generally less productive and more expensive to operate. In the late 1970s, oil production was above 5 million barrels a day. In 2000, output was on average 3.1 million barrels a day. To expand capacity back to perhaps 5 million barrels a day would require heavy capital investment that Iran presently cannot afford. It therefore has to rely on foreign investment, but for foreign oil investors to move heavily into Iran would require important changes in operating conditions. Iran would also need foreign investment to develop natural gas exports.

Taking Iranian and Iraqi interests into account

A settlement in the Gulf could be followed up by an OPEC agreement on oil prices and market shares that would take Iranian and Iraqi interests into account, meaning large quotas for the two populous countries on the basis of high prices and reduced quotas for the Arabian Peninsula exporters. Such an agreement could be fragile. The oil price could tumble if demand weakened as the agreement was being concluded. The credibility of the arrangement would depend on the low-cost producers renouncing market shares. To their advantage, spare capacity and the ensuing ability to suddenly lower oil prices would constitute a potential sanction against the more populous neighbours.

Since the oil price decline of 1986 there has been a potential conflict between the oil market strategies of Iraq, Kuwait and Saudi Arabia, all of which had an interest in marking their independence by raising doubts about their intentions, in order to make actions less predictable. The surprise factor is an important part of OPEC bargaining. Saudi Arabia still has no natural ally in the Middle East in efforts to stabilize the oil market, at any price level, not even Kuwait.

Managing oligopoly power

Managing oligopoly power in the oil market is the principal challenge for OPEC and especially the Middle Eastern core in the decades ahead. Because the supply of non-OPEC oil ultimately depends on costs and prices, OPEC oil-pricing policy in the longer run decides demand for OPEC oil, the OPEC oil market share and OPEC oil revenues. Insofar as demand for Middle East OPEC oil is a residual, made up by total world oil demand minus other supplies, it is highly sensitive to changes in demand.

Conventional wisdom is that the world's dependence on OPEC oil, especially from the Middle East, will increase markedly, so that the OPEC Middle East share of the world oil market will gradually approach their share of the world's oil reserves. Apparently, the task of managing oil prices and revenues will be less difficult over the next few decades than in the past. One prominent analysis is that world demand for oil until 2020 will grow at about twice the pace that it has since 1980, rising by more than one-half.[6] In that scenario, demand for OPEC oil is set to grow even faster, doubling between 2000 and 2020, and demand for oil from the Middle East even faster still. If these prospects materialize, OPEC, especially the Middle Eastern core, should have little reason to worry about the future, as oil demand growth will increase its market share and bargaining power. This will give room for higher oil revenues by increasing volumes and eventually also by gradually raising real oil prices. According to this forecast, volume demand for oil from the OPEC Middle East will grow at an average annual rate of 4–5 per cent, so that at even prices, oil revenues will grow faster than population. At gradually rising prices, oil revenues will permit a per capita real income growth over the next few decades in the OPEC Middle East. From this perspective, there should be little reason to worry about economic monoculture, social distress and any crisis of the rentier state. Oil seems set to help the Middle East out, as in the 1970s and early 1980s.

Because it is far from certain that the above forecast will materialize, there is no room for complacency. The evident risk, from an OPEC or Middle Eastern point of view, is that oil demand growth will not pick up as forecast, but grow at the historical low rate of about 1 per cent a year over the next few decades. With the high growth potential for non-OPEC supplies, demand for OPEC oil would increase slowly in this scenario, and demand for Middle East OPEC oil would only grow at a pace of about 1 per cent a year, as during the past decades. This is no recipe for higher oil prices, but for lower ones. In any case, oil revenues would grow slowly, at a much lower pace than population, so that per capita oil income would continue declining. Economic monoculture would intensify social problems, and make income distribution and intergenerational equity more burning issues, possibly destabilizing the rentier state. Even if demand for Middle Eastern oil should grow quickly, there is ample potential for disorder and conflict so long as the basic political problem of Iraq is not settled.

The prevailing view in the 1970s and early 1980s was that the OPEC countries, by cutting oil volumes extracted, could achieve a proportionally higher oil price rise and, apparently, raise the value of their oil reserves as well as extend their lifetime. Reducing output as prices were rising appeared to have the double benefit of supporting present revenues and securing those of tomorrow. This experience was pertinent both to the oil importers, who under the impression of resource scarcity were willing to pay higher prices for oil, and to the oil exporters, who were taught a practical lesson in the benefits of co-operation for the sake of output restraint. The lesson may have been especially welcome in the Gulf countries, which because of small populations had poor prospects of economic diversification, but could harvest a high economic rent as a result of low production costs. The paradigm of oil scarcity meant that oil exporters did not have to worry about the competitiveness of oil, or of their own oil industry. Following this rationale, Kuwait, as one example, on several occasions reduced oil output. With oil extraction according to revenue targets, high oil prices were apparently easy to defend because the higher the oil price, the lower the volume by which the oil suppliers could reach their income targets. Considerable idle capacity was not considered a major problem.

However, the paradigm of oil scarcity was short lived. High oil prices gave incentives to oil exploration and development elsewhere, especially the North Sea and the US Gulf of Mexico, and OPEC collectively lost market share. Two major oil price rises gave new life to the US and Russian oil industries and contributed to making the North Sea an important oil province, as well as providing incentives for oil exploration and development elsewhere. By the early 1980s, the spectre of oil resource scarcity was vanishing. Instead, oil prodigality became increasingly evident. For the major OPEC countries, the practical impact on oil policy was that the benefit of forsaking present output was doubtful. If the outlook for oil supplies is not scarcity, but abundance in the near future, present production does not compromise future output. Therefore, forsaking output today does not mean a gain tomorrow, but rather giving away market shares and revenues to other oil exporters, within or outside OPEC. Then, idle capacity becomes a major problem.

The paradigm shift from oil scarcity to oil abundance was manifest in the 1986 oil price collapse, triggered by the OPEC low-cost producers, essentially Kuwait and Saudi Arabia, to regain market share. With the paradigm of oil abundance, OPEC co-operation has been more difficult to achieve and the support of major non-OPEC exporters has become more important. For effective co-operation to take place in oil supplies and for the oligopolists to benefit from their position, a certain mutual confidence is required, apart from agreement on the objectives of the co-operation. This is the essential problem within OPEC and also between OPEC and the major non-OPEC oil suppliers.

This leads to the pricing risks. With considerable caution, Saudi Arabia for many years was a champion of oil price moderation. It passively opposed the quadrupling of oil prices in 1973–74, around 1980 contributed to oil price stabilization, and was instrumental in bringing down oil prices in 1985–86. In hindsight, Saudi caution proved to be correct. OPEC set a double trap for itself. High oil prices during the 1970s and early 1980s gave strong incentives to oil exploration and development, which caused resource abundance outside OPEC. Low oil prices after the mid-1980s gave equally strong incentives to cost saving through the development of technology and organization. The outcome is that the diffusion of technology and open markets make oil industry costs converge worldwide, not only between companies, but also between regions. As the cost differential diminishes, the competitive advantage of the traditional low-cost producers erodes. The Middle East still offers the least costly oil prospects, but the edge is diminishing. Insofar as the Middle East oil exporters pursue economic rent rather than market share with their policy, they make the cost difference to the next-best oil provinces irrelevant in the perspective of world oil supplies.

Increasing competition could induce leading Middle Eastern oil exporters to consider OPEC redundant,[7] insofar as the leading oil exporters would prefer the freedom of a competitive market to pursue market shares and eventually by lowering prices try to drive competitors out of the market. Therefore, quickly rising non-OPEC oil supplies entail the risk of tempting Saudi Arabia and Kuwait, and eventually Iraq, to go for market share and disregard the rest of OPEC. Consequently, to induce strongly rising oil demand, oil prices would not rise, but fall. Their falling marginal supply costs outside OPEC would tempt the low-cost producers to offset lower oil prices by higher volumes. Iraq is a likely candidate.[8] For oil demand, the constant risk is that high prices will negatively affect economic activity and indirectly depress consumption. The additional risk is that of a technological breakthrough for competing liquid motor fuels, for example in gas-to-liquids technology.

Although the Middle East has about two-thirds of the world's proven oil reserves and a reserve-to-production ratio far above that of the rest of the world, many non-OPEC oil producers have a technological edge over the OPEC countries, especially those in the Middle East. Since the early 1980s, the offshore oil industry in the US Gulf of Mexico and the North Sea has gone through a technological and organizational revolution. The immediate result has been an average annual cost reduction of 3 to 4 per cent.

The persistent cost cut has more than made up for the resource depletion, so that in the US Gulf of Mexico or the North Sea in 2001 it was comparatively less costly to develop a small oil field in deep waters than it was to develop a large oil field around 1970. Moreover, experience and new technology have improved finding rates in exploration. The improvement in technology and organization has caused reserve replacement by oil companies to improve markedly. Consequently, the output decline of mature oil provinces such as North America and the North Sea is a much more protracted process than was assumed as recently as 1990. As other areas of the world open up for the international oil industry, they will also benefit from the progress in petroleum technology and organization. This means that the cost advantage given the Middle East OPEC members as a result of their large fields is shrinking.

Improved technology and organization also reduce lead times, making non-OPEC supplies more price responsive at shorter notice. Consequently, for OPEC there is an evident risk that with high oil prices, non-OPEC supplies will increase more than expected. In the 1970s, the subsequent growth of North Sea oil output was not anticipated. Likely candidates for oil supply growth are Russia, Central Asia and parts of Africa and Latin America. The constraint is not resources, technology or capital, but access and legal and fiscal conditions. The supply from these regions is price sensitive insofar as the host countries are not rent seekers, but seeking to attract foreign investment in oil and natural gas and eventually take market shares, as did the OPEC countries in the 1960s.

With strong competition, OPEC has good reasons to show caution on oil prices. Because oil demand cannot be forced upon consumers, it has to be enticed through economic activity and competitive prices; low-cost and high-cost oil producers alike have an interest in considering demand. The high-cost oil producers have an immediate interest in demand not receding, as they are the most vulnerable to lower oil prices. The low-cost oil producers, generally with long time horizons, have a long-term interest in keeping oil prices at a level that secures demand and slows the development of backstop technologies. OPEC's choice therefore seems to be between oil price moderation that would slow down the progress of alternatives and permit an expanding oil market, and high oil prices that would limit oil demand and accelerate the progress of alternative fuels. Should Iraq realize that its possession of huge oil reserves rationally leads to a long-term view, its price interests may come to be more in tune with those of Kuwait and Saudi Arabia.

The challenge of natural gas

Consumers, utilities and governments are in a position not only to consider availability and cost effectiveness, but also other factors such as the convenience and cleanliness of the energy that they use. Natural gas is a convenient fuel and is cleaner than either oil or coal, but it is more costly to transport and handle.[9] Presently, the growth in the use of natural gas in power generation is based on the introduction of the combined cycle turbine, causing coal to lose market share.

Natural gas demand is likely to benefit from technological progress that is on its way. A breakthrough in the conversion of natural gas to liquid fuels would significantly enhance its competitiveness in relation to oil, blurring the barriers between the oil and gas markets.[10] Any advance in the use of fuel-cell vehicles is likely to enhance the demand for hydrogen or methanol based on natural gas.[11] The essential effect would be to undermine the predominance of oil in the transportation sector. The outcome would most likely be an upward pressure on gas prices and a downward pressure on oil prices. If successful gas-to-liquid technologies should do away with the prime market for oil in combustion engines, the more widespread availability of natural gas would make supplies less oligopolistic with weaker prospects for cartel formation than is the case with oil.

Progress in pipeline and Liquefied Natural Gas (LNG) technology and reductions in the costs of moving gas would further enhance competitiveness with oil. New technology is being developed for the transportation of gas, for example as compressed natural gas, permitting small-scale operations that would improve flexibility and reduce costs. The costs of conventional gas pipeline transportation are declining.[12]

The availability of natural gas is setting a ceiling on oil's share of the world energy market. In the aftermath of the high oil prices of the 1970s and 1980s, oil has found its toughest competition. The need for gas to compete against coal in power generation gives it an advantage over oil outside the transportation sector.[13] A final observation is that natural gas use not only seems to expand at the expense of coal, but also to replace fuel oil use.

The abundance of natural gas in proven reserves and potential finds gives a competitive edge, but the drawback is a trend toward longer transportation routes and higher transmission costs for incremental supplies. In North America, the major source of incremental gas supplies seems to be northern Canada and Alaska, requiring the construction of long and costly pipelines. Europe will increasingly have to import gas from offshore central Norway, Siberia, North Africa and ultimately the Middle East and Central Asia. There is little doubt about the reserve base, but longer transportation distances will put an upward pressure on delivery costs, despite improvements in the technology. In China, gas will need to be transported from Sinkiang and Siberia. In the longer run, the cost of importing LNG by tanker may set the ceiling for natural gas prices in the major markets.

To keep markets outside the transportation sector, oil will need competitive prices. Any substantial oil price increase relative to other fuels for an extended period would enhance competition, essentially from natural gas, advancing the concentration of oil use on the transportation sector. With a higher proportion of motor fuel, oil demand will be more sensitive to the level of economic activity. Abundant supplies of both oil and gas would put a downward pressure on prices unless demand picked up. In the event of a breakthrough for gas-to-liquids, the downward pressure on oil prices could be substantial. Eventually, as has happened in North America, robust demand can make the price of natural gas relative to oil increase in the final, end-user markets.

For OPEC, the rise of natural gas means heavier competition from the gas exporters, some of which, such as Russia and Norway, are already major oil exporters.[14] OPEC, or at least the member countries of North Africa and the Middle East that are able to supply the European market, will have an evident interest in co-ordinating gas export policies and eventually having an integrated approach to their oil and gas supply and pricing policies. The major OPEC Middle East oil exporters are in this position. For them, building up gas exports would diversify economic risk. In this way, OPEC would also gain in power, but at the cost of rising complexity and diversity of interests. Some of the poorer OPEC countries, such as Algeria, Libya and Iran, have large gas reserves and an evident interest in gaining both markets and a fair share of economic rent accruing from natural gas.

Defending economic rent in climate politics

International climate politics are about the costs and alternative ways of reducing CO_2 emissions. Because such measures affect demand for oil and natural gas, prices and the division of economic rent, they directly impact on the oil revenues of the OPEC countries and the export earnings and tax revenues of the Middle East oil exporters. The major risk is that climate concerns make consumer governments tax away a huge share of the economic rent. Obviously one dimension of international climate politics is the potential conflict of interests between oil-exporting and oil-importing countries.

Environmental problems, which affect our daily lives right now, have been on the political agenda since the 1960s. Prosperity leads to the desire for a better environment for the sake of improved comfort and health. Such environmental problems can be concisely defined. Causes and effects are easy to state and ultimately to correct. Various emissions of, for example, particles, sulphur and nitrogen have documented harmful effects at the local and regional levels.

The climate issue, on the other hand, concerns the long-term global temperature and entered the political agenda only in the 1980s. The climate problems are vaguer than the environmental ones, and knowledge of their causes and effects is more limited. CO_2 has been appointed the chief culprit, but the harm documented is disputed. It is difficult to correct a problem about which knowledge is inadequate, especially when rectification costs are potentially enormous. It is uncertain whether the world is facing new, serious climate problems, but fears and sentiments can be exploited politically.[15]

Facing fear and uncertainty, many politicians feel a need to take a position. Hence, they try to give the impression of doing something on climate, without knowing what measures to take and at what cost. The climate and

CO_2 issues have become political symbols. The negotiations leading to the Kyoto agreement appear more like political horse trading than a sober attempt to solve actual problems. Fulfilling the Kyoto Protocol would be costly not only for the oil importers but also for the oil exporters and other countries.[16] The climate issue can also be used as a rationale to tax oil and natural gas, transferring income or economic rent from oil exporters to oil importers. Measures envisaged are likely to cause lower demand in the industrial countries and lower oil prices worldwide.

Higher taxes on oil and gas in the consumer countries would depress international oil and gas market prices further. Thus instead of depressing oil demand, the Kyoto Protocol could actually boost it, because price elasticity of oil demand is low. With low market prices and high taxes, oil becomes a more attractive fuel for importer governments, especially in developing countries that are not bound by the Kyoto Protocol.

The alternative might be for OPEC, and especially the Middle Eastern oil exporters, to raise oil prices significantly, to capture rent rather than taking volumes. If the CO_2 issue really should be taken seriously, the most effective solution would probably be a comprehensive agreement among coal, gas and oil producers to levy a high excise tax, raising the economic rent to the benefit of the producers. The mechanism would be a carbon tax, highest on coal, lower on oil and lowest on natural gas.

Comprehensive measures aimed at curbing the use of fossil fuels could cause OPEC or the key Middle Eastern oil exporters to raise output to compensate for the price loss, aiming at market share. The temptation could be to flood the market with cheap oil, giving a strong competitive advantage to countries that do not impose high consumer taxes on crude or oil products. OPEC would lose economic rent, but some low-cost OPEC countries would gain in volume. Nevertheless, the outcome would be a transfer of income from the oil exporters to the oil importers. The effect could be a more strongly rising oil demand in developing countries.

A basic flaw of the Kyoto Protocol is that binding measures do not include developing countries such as China and India, which are large users of coal, with quickly rising oil demand, and fast-increasing CO_2 emissions. Another flaw is the exclusion of the OPEC countries, the leading oil exporters. The only hydrocarbons exporters included are Australia, Canada, Denmark, the Netherlands and Russia. For Russia, the sharp decrease in coal and oil use represents a potential to supplement gas exports by selling emission permits, because Russia is being honoured for historically inefficient energy use by a reference to 1990 emission levels. For the others, the opportunity may be to eventually buy emission permits as their oil and gas industries expand. The OPEC countries will eventually have an interest in being allocated liberal emission levels that could permit them to trade permits as their natural gas exports gradually substitute for oil exports.[17]

The potential for the trade in CO_2 emissions, both internationally and between companies, is vast, but there are many problems. The discussion is relevant insofar as both energy exporters and importers are co-signatories of Annex I of the Kyoto Protocol. These co-signatories comprise the list of those between which international trade of CO_2 quotas is envisaged, although the particular rules are still to be decided. When coupled with oil and natural gas trade, differences in abatement potential and costs can provide a remarkable complementarity between exporters and importers that could facilitate such trade. Finally, internalizing such cross-border CO_2 abatement and trade, combined with fuel substitution, could enhance both earnings and strategic advantages. Substituting natural gas for coal in power generation and transferring the abatement from gas importers to exporters could provide benefits for both sides. Power generation has to respect ever-stricter environmental regulations. The costs of CO_2 reductions will be high for the petroleum industry.

In principle, the market can allocate the emission reduction in a more efficient way than a general tax. There is, so far, hardly any experience with such trade across borders and even less across borders within one company or group of companies. Although there is a consensus that international permit trading should be an acceptable method for reducing emissions, eventual trading limits and scope remain unsettled issues. Unlimited international trading would be the least costly way to reduce CO_2 emissions, at least for the rich countries that thus could avoid or defer measures at home by buying permits from poorer countries or countries with more generous emission levels. The risk is evidently that such a trading mechanism would serve as a straitjacket, compromising abatement in the rich countries and economic development in the poorer ones, unless the latter should be able to move ahead economically using largely new, non-fossil energy. Such an evolution cannot be ruled out, but does not appear highly likely. This is why permit trading has initially been proposed for a restricted group of countries, the already-mentioned signatories of Annex I. Moreover, it is doubtful that permit trading will be unrestricted. Both volume and geographical limitations seem likely.

The immediate means of reducing CO_2 emissions is to introduce new technologies and to substitute carbon-intensive fuels with other fuels. A relevant case is the substitution of natural gas for coal in power generation. The gain could be sold in a market for permits, so that countries with high abatement costs in reality finance measures in countries with lower costs by buying permits. The market will thus set the international permit price, depending on demand and supply, and hence, distribute the gain and the burden.

In principle, international permit trading could also take place within a company or a group of companies operating in several countries. A company or a group operating in countries with different abatement costs would be able to internalize the difference as a gain, by carrying out the abatement where it is the least costly and have it credited where it is the most costly. In practice, this facility will depend upon the organization of permit trading.

As the details of international permit trading are still to be settled, this discussion should also consider the options of both competitive and monopolistic permit trading.[18]

A competitive trading model implies that emission permits are bought and sold by individual firms and possibly local and regional authorities. Decentralized trading means that no single seller or buyer can influence the price by withholding permits from the market, nor will there be an incentive to flood the market with permits, because the price will reflect the marginal cost of CO_2 abatement within the trading area. The condition is that central governments that have negotiated aggregate national emission levels subsequently distribute or sell permits to private parties within the country. With strictly national trading, the value of permits would reflect the marginal abatement cost. With cross-border trading, however, the value of permits would reflect both marginal abatement costs in the buyer country and the international value of the permit traded. This core of international permit trading seems set to emerge, possibly through an institutionalized permit exchange.

From a dynamic perspective, the value of permits seems set to increase, because economic growth and rising energy demand will put more pressure on constant emission limits. Hence, buying permits could permit expanding energy use and thus higher economic growth than otherwise would have been allowable. Against this backdrop, international permit trading provides stronger incentives for countries with relatively generous emission levels, such as Russia, to restrict emissions.

With decentralized permit trading, firms would have incentives to abate emissions wherever this was most cost effective within their organization. The purpose could be to replace energy-intensive lines by expanding other activities with a higher value added in relation to emissions, and eventually to sell permits as a source of revenues. Multinational firms operating in several countries would also have incentives to abate emissions in countries where the permit cost is modest and have the gains credited in a country with higher permit costs. The condition is an internationally recognized accounting procedure, in eventual conjunction with an international permit exchange. Hence, multinational firms might internalize the gains from cross-border emission abatement, saving transaction costs. The risk is that in countries with generous emission limits, again Russia is an example, decentralized sales of permits would flood the market, bringing the international price down to a level where total revenues from emission sales actually fell with rising sales volumes.

The alternative would be for governments to monopolize permit trading. Apparently, such a procedure could be in the interest of some countries with generous emission levels as it could avoid excessive permit sales and instead attract foreign investment in energy-intensive industries. For the prospective buyers, this would raise the price of permits well above the level of decentralized trading, providing stronger abatement incentives. This might be a more effective way of abating emissions in prospective buyer countries, but the gain could be offset by transfers of industrial activity. Insofar as countries with generous emission levels did not make full use of their permits or sold the remainder in an international market, they would represent a harbour for industries seeking to overcome emission restrictions.[19] Again, Russia is the case in point with actual emissions about 30 per cent below the 1990 level, which is also the 2010 target. Indeed, permits unused are unlikely to remain so for long. This potential for industrial transfer has not been much discussed, so far.

With monopolized permit trading, firms would have to bid to their own government or to foreign governments, either directly or indirectly through an international exchange. Government-to-government permit trading would carry a risk of politicization and eventual conflict because of close and complex bilateral arrangements. With monopolized permit selling only, the prospective buyer firms would risk becoming the hostages of a few foreign governments that would be in a position not only to raise permit prices, but also to demand other favours.

For this reason, decentralized permit trading seems preferable. The advantages are flexibility and cost-effectiveness. The necessary conditions are accountability and transparency as well as an institutionalized exchange mechanism defining the roles and obligations of the private parties participating. Such an exchange would have buyers and sellers of credits. Integrated firms could use transfer prices set in an open market.

If combined with an international excise carbon tax regime, a system of emission permit trading would provide strong incentives for substituting natural gas for coal, essentially in power generation. For global greenhouse gas emissions, it would represent a gradual solution, not a dramatic one. OPEC and the leading Middle Eastern oil exporters are likely to face these issues for many years. Their major interest lies in avoiding a CO_2 tax in the consuming countries that would depress world market oil and natural gas prices, as opposed to an energy tax that would hit substitutes equally. The preference for the oil exporters would be a carbon tax at the production stage that would put a floor under international oil and natural gas prices. The fiscal measure could be an excise tax levied on carbon extraction from the ground, favouring natural gas over oil, and oil over coal. Excise taxes essentially represent a cost element, contributing to a floor below which the market value of oil does not fall. A historical precedent is the OPEC countries' royalties levied on oil production in the 1950s and 1960s.[20] In this respect, oil exporters and oil importers have radically different interests.

The position of the United States is crucial in this respect. As it is the world's largest user and importer of oil and natural gas, US taxes and duties can influence world market prices. So far, the United States has opposed any carbon taxes or gasoline taxes that would raise consumer prices. Even if the Clinton administration favoured such measures, they were almost unanimously rejected by Congress. Therefore, the Bush Jr administration's refusal to sign the Kyoto Protocol reflects a US consensus that is unlikely to change, even with a rising dependence on oil imports and at least an indirect dependence on the Middle East for oil market stability.

The background is the structure of the US economy, in particular the transportation system, which makes high gasoline prices carry a larger social cost than in Europe or Japan. By refusing to tax gasoline substantially or to impose a carbon tax, the United States keeps domestic oil product prices comparatively low, and at the same time props up world market oil prices, helping OPEC. By refusing to sign the Kyoto Protocol and enter into international carbon emission permit trading, the United States, as potentially the world's largest buyer of such permits, has reduced their market value to low levels. Granting Russia higher trading quotas at the 2001 Marrakesh meeting has, with the United States absent from the market, caused further price decline, compromising the economics of measures to really curb carbon emissions or conserve energy.

Managing oil industry diversification

The OPEC countries, and also the Middle East oil exporters, need to diversify their economies to create an alternative income base that can supplement and reduce dependence on oil revenues, and provide employment. The OPEC oil industry also needs to diversify. Since the wave of nationalization in the 1970s, national oil companies, often in a monopoly position, dominate the oil industry in most OPEC countries. With some exceptions, these companies do not operate outside their national territories. Even if the oil industry nationalization in the 1970s can be seen as an important step in the economic and political emancipation of the oil-exporting countries, a generation later it is time to review oil industry organization.

In the oil industry, as in other fields of business, monopolies in the longer run become inefficient, with high internal costs and slow responses to changes in technology and markets. This is also the case with the OPEC national oil companies, which are often run more as parts of public bureaucracies than as independent businesses. Providing employment is a high priority in all OPEC countries, and in doing so the national oil companies internalize some of the economic rent, raising the cost of oil operations and discarding some of the resource-based competitive advantage over non-OPEC oil.

By operating essentially within national boundaries, the national oil companies of the OPEC countries are effectively undiversified. Their upstream operations, confined to a specific country, are highly exposed to the geological risk of the particular area. By confining operations to one country they limit their ability to learn and connect to the dynamic development of technology and organization that takes place in the international oil industry. By remaining essentially upstream operations, selling crude oil, they are more exposed to oil market risk than are vertically integrated companies. Because of slack management, high costs and lack of diversification, the OPEC national oil companies would not be highly valued as investment objects by the standard international financial markets. Unless the explicit objective of the national oil company is to provide employment and job security for a technocratic elite, the government owner does not get an adequate return on oil investment. With rising population and higher income requirements, the efficient use of resources becomes a more urgent concern in the OPEC Middle Eastern oil-exporting countries.

The remedy is not to revert to the old pattern, with the large multinational oil companies dominating the OPEC oil industries, but rather to find a new balance of pluralism and competition. Opening up the upstream oil industry to foreign investment would be an essential step to attract capital, technology and expertise, and to ensure competition for the national oil companies. The effectiveness of such an opening-up would depend on access. Any selectivity or limitation on the choice of foreign investors would compromise competition and the bargaining position of the host country. The OPEC countries, including the Middle East oil exporters, need the resources of both large multinational oil companies and smaller, specialized upstream oil companies. A sensible complementary step would be to open up the upstream oil industry to private domestic companies. The OPEC countries, especially the Middle East oil exporters, have developed a considerable pool of talent in upstream oil matters. Human resources are available for newcomers in the oil industry and private capital would be willing to invest, provided fiscal terms were acceptable.

The next step would be to consider vertical integration. Even if economic rent is usually collected upstream in the oil industry, there are good reasons for oil-exporting countries to let their national oil companies invest downstream. Traditionally, vertical integration has been the strategy preferred by oil companies serving large markets, to secure oil supplies and capture a larger part of the economic rent.[21] With the consolidation of the international companies through mergers and acquisitions, the strengthening of oligopoly in the major markets and consequent prospects for more economic rent downstream, there are good arguments for the national oil companies of the OPEC countries to integrate vertically downstream.[22] This would both diversify risk and put them in more direct touch with end-user markets. The national oil companies of Kuwait and Venezuela have already invested downstream on a large scale. The question is to what extent it would be beneficial and possible for OPEC countries to invest in the large international oil companies. The UK government in the 1980s prevented Kuwait from keeping a 20 per cent share in BP. It is an open question what share the French or the US government, for example, would permit an OPEC country to take in TotalFinaElf or ExxonMobil. This would not prevent a more selective investment, aimed at a large share in specific oil product markets.

Partly privatizing the national oil companies would be the logical follow-up. The Middle East oil exporters no longer need wholly state-owned oil companies to control activities. The dominant position of state-owned companies can be an obstacle to government control insofar as they obstruct competition and transparency. Twenty-five years after most OPEC countries took over their oil industries, there is a good case for privatization.

The major justification for establishing national oil companies was that they would give governments a better control over oil activities. They would provide direct instruments for implementing government oil policy. They would also increase government expertise in and insight into matters relating to oil. These considerations have, at least implicitly, been decisive when organizing close contacts between the state oil companies and the ministries to which they are in principle accountable.

Using a state oil company as a tool for government oil policy implies that the government has control and the necessary insight. The expertise and insight arising from direct participation in oil activities first go to the state oil company.[23] The government gets the relevant information only in the second instance. In the process of exchanging information between the ministry and the private operators, the state oil company has the role of intermediary. The intermediate position gives a potential for selection. This implies a potential for deliberately influencing the flows of information to enhance asymmetry. In the transfer of information about oil activities to the government, the volume implies selection. This selection can easily become a deliberate screening. In the transfer of information from the government to those undertaking oil activities, some practical interpretation and precision is often required. This again can easily become a deliberate reorientation.

Within a system of state participation, the state oil companies occupy a strategic role, which in many ways gives them the advantage over both government and business.[24] In relation to the government, the operational position of the state oil companies gives them evident advantages in the matter of access to relevant information. They generally have greater resources to collect and process information than their formally superior government organizations. In this way, state oil companies are in the same position as large private business organizations. They can be selective in the feedback of information and have the potential to keep the government less than fully informed and to pursue distinct strategic interests.

State oil companies also have an important advantage in relation to large private businesses. The government's responsibility in any case implies closer links of communication with nationalized than private companies. If nationalized companies are intended to perform particular tasks for the government, as is the case with the state oil companies, the links of communication are likely to be close. As they are able to communicate more directly with government, they are also better able to influence government policy. This can be called a political gain of nationalization. In addition, state oil companies usually have access to low-interest treasury funds, which can make them view their capital costs as being lower than those of private oil companies.[25] This can imply a lower discount rate, giving an enhanced discretion in commercial ventures, which can also be used for long-term strategic purposes.

Correspondingly, in relation to the other oil companies active in exploration and production in the country, the state oil company has the obvious advantage of representing the government. The opinion of the state oil company is not only the opinion of an oil company, but also to a considerable extent the opinion of the state. A state oil company can use its strategic position to build up a position of power by influencing government policy and by substituting itself for government in relation to private oil companies. There is a definite risk that the active use of a state oil company in a system of state participation leads to a gradual reversal of the process of government, so that real decision making is transferred after some time from government agencies to state oil companies and the role of government is consequently reduced to that of endorsing decisions already taken elsewhere.

Such a development is harmful to the government's economic interests. It is also directly contrary to the principles of accountability and of the government's responsibility. The advantages for the state oil companies, as large organizations, give them a much better control of their environment so that they enjoy greater external stability.[26] They have a potential for political influence even in the context of developed economies with mature democratic political systems. In developing economies with less mature and less democratic political systems, as in the Middle East, the potential is much larger.

An explicit objective of government policy has been to create efficient and dynamic state oil companies. An important aspect of dynamism and efficiency is the desire for independence from outside interference, in this case from the government-owner. The question is what the governments can do to reduce this risk of government reversal. For the government to compete with the state oil companies in the matter of information seems futile for reasons of cost and organization. A constant reorganization of the state oil companies would reduce the risk, but would also be detrimental to efficiency. Detailed supervision also impedes efficiency, leading as it does to even greater bureaucratization and to closer contacts, which might ultimately cause a reversal of the control. The best solution seems to be privatization combined with pluralism so that competition and market forces provide transparency and control. This does not impede the government from retaining a majority or minority share.

The dominant position of the national oil companies in the Middle Eastern oil-exporting countries means that their eventual privatization would imply a significant move away from a centralized state-run economy toward a more decentralized and market-based economy. By reason of the consequent enhanced transparency and accountability, it would represent an important step toward a more open society.

No taxation without representation

Today there is no Middle Eastern democracy, but there are several countries whose citizens enjoy some measure of freedom. Examples are Egypt, Iran, Kuwait, Lebanon, Morocco and Yemen. In none of these cases, with the partial exception of Iran, are rulers really accountable to democratically elected assemblies. In practice, political succession does not take place according to constitutional procedures, but through natural death, murder or *coup d'état*. Many Arab states lack representative institutions able to balance opposing interests and elaborate compromises. The institution of censorship is practised in all Arab countries except Lebanon. It represses the opportunity of dialogue between the rulers and the ruled. In Iran, the substitute for censorship is the arbitrary closure of publications, with consequent strong incentives for self-censorship.

In the oil-exporting countries of the Middle East, oil revenues have provided a substitute for democracy. Because the rulers did not have to tax their subjects, they have not needed to be accountable to citizens and representative governments have been considered redundant.[27] The rulers have implicitly encountered demands for democracy by turning around the rallying slogan from the American War of Independence and stating: 'No representation without taxation'. Oil revenues are an important reason why the wave of democracy that in the 1980s and 1990s swept over most of the world has only to a limited extent reached the Middle East, so that oil is partly responsible for the retarded political and institutional development of the region.[28]

Oil revenues are no longer plentiful, but the political consequences of the new economic situation have yet to materialize. Iran is making important attempts at institutionalized representative government, although without any linear progress. The state in Saudi Arabia and most certainly in Iraq will need more money than can come from oil revenues and user fees. It will need to tax the citizens, but also give them a participation in running government.

The root of the problem is in the pre-oil societies of the Middle East, where autocratic rulers could consider entire countries as their private domain or private property. The oil wealth was not considered to belong to the nation, but to the ruler. This tradition was often encouraged by the Western powers. For Western oil interests it was more advantageous to deal with and eventually corrupt or manipulate a ruling individual or family, rather than deal with more complex representative institutions defending national interests. This is why Western powers have repeatedly not encouraged democracy in the oil-exporting countries, but rather actively opposed it whenever it might threaten their oil interests.[29] The first example was British reticence at the first Iranian revolution in 1905–11, the most recent is US support for maintaining the status quo in Saudi Arabia and tacit French support for the suspension of Algeria's elections in 1992. Other examples are British support for the Iraqi Hashemite monarchy until 1955 and US support for the shah's regime in Iran until 1979.

The responsibility for the lack of democracy in the Middle East oil-exporting countries lies no longer with the West, however, but with local rulers. The new class has collectively taken over the bad habits of the former individual rulers, taking power for granted and considering the country as property. The common feature of the new class under the shah in Iran, among the FLN in Algeria and among the Baath party in Iraq has been and is the will to stay in power and keep privileges, regardless of any consequences, means required or lack of justification. They have all chosen to drive their respective countries to catastrophe rather than give up power. Only time will show to what extent this also applies to the combined royal and technocratic new class in Saudi Arabia. Oil is a major factor in this respect, providing both money and foreign support.

In all major Middle East oil-exporting countries, corruption has been or still is endemic, among both the old rulers and the new class. A sizeable proportion of the oil revenues has gone into private pockets. In Iran under the shah, the new class combined a low degree of industrial efficiency with a high degree of personal greed. The military was at least as corrupt as the civilian administration.[30] The same seems to hold true for Iraq and Saudi Arabia today.

Corruption shows the parasitic and actively counterproductive role of the new class, in Iraq not least the military officers, and their waste of the country's resources. The imports and the resulting profits are paid for by oil and gas exports. Some sources indicate that the standard personal commission on military contracts in Saudi Arabia is 30 per cent. With one-third of the budget allocated to military expenditure, this means up to 10 per cent of the Saudi budget represents a personal profit.[31] The most likely profiteers are the immediate family and friends of the princely defence minister.[32] The result is a waste of the nation's oil wealth.

The evil is the lack of accountability of the rulers, especially touching oil and natural gas revenues, whether they are princes, technocrats, clerics or military officers. This problem will have to be settled before the Middle Eastern oil exporters can embark on a more peaceful and prosperous path of development. Apart from the benefits in terms of individual freedom, democracy is also the most efficient way to make various and opposing economic interests co-operate. From the perspective of political transaction cost, in the longer run democracy is a much more efficient way of ruling a country than an autocratic government. Just as a market is the most efficient way for an economic system to establish a balance between supply and demand, political freedom of expression and association together with representative government is the most efficient way to establish a balance between the various interests and points of view.

The collapse of communist rule in the Soviet Union and Eastern Europe and its dilution in China prove that centralist, autocratic rule is incompatible with an advanced economy. In the age of the computer, managerial and political decision making has to be decentralized in order to be effective. Autocratic management of firms or nations is risky and counterproductive. Practical considerations favour democracy, in addition to ideal ones, not least in the Middle East.

Insofar as democracy can improve the distribution of wealth and income and reduce waste, it is economically beneficial. By contrast, insofar as autocratic government causes a worse distribution of wealth and income and increases waste, it is economically harmful. The traditional point of view is that Islam as a comprehensive set of beliefs and practical rules, based on a transcendental revelation, is incompatible with modern democracy. This serves to justify autocratic and corrupt government as well as fanatical terrorism. A different point of view is that Islam's principles are compatible with those of democracy, respecting the aspirations of the people and emphasizing the duty of leaders to consult with them.[33] This amounts to the accountability of the rulers to the people. In a modern society, this consultation can most effectively be organized through representative assemblies, based on free elections and the freedom of expression and organization.

From this perspective, the autocratic governments of the Middle East are breaking with the economic and political principles of modern society. This seems to be grasped by an increasing number of the people concerned, especially the young. The temporary outcome is that insufficient oil revenues in immature and unstable political systems cause conflicts of distribution and priorities to be settled outside the institutions, at times violently.

The erroneous choice of economic strategy in the leading Middle East oil-exporting countries shows the high subjective risk associated with autocratic rulers. In the case of Iraq the risk propensity of autocratic government has also led the country into two disastrous wars within ten years. The combined economic and ideological pressures on the political systems of all the oil exporters of the Middle East are such that changes are likely to come. Mounting population pressure makes intergenerational conflict more acute. The chances are that oil policies will be affected. Political transition seems to be the condition for economic development outside oil. From this perspective, any income squeeze of the Middle Eastern oil exporters may in the longer run turn out to be politically beneficial, provided the transition from rent-based autocracy to tax-based democracy can be managed peacefully.

Conclusion: Structural instability

The Middle East is going to remain a region of acute importance to the world, not only because of oil, but also because of political instability. In the future Middle East, the political balance is unlikely to be much different from what it was before the Iraqi occupation of Kuwait on 2 August 1990, meaning that a stronger Iraq seems likely. A weaker US presence, through withdrawal or through worsened relations with Saudi Arabia, is likely to further strengthen Iraq's prospects of regional power. Even with Iraq's arsenals destroyed, the country will retain a population larger than that of the Gulf States, including Saudi Arabia, keeping a central geographical position. Population, education and military training will make Iraq at least a political challenge to neighbours.

Iran will stay by far the most populous country of the region, perhaps with an increasing ideological appeal.

It will be in the interest of Saudi Arabia, the Emirates and eventually Kuwait not to provoke these two countries, nor to act contrary to their basic interests in the oil market. A permanent US military presence in Saudi Arabia is a poor substitute for good relations with Iran and Iraq and probably even a political liability for the regime. Improved relations between Iran and Saudi Arabia make a promising sign that both countries realize that the countries concerned, not outside powers, must settle basic regional problems.

Even if outside powers have exercised and still exercise influence in the Middle East, the region has a considerable potential for instability without any external interference. Iraq remains the key. In 1991, Iraq was defeated by a coalition of external powers and Middle Eastern neighbours. This was politically possible because the Soviet Union was in the final stage of disintegration and could no longer play a significant part in the Middle East. The alternative to fighting Iraq, if the Soviet Union had still been a potent force in the Middle East, would have been to tolerate the seizure of Kuwait, in which case Iraq would have represented a military menace to all its neighbours, including Iran, Saudi Arabia and Syria, and perhaps even Turkey. Some neighbours might have accepted with regret Iraqi domination of the Middle East and the Gulf. Others would have taken measures and made an alliance to resist Iraq. Likely candidates for the latter category are Iran and Syria, perhaps assisted by Saudi Arabia and Turkey. For the United States the alternative to fighting Iraq in 1991 could have been to make a tacit alliance with Iran and perhaps even Syria. The outcome might not have been lasting Iraqi domination of the Middle East and the Gulf, but another war later in the 1990s, perhaps longer lasting and bloodier than the Gulf War, and with more protracted oil supply disruptions.

Even if Iraq is essential it is not the only risk factor in the Middle East. Population growth, generational change and insufficient oil revenues impose economic change and political transition. The Iraqi menace is no reason for neighbouring countries to postpone or dilute reforms. On the contrary, progress toward a market economy and political democracy would make Iran, Kuwait and Saudi Arabia more cohesive and resilient societies, better able to resist subversion or aggression and therefore more stable partners.

The multiple economic and political pressures that influence oil prices make their stability unlikely. The idea of oil price stability, even when managed by OPEC without serious internal conflicts, has turned out to be an illusion. Another point is that the world economy hardly needs stable or rigid oil prices. Because of their macro-economic impact through trade balances and inflation rates oil price flexibility can be an advantage. An oil price rise acts as a tax increase on consumers, and a fall acts as a tax relief. The issue is how and when to apply such a worldwide macro-economic tool. Because oil consumption is closely linked to the level of economic activity, a protracted boom will lead to rising oil demand and bottlenecks in the oil supply system, with upward price pressure. Conversely, an economic recession will lead to falling oil demand, an oil glut and downward price pressure. Since 1970, oil prices have indeed acted as a worldwide macro-economic regulator, but it has been applied brutally and at awkward times, more triggered by political events than by economic conditions. The risk persists.

The OPEC idea of an oil price target zone of $22–28 a barrel represents a breakthrough in oil-pricing strategy, adapting to fluctuating circumstances in the oil market as in the world economy. To enhance effectiveness the range should be widened and OPEC membership extended. With a larger number of oil exporters participating, the chances are that the oil supply changes that trigger oil price moves would be more moderate and be applied more in tune with the level of activity in the world economy. None of this is feasible unless Middle Eastern oil supplies are reasonably secure.

Securing oil supplies demands comprehensive political reform in the Middle East and the promotion of democracy and peace. Today, there is hardly any Arab or Middle Eastern democracy. The Middle East is the world's most militarized region with a huge and complex conflict potential. Promoting democracy in the Middle Eastern oil-exporting countries is in the West's interest, although it would mean discontinuing support for old friends and would involve transitory risks. It would also mean building institutions to secure the rule of law, with an independent judiciary, freedom of expression and assembly, including the right to organize independent labour unions, which could help reduce the disparities of wealth and income, and promoting a private sector to provide alternative income sources and jobs. Such measures would come at the expense of the West's old friends, but could make many new young ones. Oppressive regimes that leave no hope for peaceful change foster terrorism and should be condemned and contested by the West.[34] The risk for the West is that oppressive governments will use terrorism as a pretext for more oppression, provoking more opposition, instability and eventually more terrorism. From this perspective, consistently promoting democracy and the rule of law is also the best strategy for the West to simultaneously combat terrorism and secure oil supplies.

Likewise, promoting peace in the Middle East is in the West's interest as it can stabilize oil supplies, although it would mean taking Arab interests seriously, putting pressure on Israel to give up Palestinian land and terminating sanctions that hit Iraq's civilian population, not the rulers. Promoting peace would also mean discontinuing massive arms sales and actively engaging in a policy of regional disarmament that would include both Iraq and Israel. Finally, promoting peace and securing oil supplies would mean including Iran, Iraq and Libya in a framework of regional co-operation, not excluding them, as has been US policy until now. By changing policies in this direction, the West can hope to reduce the motivation and potential for terrorism, enhancing the basis for economic and political co-operation and interdependence, as well as securing oil supplies.

The interest of the West, particularly of the United States, is to secure oil supplies and to prevent new terrorist attacks. The task is not only to eradicate terrorist networks but also their background and motives. In the

twenty-first century, US policy towards the Middle East represents in many
Arab eyes a continuation of twentieth-century British and French colonial-
ism.[35] Economic, political and social reforms are the only way to channel
popular resentment against present conditions and rulers into a secular and
liberal movement, removing the reasons for religious fanaticism and
terrorism. Securing oil supplies and reducing the terrorist risk requires
treating the members of the Arab and Muslim world as equals with the
same rights to independence, democracy and prosperity as Americans and
Europeans.

Saudi Arabia's initiative of February 2002 for peace between Israel and
all Arab states indirectly aimed to reduce the political risk over Middle
Eastern oil supplies. Even if the Saudi rulers would welcome Saddam
Hussein being replaced, the conjecture of a US-led attack on Iraq and an
enduring, intensifying conflict in Palestine appeared perilous for political
stability in the moderate Arab countries, and could also compromise Saudi
Arabia's relations with the United States over oil. Consequently for Saudi
Arabia, the United States would need to earn credentials of justice by
effectively helping the Palestinian cause before taking on Iraq. A peaceful
settlement in Palestine would politically weaken the hardliners in Baghdad
as well as in Teheran. Reduced regional tension would highlight the
monstrous absurdity of the present Iraqi regime. Terminating the Israeli–
Palestinian conflict would strengthen the liberal faction in Iran over the
conservative hardliners who have a stake in enmity to Israel and therefore
in the conflict not being settled. A more moderate Iran would be a more
co-operative partner for Saudi Arabia in the Gulf as in OPEC.

A more peaceful Middle East would permit general disarmament and
free resources for better purposes, which is pertinent to the strained Saudi
budget. More peaceful conditions would enhance regional trade and
economic co-operation. As for oil, improved relations between Iran, Iraq
and Saudi Arabia would strengthen co-operation in OPEC and help
stabilize oil prices. As for oil supplies, concerns over reserves, costs and
depletion rates indicate that Russia is unlikely ever to replace Saudi Arabia
as the ultimate producer. Consequently, the West will remain dependent
upon oil from the Middle East and especially Saudi Arabia, whatever the
state of affairs between Israel and the Palestinians.

NOTES

Chapter 1: The necessity of oil

1   Steven Simon and Daniel Benjamin, 'Myths of American misdeeds', *Financial Times*, 2 October 2001.
2   Roula Khalaf, 'Why they hate us', *Financial Times*, 5 October 2001.
3   Dominique Moïsi, 'Tragedy that exposed a groundswell of hatred', *Financial Times*, 24 September 2001.
4   Heather Deegan, *The Middle East and Problems of Democracy* (Boulder, CO: Lynne Reiner, 1994), p 6.
5   Saïd K. Aburish, *A Brutal Friendship* (London: Indigo, 1997), pp 109ff.
6   Marwan Bishara, *Palestine/Israël: la paix ou l'apartheid* (Paris: Éditions La Découverte, 2001), p 35.
7   Mary Chartouni-Dubrarry, 'Proche-Orient: le compte à rebours', in Thierry de Montbrial and Pierre Jacquet (eds), *Ramses 2002* (Paris: Dunod, 2001), pp 141–58.
8   'Sharon's unstated mission to topple Arafat's regime', *Financial Times*, 10 November 2001.
9   'Russia becoming an oil ally', *The New York Times*, 18 October 2001.
10 'Goodbye, OPEC', *Jane's Foreign Report* 2668 (6 December 2001).
11 Yasser Hawary, 'Vers un désordre mondial permanent?', *Arabies* 189 (January 2002), p 14.
12 'US dismay with Saudis fuels talk of a pullout', *The New York Times*, 16 January 2001.
13 'Saudis may seek US exit', *The Washington Post*, 18 January 2001.
14 Seymour M. Hersh, 'The Iraq hawks: can their war plan work?', *The New Yorker*, 24 December 2001.
15 Michael T. Klare, *Resource Wars* (New York: Henry Holt and Company, 2001), p 63.
16 David E. Spiro, *The Hidden Hand of American Hegemony* (London: Cornell University Press, 1999), p 121.
17 'Économie: les scénarios', *L'Expansion*. 653 (27 September 2001), pp 64–8.
18 Quentin Peel, 'Washington's balancing act', *Financial Times*, 1 October 2001.
19 'U.S. rebukes Israeli leader as coalition tensions rise', *Financial Times*, 6–7 October 2001.
20 'A nation challenged: ally's future; US pondering Saudis' vulnerability', *The New York Times*, 4 November 2001.
21 David Buchan, 'OPEC's dilemma', *Financial Times*, 24 September 2001.
22 'Saudi Arabia: The double act wears thin', *The Economist*, 29 September 2001, pp 22–3.
23 Susan Strange, *States and Markets* (London: Pinter Publishers, 1988), p 187.
24 Philip L. Verleger, Jr, *Adjusting to Volatile Energy Prices* (Washington, DC: Institute for International Economics, 1993), p 28.
25 Hullar Durgin, 'US administration faces crisis over energy policy', *Financial Times*, 6 December 2000.
26 Bernard C. Beaudreau, *Energy and the Rise and Fall of Political Economy* (London: Greenwood Press, 1999), p 7.

27   Bernard C. Beaudreau, *Energy and Organisation* (London: Greenwood Press, 1998), p 3.
28   Gary S. Becker, *The Economic Approach to Human Behaviour* (Chicago: The University of Chicago Press, 1978), p 187.
29   Beaudreau: *Energy and Organisation*, p 10.
30   Vaclav Smil, *Energy in World History* (Boulder, CO: Westview Press, 1994), pp 158ff.
31   Jean-Claude Debeir, Jean-Paul Deléage and Daniel Hémery, *In the Servitude of Power* (London: Zed Books, 1991), pp 108ff.
32   John Mitchell with Koji Morita, Norman Selley and Jonathan Stern, *The New Economy of Oil* (London: The Royal Institute of International Affairs, 2001), p 25.
33   Rögnvaldur Hanneson, *Petroleum Economics* (London: Quorum Books, 1998), p 3.
34   A.F. Alhajji and David Huettner, 'The target revenue model and the world oil market: empirical evidence from 1971 to 1994', *The Energy Journal* 21/2 (2000), pp 121–44.
35   Robert Cooter and Thomas Ulen, *Law and Economics* (New York: Addison Wesley, 2000), p 7.
36   George Philip, *Oil and Politics in Latin America* (Cambridge: Cambridge University Press, 1982), pp 1ff.
37   Dag Harald Claes, *The Politics of Oil-Producer Cooperation* (Boulder, CO: Westview Press, 2001), p 7.
38   Robert B. Ekelund, Jr and Robert D. Tollison, *Politicized Economies* (College Station: Texas A & M College Press, 1997), p 28.
39   Kenneth W. Dam, *Oil Resources* (Chicago: The University of Chicago Press, 1976), pp 4ff.
40   Christopher Tugendhat and Adrian Hamilton, *Oil – The Biggest Business* (London: Eyre Methuen, 1975), pp 24ff.
41   J.W. Anderson, *The Surge in Oil Prices: Anatomy of a Non-Crisis*, Discussion Paper (Washington, DC: Resources for the Future, 2001), pp 2–3.
42   'Cheap oil: The next shock?', *The Economist*, 6 March 1999, pp 23–5.
43   Paul Stevens, 'Oil and the Gulf', in Gary Sick and Lawrence G. Potter (eds), *The Persian Gulf at the Millennium* (New York: St Martin's Press, 1997), pp 83–114.
44   Kate Gillespie and Clement M. Henry, 'Introduction', in Kate Gillespie and Clement M. Henry (eds), *Oil in the New World Order* (Gainsville: University Press of Florida, 1995), pp 1–20.
45   *National Energy Policy* (Washington, DC: The White House, 2001), p viii.
46   Gregory P. Nowell, *Mercantile States and the World Oil Cartel 1900–1939* (London: Cornell University Press, 1994), p 148.
47   Ed Shaffer, *The United States and the Control of World Oil* (London: Croom Helm, 1983), pp 40ff.
48   Matthew Jones and David Buchan, 'Tapping rich stores of offshore co-operation', *Financial Times*, 22 December 2000.
49   Manuel Castells, *The Rise of the Network Society* (London: Blackwell, 1996), p 386.
50   Jean Gaudrey, *Nouvelle Économie, nouveau mythe?* (Paris: Flammarion, 2000), pp 38ff.
51   Richard Rosecrance, *The Rise of the Virtual State* (New York: Basic Books, 1999), p 13.
52   Marie N. Fagan, 'Resource depletion and technical change: effects on U.S. crude oil finding costs from 1977 to 1994', *The Energy Journal* 18/4 (1977), pp 91–108.
53   Maurice A. Adelman, 'Modeling world oil supply', *The Energy Journal* 14/1 (1993), pp 1–33.
54   Mitchell with Morita, Selley and Stern: *The New Economy of Oil*, p 48.
55   Carroll L. Wilson (ed), *Energy: Global Prospects 1985–2000*, Report of the Workshop on Alternative Energy Strategies (New York: McGraw-Hill, 1977), pp 167ff.
56   Jahangir Amuzegar, *Managing the Oil Wealth* (London: I.B. Tauris, 1999), pp 48ff.
57   Geoffrey Kemp and Robert Harkavi, *Strategic Geography and the Changing Middle East* (Washington, DC: Brookings Institution Press, 1997) pp 373ff.

58 'Bush energy plan: the international dimension', *Middle East Economic Survey*, 28 May 2001, pA7.

59 Ian W.H. Parry, *Are Gasoline Taxes in Britain Too High?* (Washington, DC: Resources for the Future, 2001), p 10.

60 John Roberts, *Visions and Mirages* (Edinburgh: Mainstream Publishing, 1995), pp 23ff.

61 Philippe Fargues, 'Demographic explosion or social upheaval', in Ghassan Salamé (ed), *Democracy without Democrats* (London: I.B. Tauris, 1994), pp 156–79.

62 R. Stephen Humphreys, *Between Memory and Desire*, paperback edn (Berkeley: University of California Press, 2001), p 22.

63 Robert Gilpin, *The Challenge of Global Capitalism* (Princeton, NJ: Princeton University Press, 2000), pp 71–2.

64 Becker: *The Economic Approach to Human Behaviour*, p 134.

65 Franz Wirl, *The Economics of Conservation Programs* (London: Kluwer Academic Press, 1997), p 24.

66 Chauncey Starr, *Energy Planning – A Nation at Risk* (Palo Alto, CA: Electric Power Research Institute, 1977), p 2.

67 William W. Hogan and Alan S. Manne, *Energy–Economy Interactions: The Fable of the Elephant and the Rabbit* (Palo Alto, CA: Energy Modeling Forum, Stanford University, 1977), pp b-2ff.

68 Beaudreau: *Energy and Organisation*, p 27.

69 Robert S. Dohner, 'Energy prices, economic activity and inflation', in Knut Anton Mork (ed), *Energy Prices, Inflation and Economic Activity* (Cambridge, MA: Ballinger, 1981), pp 7–41.

70 Dale W. Jorgenson, 'The great transition: energy and economic change', *The Energy Journal* 7/5 (1986), pp 1–13.

71 Clare P. Doblin, 'Declining energy intensity in the U.S. manufacturing sector', *The Energy Journal* 9/2 (1988), pp 109–35.

72 Wirl: *The Economics of Conservation Programs*, p 24.

73 Nathan Rosenberg, *Exploring the Black Box* (Cambridge: Cambridge University Press, 1994), p 163.

74 Sam Schurr, 'Energy efficiency and productive efficiency: some thoughts based on the American experience', *The Energy Journal* 3/3 (1982), p 8.

75 Lee Schipper and Stephen Myers, *Energy Efficiency and Human Activity* (Cambridge: Cambridge University Press, 1992), pp 84ff.

76 Becker: *The Economic Approach to Human Behaviour*, p 89–90.

77 *Annual Energy Outlook 1996* (Washington, DC: Energy Information Administration, 1996), p 14.

78 Lee Schipper et al., 'Linking life-styles and energy use: a matter of time?', *Annual Review of Energy* 14 (1989), pp 273–320.

79 Richard C. Carlson, Willis W. Harman, Peter Schwartz, and associates, *Energy Futures, Human Values and Lifestyles* (Boulder, CO: Westview Press, 1982), p 55.

80 Theodore Modis, *Predictions* (New York: Simon and Schuster, 1992), p 69.

81 Smil: *Energy in World History*, pp 158–9.

82 Jean-Marie Martin, 'Le changement des technologies de l'énergie: genèse, modalités et hypothèses explicatives', in Bernard Bourgeois, Dominique Finon and Jean-Marie Martin (eds), *Énergie et changement technologique* (Paris: Éditions Économica, 2000), pp 17–61.

83 Tim Ford, 'Fuel cell-vehicles offer clean and sustainable mobility for the future', *Oil and Gas Journal* 97/50 (13 December 1999), pp 130–7.

84 George Couvaras, 'Gas to liquids: a paradigm shift for the oil industry?', *Oil and Gas Journal* 97/50 (13 December 1999), pp 124–6.

85   DeAnne Julius and Afsaneh Mashayeki, *The Economics of Natural Gas* (Oxford: Oxford Institute for Energy Studies, 1990), p 10.
86   Hillard G. Huntington, 'Crude oil prices and U.S. economic performance: where does the asymmetry reside?', *The Energy Journal* 19/4 (1998), pp 107–32.
87   Gilpin: *The Challenge of Global Capitalism*, p 71.
88   Castells: *The Rise of the Network Society*, pp 203ff.
89   Mary Ann Heiss, *Empire and Nationhood* (New York: Colombia University Press, 1997), p 221.
90   Robert L. Bradley, Jr, *Oil, Gas, and Government*, vol I (London: Rowmand and Littlefield, 1996), pp 57ff.
91   Alessandro Roncaglia, *The International Oil Market* (London: Macmillan, 1985), p 9.
92   John M. Blair, *The Control of Oil* (New York: Pantheon Books, 1976), pp 25ff.
93   Simon Bromley, *American Hegemony and World Oil* (University Park: The Pennsylvania State University Press, 1991), pp 82ff.
94   Charles E. Lindblom, *Politics and Markets* (New York: Basic Books, 1977), pp 76ff.
95   John D. Wirth, 'Introduction', in John D. Wirth (ed), *Latin American Oil Companies and the Politics of Energy* (London: University of Nebraska Press, 1985), pp ix–xxxix.
96   Tugendhat and Hamilton: *Oil – The Biggest Business*, pp 24ff.
97   *Energy Security, A Report to the President of the United States* (Washington, DC: US Department of Energy, 1987), pp 8ff.
98   Martin Sæter, 'Oljen og de politiske samarbeidsformer', *Internasjonal Politikk* 2B (1975), pp 397–421.
99   Edward N. Krapels, *Oil Crisis Management* (London: The Johns Hopkins University Press, 1980), pp 36ff.
100 Ian Seymour, *OPEC: Instrument of Change* (London: Macmillan, 1980), p 132.
101 Anthony Sampson, *The Seven Sisters* (London: Hodder and Stoughton, 1975), pp 3ff.

Chapter 2: Foreign powers and Middle Eastern oil

1   Charles Sèbe and William Le Bras, *Indomptable Iraq* (Paris: Le Sémaphore, 1999), p 111.
2   Kate Gillespie and Clement M. Henry, 'Introduction', in Kate Gillespie and Clement M. Henry (eds), *Oil in the New World Order* (Gainsville: University Press of Florida, 1995), p 12.
3   Paul Stevens, 'Oil and the Gulf', in Gary Sick and Lawrence G. Potter (eds), *The Persian Gulf at the Millennium* (New York: St Martin's Press, 1997), p 87.
4   Bahgat Korany, 'The Arab world and the new balance of power in the new Middle East', in Michael C. Hudson (ed), *Middle East Dilemma* (New York: Columbia University Press, 1999), pp 35–59.
5   Gregory P. Nowell, *Mercantile States and the World Oil Cartel 1900–1939* (London: Cornell University Press, 1994), p 12.
6   Saïd K. Aburish, *A Brutal Friendship* (London: Indigo, 1997), pp 69ff.
7   John D. Wirth, 'Introduction', in John D. Wirth (ed), *Latin American Oil Companies and the Politics of Energy* (London: University of Nebraska Press, 1985), pp ix–xxxix.
8   Georges Corm, *Le Proche-Orient éclaté* (Paris: Éditions Gallimard, 1991), pp 82ff.
9   Jahangir Amuzegar, *Managing the Oil Wealth* (London: I.B. Tauris, 1999), p 199.
10   Christopher Tugendhat and Adrian Hamilton, *Oil – The Biggest Business* (London: Eyre Methuen, 1975), pp 82ff.
11   *Ibid.*, pp 73ff.
12   Brian McBeth, *British Oil Policy 1919–1939* (London: Frank Cass, 1985), pp 24ff.
13   Simon Bromley, *Rethinking Middle East Politics* (Cambridge: Polity Press, 1994), p 74.
14   *Ibid.*
15   David Fromkin, *A Peace to End All Peace* (New York: Avon Books, 1989), p 375.

16 McBeth: *British Oil Policy 1919–1939*, p 32.
17 Ofra Bengio, 'Iraq's Shi'a and Kurdish communities: from resentment to revolt', in Amatzia Baran and Barry Rubin (eds), *Iraq's Road to War* (New York: St Martin's Press, 1993), pp 51–66.
18 Edith and E.F. Penrose, *Iraq, International Relations and National Development* (London: Ernest Benn, 1978), pp 87ff.
19 Alan Richards and John Waterbury, *A Political Economy of the Middle East* (Boulder, CO: Westview Press, 1990), p 146.
20 *Ibid.*, p 255.
21 Phebe Marr, *The Modern History of Iraq* (Boulder, CO: Westview Press, 1985), pp 247ff.
22 *Ibid.*, p 248.
23 Peter Sluglett and Marion Farouk-Sluglett, 'Iraq', in *The Middle East, the Arab World and Its Neighbours* (London: Times Books, 1991), pp 84–107.
24 Alvin Z. Rubinsten, 'Soviet policy in the Middle East: perspectives from three capitals', in Robert H. Donaldson (ed), *The Soviet Union in the Third World: Successes and Failures* (London: Croom Helm, 1981), pp 150–60.
25 Robert O. Freedman, 'Soviet policy toward Ba'athist Iraq', in Donaldson: *The Soviet Union in the Third World*, pp 161–91.
26 Fromkin: *A Peace to End All Peace*, p 558.
27 Roger Owen and Sevket Pamuk, *A History of Middle East Economies in the Twentieth Century* (London: I.B. Tauris, 1998), p 230.
28 Richard N. Schofield, 'Border conflicts: past, present and future', in Gary Sick and Lawrence G. Potter (eds), *The Persian Gulf at the Millennium* (New York: St Martin's Press, 1997), pp 127–65.
29 Marise Fabriès-Verfaille, *L'Afrique du Nord et le Moyen-Orient dans le nouvel espace mondial* (Paris: Presses Universitaires de France, 1998), pp 191ff.
30 R. Stephen Humphreys, *Between Memory and Desire*, paperback edn (Berkeley: University of California Press, 2001), p 79.
31 Amuzegar: *Managing the Oil Wealth*, p 135.
32 *Ibid.*, p 39.
33 John Roberts, 'Piercing together the peace jigsaw', *The Energy Compass*, 14 December 1990.
34 Amuzegar: *Managing the Oil Wealth*, p 136.
35 Hussein J. Agha and Ahmad S. Khalidi, *Syria and Iran* (London: The Royal Institute of International Affairs, 1995), p 9.
36 Geoffrey Kemp and Jeremy Pressman, *Point of No Return* (Washington, DC: Brookings Institution Press, 1997), p 120.
37 Mostafa Dolatyar and Tim S. Gray, *Water Politics in the Middle East* (London: Macmillan, 2000), p 143.
38 Guy Dinmore, 'Iran's unsteady ship', *Financial Times*, 12 December 2000.
39 Marcel Pott, *Allahs falsche Propheten* (Cologne: Bastei Lübbe, 2001), p 242.
40 Kemp and Pressman: *Point of No Return*, p 131.
41 Hassan Tahsin, 'Unhappy state of Arab–US ties', *Arab News*, 13 February 2002.
42 Roula Khalaf, 'Winds of change', *Financial Times*, 11 February 2002.
43 Gillespie and Henry: 'Introduction', pp 1–17.
44 Christopher Piening, *Global Europe* (London: Lynne Rienner, 1997), pp 69ff.
45 Pierre Péan and Jean-Pierre Séréni, *Les Émirs de la République* (Paris: Éditions du Seuil, 1982), pp 56ff.
46 B.A. Roberson, 'Introduction', in B.A. Roberson (ed), *The Middle East and Europe* (London: Routledge, 1998), pp 1–19.
47 Geoffrey Kemp and Robert E. Harkavy, *Strategic Geography and the Changing Middle East* (Washington, DC: Brookings Institution Press, 1997), pp 373ff.

48   Simon Bromley, *American Hegemony and World Oil* (University Park: The Pennsylvania State University Press, 1991), pp 69ff.
49   Nowell: *Mercantile States*, pp 112ff.
50   Charles K. Ebinger (ed), *The Critical Link: Energy and National Security in the 1990s* (Cambridge, MA: Ballinger, 1982), pp 173ff.
51   Patrick Criqui, 'Un nouveau partage de la rente', *Le Monde*, 25 September 1990, p 27.
52   Antoine Ayoub, *Le Pétrole – économie et politique* (Paris: Éditions Économica, 1996), p 145.
53   *National Energy Strategy* (Washington, DC: Government Printing Office, 1991), p 5.
54   Semih Vaner, 'Turquie: la démocratie ou la mort', *Politique Étrangère* 4 (1998), pp 763–78.
55   Robert Cottrell, 'The sweet smell of Russian oil', *Financial Times*, 1 February 2002.
56   Robert Cottrell, 'Putin's risky strategy', *Financial Times*, 12 February 2002.
57   *Energy Security: Evaluating U.S. Vulnerability to Oil Supply Disruptions and Options for Mitigating Their Effects* (Washington, DC: General Accounting Office, 1996), p 5.
58   Jan H. Kalicki, 'Caspian energy at the crossroads', *Foreign Affairs* 80/5 (September–October 2001), pp 32–9.
59   'Ganz neue Landkarten', *Wirtschaftswoche* 41 (10 October 2001), pp 32–9.
60   Ahmed Rashid, *Taliban* (London: I.B. Tauris, 2000), pp 157ff.
61   Ottar Skagen, *Caspian Gas* (London: The Royal Institute of International Affairs, 1987), p 1.
62   Frédéric Grare, 'La nouvelle donne énergétique autour de la mer Caspienne: une perspective géopolitique', in *La Caspienne: une nouvelle frontière*, Cahiers d'études sur la Méditerranée orientale et le monde turco-iranien 23 (Paris: Édisud, 1997), pp 15–38.
63   In this context, the term Central Asia will include Azerbaijan, even if it is geographically a Caucasian republic. The justification is that Azerbaijan is Muslim and has oil.
64   Martha Brill Olcott, 'Pipelines and pipe dreams: energy development and Caspian society', *Journal of International Affairs* 53/1 (Fall 1999), pp 305–25.
65   John Barham, 'East–west pipeline: oil and gas to be transported through Turkey', *Financial Times*, 3 March 1998.
66   Darrel Slider, 'Democratisation in Georgia', in Karen Dawisha and Bruce Parrott (eds), *Conflict, Cleavage and Change in Central Asia and the Caucasus* (Cambridge: Cambridge University Press, 1997), pp 155–98.
67   Muriel Atkin, 'Thwarted democratisation in Tajikistan', in Dawisha and Parrott: *Conflict, Cleavage and Change*, pp 277–311.
68   Michael Ochs, 'Turkmenistan: the quest for stability and control', in Dawisha and Parrott: *Conflict, Cleavage and Change*, pp 312–59.
69   Terry Lynn Karl, *The Paradox of Plenty* (London: University of California Press, 1997), pp 44ff.
70   Grare: 'La nouvelle donne énergétique', pp 22ff.
71   Ian Cuthberson, 'Notre destin est en train de se jouer en Asie centrale', *Le Temps Stratégique*, September 1995, pp 30–45.
72   Vicken Cheterian, 'Sea or lake: a major issue for Russia', in *La Caspienne: une nouvelle frontière*, pp 103–125.
73   Olivier Roy, *La Nouvelle Asie centrale* (Paris: Éditions du Seuil, 1997), pp 243ff.
74   Grare: 'La nouvelle donne énergétique', p 32.
75   *Ibid.*, p 34.
76   Roy: *La Nouvelle Asie centrale*, pp 291ff.
77   Mohammad Reza-Djalili, 'Perspectives iraniennes', in *La Caspienne: une nouvelle frontière*, pp 127–41.
78   Grare: 'La nouvelle donne énergétique', p 27.
79   Roy: *La Nouvelle Asie centrale*, p 292.
80   Cheterian: 'Sea or lake: a major issue for Russia', p 115.

81 Lowell Bezanis, 'Joining forces with Iran and Russia', *Transition*, 11 September 1995, pp 70–3.

82 Stephen Blank, 'The United States and Central Asia', in Roy Allison and Lena Jonson (eds), *Central Asian Security* (Washington, DC: Brookings Institution, 2001), pp 127–51.

83 Ariel Cohen, 'Odessa–Brody pipeline creates new option for export of Caspian Basin resources', *EurasiaNet*, 11 December 2001, www.eurasianet.org

84 'Russia wins the war', *The New York Times*, 23 December 2001.

85 'Opec at bay', *Financial Times*, 19 November 2001.

86 Taras Kuzio, 'Nato reevaluates strategic considerations in Caucasus, Central Asia', *EurasiaNet*, 17 December 2001, www.eurasianet.org

87 Kenan Aliyev, 'US envoy cautions that window could close on a Karabakh settlement', *EurasiaNet*, 14 January 2002, www.eurasianet.org

88 Michael Lelyveld, 'Caspian: Moscow attempts to set sea borders', *EurasiaNet*, 12 January 2002, www.eurasianet.org

89 Nailia Sohbetqizi, 'Pragmatism guides Russian-Azerbaijani deal making', *EurasiaNet*, 11 January 2002, www.eurasianet.org

90 Haroutiun Khachatrian, 'Armenian leaders restrained on Karabakh peace prospects', *EurasiaNet*, 12 December 2001, www.eurasianet.org

91 Parker T. Hart, *Saudi Arabia and the United States* (Bloomington: Indiana University Press, 1998), p 8.

92 *National Energy Strategy*, p 4.

93 Pierre Terzian, *Le Gaz naturel* (Paris: Éditions Économica, 1998), pp 15ff.

94 Mamoun Fundy, *Saudi Arabia and the Politics of Dissent* (London: Palgrave, 1999), p 46.

95 Joseph A. Kechichian, *Succession in Saudi Arabia* (London: Palgrave, 2001), p 142.

96 'A Saudi prince with an unconventional idea: elections', *The New York Times*, 28 November 2001.

97 Fundy: *Saudi Arabia and the Politics of Dissent*, p 115.

98 Kenneth Katzman, *Searching for Stable Peace in the Persian Gulf* (Carlisle, PA: US Army War College, 1998), pp 19ff.

99 Yasser Hawatmeh, 'Tout empire périra', *Arabies*, June 1997, p 5.

100 'Angry Saudis step up pressure on Israel', *Financial Times*, 4 July 1997.

101 Charles Zorgbibe, *La Méditerranée sans les Grands?* (Paris: Quadrige/Presses Universitaires de France, 1997), pp 196ff.

102 Françoise Nicolat and Pierre Jacquet, 'L'actualité économique internationale', in Thierry de Montbrial and Pierre Jacquet (eds), *Ramses 99* (Paris: IFR/Dunod, 1998), pp 135–64.

103 Ayoub: *Le Pétrole – économie et politique*, pp 47ff.

104 Roula Khalaf, 'Saudi suspicions', *Financial Times*, 16 November 2001.

105 Jon B. Alterman, 'The Gulf States and the American umbrella', *Middle East Review of International Affairs (MERIA)* 4/4 (December 2000).

Chapter 3: Oil supplies, OPEC, oligopoly and politics

1 Daniel Yergin, *The Prize* (New York: Simon and Schuster, 1991), p 432.

2 Robert B. Ekelund, Jr and Robert D. Tollison, *Politicized Economies* (College Station: Texas A & M College Press, 1997), p 28.

3 P.S. Dasgupta and G.M. Heal, *Economic Theory and Exhaustible Resources* (Cambridge: Cambridge University Press, 1979), pp 156ff.

4 Bob Tippee, *Where's the Shortage?* (Tulsa, OK: PennWell Books, 1993), pp 116ff.

5 F.M. Scherer, *Industry, Structure, Strategy, and Public Policy* (New York: HarperCollins, 1996), p 81.

6 Tippee: *Where's the Shortage?*, pp 74ff.

7 Paul H. Frankel, *Essentials of Petroleum* (London: Frank Cass, 1969), p 58.

8   Daniel Johnston, *International Petroleum Fiscal Systems and Production Sharing Contracts* (Tulsa, OK: PennWell Books, 1994), pp 274ff.
9   Peter F. Cowhey, *The Problems of Plenty: Energy Policy and International Politics* (Berkeley: University of California Press, 1985), pp 30–1.
10 Richard A. Manning, *The Asian Energy Factor* (New York: Palgrave, 2000), p 25.
11 Michael C. Lynch, *Crying Wolf: Warnings about Oil Supplies* (New York: Council on Foreign Relations, 1998), p 5.
12 Colin C. Campbell, *The Coming Oil Crisis* (Brentwood, England: Multi-Science Publishing and Petro-Consultants, 1997), p 7.
13 Kenneth S. Deffeyes, *Hubbert's Peak* (Princeton, NJ: Princeton University Press, 2001), p 133.
14 Antoine Ayoub, *Le Pétrole – économie et politique* (Paris: Éditions Économica, 1996), pp 47ff.
15 Fiona Venn, *Oil Diplomacy in the Twentieth Century* (London: Macmillan, 1986), pp 142ff.
16 Robert Axelrod, *The Complexity of Co-operation* (Princeton, NJ: Princeton University Press, 1997), p 11.
17 Robert Axelrod, *The Evolution of Co-operation* (New York: Basic Books, 1984), p 8.
18 Scherer: *Industry Structure, Strategy and Public Policy*, pp 83ff.
19 *Ibid.*, p 85.
20 Thomas C. Schelling, *The Strategy of Conflict* (Cambridge, MA: Harvard University Press, 1980), p 5.
21 Tippee: *Where's the Shortage?*, p 265.
22 Jahangir Amuzegar, *Managing the Oil Wealth* (London: I.B. Tauris, 1999), p 195.
23 F. Gregory Cause III, 'Saudi Arabia over a barrel', *Foreign Affairs* 79/3 (May/June 2000), pp 80–94.
24 F. Gregory Cause III, *Oil Monarchies* (New York: Council on Foreign Relations Press, 1994), pp 42ff.
25 *Ibid.*, p 43.
26 Peter Pawerlka, 'Der Irak als „Rentierstaat"', in Peter Pawerlka, Isabella Pfaff and Hans-Georg Wehling (eds), *Die Golfregion in der Weltpolitik* (Stuttgart: Verlag W. Kohlhammer, 1991), pp 109–43.
27 Thomas Bierschenk, 'Die Golfstaaten: politische Stabilität trotz ökonomischem Wandel', in Pawerlka, Pfaff and Wehling: *Die Golfregion in der Weltpolitik*, pp 95–108.
28 Roger Owen and Sevket Pamuk, *A History of Middle East Economies in the Twentieth Century* (London: I.B. Tauris, 1998), p 207.
29 Ådne Cappelen and Robert Choudhury, *The Future of the Saudi Arabian Economy* (Oslo: Central Bureau of Statistics, 2000), p 17.
30 R. Stephen Humphreys, *Between Memory and Desire* (Berkeley: University of California Press, 1999), p 113.
31 Alan Richards and John Waterbury, *A Political Economy of the Middle East* (Boulder, CO: Westview Press, 1990), pp 353ff.
32 Humphreys: *Between Memory and Desire*, p 13.
33 Source: SIPRI Military Expenditure Database.
34 Humphreys: *Between Memory and Desire*, p 11.
35 'MENA Still World's Leading Arms Market', *Middle East Economic Survey* 43/47 (20 November 2000).
36 Jacqueline S. Ismael, *Kuwait: Dependency and Class in a Rentier State* (Gainesville: University Press of Florida, 1993), pp 81ff.
37 Karim Pakravan, 'The emerging private sector: new demands on an old system', in Gary Sick and Lawrence G. Potter (eds), *The Persian Gulf at the Millennium* (New York: St Martin's Press, 1997), pp 115–26.
38 *Middle East Oil and Gas* (Paris: International Energy Agency, OECD, 1995), pp 25ff.

39 Giacomo Luciani, 'The oil rent, the fiscal crisis of the state and democratisation', in Ghassan Salamé (ed), *Democracy without Democrats* (London: I.B. Tauris, 1994), pp 130–55.
40 Kiren Aziz-Chaudhry, 'Economic liberalisation and the lineages of the rentier state', in Nicholas S. Hopkins and Saad Eddin Ibrahim (eds), *Arab Society* (Cairo: The American University in Cairo Press, 1997), pp 345–58.
41 Amuzegar: *Managing the Oil Wealth*, p 132.
42 Jahangir Amuzegar, *Iran's Economy under the Islamic Republic* (London: I.B. Tauris, 1993), p 277.
43 Amuzegar: *Managing the Oil Wealth*, p 133.
44 Aziz-Chaudhry: 'Economic liberalisation and the lineages of the rentier state', p 368.
45 Ridha Kéfi, 'Après Bachar, Qossai?', *Jeune Afrique – l'Intelligent*, 28 August 2001, pp 34–7.
46 Anthony H. Cordesman and Ahmed S. Hashim, *Iraq* (Boulder, CO: Westview Press, 1997), p 127.
47 Phebe Marr, *The Modern History of Iraq* (Boulder, CO: Westview Press, 1985), pp 247ff.
48 Fadhil Al-Chalabi and Adnan Al-Janabi, 'Optimum production and pricing policies', *Journal of Energy and Development*, Spring 1979, pp 229–58.
49 Anthony H. Cordesman, *Saudi Arabia* (Boulder, CO: Westview Press, 1997), p 51.
50 Cappelen and Choudhury: *The Future of the Saudi Arabian Economy*, pp 8ff.
51 Cause: 'Saudi Arabia over a barrel', pp 80–94.
52 Hani Z. Yamani, *To Be a Saudi* (London: Janus Publishing Company, 1997), pp 98ff.
53 Scherer: *Industry, Structure, Strategy, and Public Policy*, p 84.
54 Joan Edelman Spero, *The Politics of International Economic Relations* (London: Routledge, 1992), pp 271ff.
55 Ian Seymour, *OPEC: Instrument of Change* (London: Macmillan, 1980), p 37.
56 *Ibid.*, p 53.
57 A.F. Alhajji and David Huettner, 'OPEC and world crude oil markets from 1973 to 1994: cartel, oligopoly or competitive?', *The Energy Journal* 21/3 (Autumn 2000), pp 31–60.
58 *Ibid.*
59 Maurice A. Adelman, *The Genie out of the Bottle* (Cambridge, MA: The MIT Press, 1996), p 36.
60 Alhajji and Huettner: 'OPEC and world crude oil markets from 1973 to 1994', p 32.
61 A.F. Alhajji and David Huettner, 'The target revenue model and the world oil market: empirical evidence from 1971 to 1994', *The Energy Journal* 21/2 (2000), pp 121–44.
62 A.F. Alhajji and David Huettner, 'OPEC and other commodity cartels: a comparison', *Energy Policy* 28 (2000), pp 1151–64.
63 Douglas B. Reynolds, 'Modeling OPEC behavior: theories of risk aversion for oil producer decisions', *Energy Policy* 27 (1999), pp 901–12.
64 Grethe Værnøe, 'OPEC-Kartell eller fagforening?', *Samtiden* 2 (1975), pp 65–78.
65 Dag Harald Claes, *The Politics of Oil-Producer Cooperation* (Boulder, CO: Westview Press, 2001), p 281.
66 Heike Pleines, 'Corruption and crime in the Russian oil industry', in David Lane (ed), *The Political Economy of Russian Oil* (London: Rowman and Littlefield, 2000), pp 75–96.
67 John Erik Fossum, *Oil, the State and Federalism* (Toronto: Toronto University Press, 1992), pp 17ff.
68 'Russian oil chief rejects Opec calls for export cuts', *Financial Times*, 19 November 2001.
69 'Opec at bay', *Financial Times*, 19 November 2001.
70 Claes: *The Politics of Oil-Producer Cooperation*, p 326.
71 Fossum: *Oil, the State and Federalism*, p 25.

Chapter 4: The political economy of oil prices

1 Maurice A. Adelman, *The Economics of Petroleum Supply* (Cambridge, MA: The MIT Press, 1993), pp 305ff.

2 P.S. Dasgupta and G.M. Heal, *Economic Theory and Exhaustible Resources* (Cambridge: Cambridge University Press, 1979), pp 156ff.

3 This is the famous rule of Harold Hotelling, established in 1931, quoted in Dasgupta and Heal: *Economic Theory and Exhaustible Resources*, p 156.

4 Djavad Saleh-Isfahani, 'Models of the oil market revisited', *The Journal of Energy Literature*, Summer 1995, pp 3–21.

5 C.J. Campbell, *The Golden Century of Oil* (Dordrecht: Kluwer Academic Publishers, 1991), pp 15ff.

6 Paul H. Frankel, *Essentials of Petroleum*, 2nd edn (London: Frank Cass, 1969), pp 18ff.

7 A.F. Alhajji and David Huettner, 'The target revenue model and the world oil market: empirical evidence from 1971 to 1994', *The Energy Journal* 21/2 (2000), pp 121–44.

8 F.M. Scherer, *Industry, Structure, Strategy, and Public Policy* (New York: HarperCollins, 1996), pp 83ff.

9 *Ibid.*, p 85.

10 Maurice A. Adelman, 'Mineral depletion, with special reference to petroleum', *Review of Economics and Statistics*, February 1990, pp 1–10.

11 Daniel Johnston, *International Petroleum Fiscal Systems and Production Sharing Contracts* (Tulsa, OK: PennWell Books, 1994), p 263.

12 Dasgupta and Heal: *Economic Theory and Exhaustible Resources*, pp 156ff.

13 Kenneth W. Dam, *Oil Resources* (Chicago: The University of Chicago Press, 1976), pp 4ff.

14 Petter Nore, *The Norwegian State's Relationship with the International Oil Companies over North Sea Oil, 1965–1975*, unpublished PhD thesis (London: School of Social Sciences, Division of Economics, Thames Polytechnic, 1979), p 308.

15 Alfred Marshall, *Principles of Economics*, 8th edn (London: Macmillan, 1994), pp 523ff.

16 David W. Pearce and E. Kerry Turner, *Economics of Natural Resources and the Environment* (Baltimore: The Johns Hopkins University Press, 1990), pp 288ff.

17 Edmund S. Phelps, *Political Economy* (New York: W.W. Norton & Company, 1985), pp 130–1.

18 Jack Hirshleifer, *Price Theory and Applications* (Englewood Cliffs, NJ: W.W. Norton & Company, 1988), pp 376ff.

19 *Background Report on Petroleum Production Taxation* (Canberra: Australian Government Publishing Service, 1990), p 12.

20 *Ibid.*, p 14.

21 Maurice A. Adelman, *The World Petroleum Market* (Baltimore: The Johns Hopkins University Press, 1972), p 6.

22 Paul A. Samuelson, *Economics* (New York: McGraw-Hill, 1970), pp 369ff.

23 Hirshleifer: *Price Theory and Applications*, p 377.

24 Dam: *Oil Resources*, pp 4ff.

25 William G. Shepherd, *The Economics of Industrial Organisation* (Englewood Cliffs, NJ: Prentice Hall, 1979), pp 172ff.

26 Scherer: *Industry Structure, Strategy and Public Policy*, p 112.

27 Edith Penrose, *The Growth of Firms, Middle East Oil and Other Essays* (London: Frank Cass, 1971), p 158.

28 Christopher Tugendhat and Adrian Hamilton, *Oil – The Biggest Business* (London: Eyre Methuen, 1975), p 11.

29 *Ibid.*, p 100.

30 John M. Blair, *The Control of Oil* (New York: Pantheon Books, 1976), p 63.
31 Hossein Razavi and Fereidun Fesharaki, *Fundamentals of Petroleum Trading* (London: Praeger, 1991), p 19.
32 Bob Tippee, *Where's the Shortage?* (Tulsa, OK: PennWell Books, 1993), pp 224ff.
33 S. Gürcan Gülen, 'Efficiency in the crude oil futures market', *Journal of Energy Finance and Development* 3/1 (1998), pp 13–22.
34 Jaun A. Siu and John Fred Weston, 'Restructuring the U.S. oil industry', *Journal of Energy Finance and Development* 1/2 (1996), pp 113–32.
35 John Wood-Collins, 'Mergers, size and value', *Oxford Energy Forum* 1 (May 2000), pp 11–12.
36 BP Amoco, 'This is how we compete with OPEC', *Petrostrategies*, 19 July 1999.
37 Adam Sieminski and J.J. Traynor, 'Mergers, size and value', *Oxford Energy Forum* 1 (May 2000), pp 12–15.
38 *Exploding the myth* (London: HSBC, 2001), p 4.
39 Kathleen L. Abdallah, 'The changing structure of the international oil industry', *Energy Policy* 23/20 (1995), pp 871–7.
40 Paul Stevens, 'Strategic positioning in the oil industry: trends and options', in Paul Stevens (ed), *Strategic Positioning in the Oil Industry* (Abu Dhabi: The Emirates Center for Strategic Studies and Research, 1998), pp 1–24.
41 *Background Report on Petroleum Production Taxation*, p 12.
42 *Ibid.*
43 *Ibid.*, p 14.
44 *Ibid.*
45 Maurice A. Adelman, *The Genie out of the Bottle* (Cambridge, MA: The MIT Press, 1996), p 63.
46 Jens Evensen, *Oversikt over oljepolitiske spørsmål* (Oslo: Ministry of Industry, 1971), p 35.
47 Adelman: *The Genie out of the Bottle*, p 63.
48 *Ibid.*, p 197.
49 Jahangir Amuzegar, *Managing the Oil Wealth* (London: I.B. Tauris, 1999), p 45.
50 Ulrich Bartsch and Benito Müller, *Fossil Fuels in a Changing Climate* (Oxford: Oxford University Press, 2000), p 9.
51 Giancarlo Pireddu and Jean-Christian Dufournaud, *Eco-Taxes in the Italian Age Model: Double Dividend Effects and the Distribution of Tax Burden* (Milan: Scuola Superiore Enrico Mattei, 1995), p 1.
52 Samuel Fankhauser, *Valuing Climate Change* (London: Earthscan, 1995), p 101.
53 William D. Nordhaus, 'Optimal greenhouse gas reductions and tax change in the "DICE" model', *American Economic Review, Papers and Proceedings* 2 (1993), pp 27–50.
54 Alan S. Manne and Richard G. Richels, 'The Kyoto Protocol: a cost-effective strategy for meeting environmental objectives?', *The Energy Journal*, Special Issue 1999: 'The costs the Kyoto Protocol: a multi-model evaluation', pp 1–23.

Chapter 5: The persistent political risks

1 R. Stephen Humphreys, *Between Memory and Desire*, paperback edn (Berkeley: University of California Press, 2001), p 105.
2 Jahangir Amuzegar, *Managing the Oil Wealth* (London: I.B. Tauris, 1999), p 38.
3 *Ibid.*, p 39.
4 Bahgat Kurany, 'The Arab world and the new balance of power in the new Middle East', in Michael C. Hudson (ed), *Middle East Dilemma* (New York: Columbia University Press, 1999), pp 35–59.
5 William B. Quandt, 'The Middle East in 1990', *Foreign Affairs, America and the World* 70/1 (1990/91), pp 49–69.

6   *World Energy Outlook 2000* (Paris: OECD/IEA, 2000), p 77.

7   Elin Berg, Snorre Kverndokk and Knut Einar Rosendahl, 'Gains from cartelisation in the oil market', *Energy Policy* 25/13 (1997), pp 1075–81.

8   Paul Stevens, 'Oil prices', *Energy Policy* 24/5 (1996), pp 391–402.

9   Jerome D. Davis, *Blue Gold: The Political Economy of Natural Gas* (London: George Allen and Unwin, 1984), p 10.

10 George Couvaras, 'Gas to liquids: a paradigm shift for the oil industry?', *Oil and Gas Journal* 97/50 (13 December 1999), pp 124–6.

11 Tim Ford, 'Fuel cell-vehicles offer clean and sustainable mobility for the future', *Oil and Gas Journal* 97/50 (13 December 1999), pp 130–7.

12 Adolf H. Feizlmayr and Colin McKinnon, 'Lower costs, environmental protection drive future pipeline technologies', *Oil and Gas Journal* 97/50 (13 December 1999), pp 83–9.

13 Jean-Pierre Pauwels, *Géopolitique de l'approvisionnement énergétique de l'Union Européenne au XXIe siècle* (Brussels: Bruylant, 1997), pp 94ff.

14 Øystein Noreng, 'The world natural gas market and its implications for the world oil market', in *The Future of Natural Gas in the World Energy Market* (Abu Dhabi: The Emirates Center for Strategic Studies and Research, 2001), pp 85–109.

15 David G. Victor, *The Collapse of the Kyoto Protocol* (Princeton, NJ: Princeton University Press, 2001), p 24.

16 William Nordhaus and Joseph G. Boyer, 'Requiem for Kyoto: an economic analysis', *The Energy Journal*, Special Issue 1999: 'The costs the Kyoto Protocol: a multi-model evaluation', pp 93–130.

17 Ulrich Bartsch and Benito Müller, *Fossil Fuels in a Changing Climate* (Oxford: Oxford University Press, 2000), p 225.

18 Christopher N. MacCracken et al., 'The economics of the Kyoto Protocol', *The Energy Journal*, Special Issue 1999: 'The costs the Kyoto Protocol: a multi-model evaluation', pp 25–71.

19 Warwick J. McKibbin et al., 'Emissions trading, capital flows and the Kyoto Protocol', *The Energy Journal*, Special Issue 1999: 'The costs the Kyoto Protocol: a multi-model evaluation', pp 287–333.

20 Maurice A. Adelman, *The Genie out of the Bottle* (Cambridge, MA: The MIT Press, 1996), p 63.

21 Giacomo Luciani and Mario Salustri, 'Vertical integration as a strategy for oil security', in Paul Stevens (ed), *Strategic Positioning in the Oil Industry* (Abu Dhabi: The Emirates Center for Strategic Studies and Research, 1998), pp 23–44.

22 Majid A. Al-Moneef, 'International downstream integration of national oil companies', in Stevens: *Strategic Positioning in the Oil Industry*, pp 45–60.

23 Kenneth W. Dam, *Oil Resources* (Chicago: The University of Chicago Press, 1976), p 140.

24 Jean-Jacques Laffont, *Incentives and Political Economy* (Oxford: Oxford University Press, 2000), p 35.

25 Dam: *Oil Resources*, p 130.

26 Stephanie M. Hoopes, *Oil Privatization, Public Choice and International Forces* (London: Macmillan, 1997), p 83.

27 Jill Crystal, *Oil and Politics in the Gulf* (Cambridge: Cambridge University Press, 1990), pp 6ff.

28 John Waterbury, 'Democracy without democrats? The potential for political liberalization in the Middle East', in Ghassan Salamé (ed), *Democracy without Democrats* (London: I.B. Tauris, 1994), pp 23–47.

29 Simon Bromley, *American Hegemony and World Oil* (University Park: The Pennsylvania State University Press, 1991), pp 90ff.

30 Robert Graham, *Iran: The Illusion of Power* (London: Croom Helm, 1978), pp 89ff.

31 Alain Gresh, 'Fin de règne en Arabie saoudite', *Le Monde Diplomatique*, August 1995, pp 1 and 8–9.

32 *Ibid.*, p 9.

33 Yann Richard, 'La constitution de la république islamique d'Iran et l'état-nation', in *État moderne, nationalismes et islamismes* (Paris: Édisud, 1994), pp 151–61.

34 Anwar Ibrahim, 'Growth of democracy is the answer to terrorism', *International Herald Tribune*, 11 October 2001.

35 Marcel Pott, *Allahs falsche Propheten* (Cologne: Bastei Lübbe, 2001), p 334.

FIGURE DATA IN TABULAR FORM

Table/Figure 1: Oil prices 1970–2000
Source: Energy Information Administration (EIA) 2001

Brent US$/bbl	Nominal	US$ 2001
1970	2.0	9.2
1972	2.8	12.0
1974	11.0	39.7
1976	12.8	40.0
1978	13.9	37.9
1980	35.0	75.5
1982	33.3	61.3
1984	29.8	51.0
1986	14.4	23.4
1988	14.8	22.3
1990	23.7	32.2
1992	19.4	24.5
1994	16.0	19.2
1996	20.8	23.6
1998	13.1	14.3
2000	24.5	25.3

Table/Figure 2: OPEC Middle East population 1970–2000
Source: The World Bank 2001

Million	1970	1975	1980	1985	1990	1995	2000
Iran	28.43	33.21	39.12	47.10	54.40	58.95	65.62
Iraq	9.36	11.02	13.01	15.32	18.08	20.78	22.68
Kuwait	0.74	1.01	1.38	1.71	2.13	1.59	1.97
Qatar	0.11	0.17	0.23	0.36	0.49	0.66	0.74
Saudi Arabia	5.75	7.25	9.37	12.38	15.80	18.98	22.02
UAE	0.22	0.51	1.04	1.38	1.84	2.34	2.37

Table/Figure 3a: OPEC Middle East oil extraction per capita 1970–2000
Sources: BP Amoco Statistical Review of World Energy 2001; The World Bank 2001

Barrels per day	1970	1975	1980	1985	1990	1995	2000
Iran	0.13	0.16	0.04	0.05	0.04	0.06	0.06
Iraq	0.17	0.21	0.19	0.09	0.11	0.03	0.12
Kuwait	4.02	2.07	1.20	0.60	0.55	1.30	1.09
Qatar	3.26	2.56	2.06	0.84	0.84	0.67	1.07
Saudi Arabia	0.66	0.98	1.06	0.27	0.41	0.43	0.42
UAE	3.55	3.30	1.64	0.87	1.15	0.95	1.06

Table/Figure 3b: OPEC Middle East oil output value per capita 1970–2000
Sources: Energy Information Administration (EIA) 2001; BP Amoco Statistical Review of World Energy 2001; The World Bank 2001

Thousand US$	1970	1975	1980	1985	1990	1995	2000
Iran	0.30	2.01	2.09	0.78	0.50	0.41	0.33
Iraq	0.36	2.56	2.05	1.53	0.99	0.18	0.87
Kuwait	8.79	25.29	22.66	10.12	4.89	8.90	7.94
Qatar	7.13	30.94	27.42	14.24	7.39	4.63	8.58
Saudi Arabia	1.45	11.92	11.07	4.64	3.59	2.97	2.62
UAE	7.75	40.27	19.70	14.66	10.16	6.54	7.94

Table/Figure 4: OPEC Middle East oil exports 1970–2000
Sources: Energy Information Administration (EIA) 2001; BP Amoco Statistical Review of World Energy 2001

Billion US$	1970	1975	1980	1985	1990	1995	2000
Iran	8.44	66.69	81.61	36.80	27.03	24.31	21.90
Iraq	3.41	28.20	26.71	23.44	17.85	3.74	20.40
Kuwait	6.54	25.47	31.16	17.33	10.40	14.11	16.20
Qatar	0.79	5.29	6.28	5.10	3.59	3.03	6.60
Saudi Arabia	8.31	86.46	103.79	57.39	56.72	56.45	59.60
UAE	1.71	20.33	20.55	20.21	18.73	15.32	19.10

Table/Figure 5: World oil product category consumption 1972–2000
Source: BP Amoco Statistical Review of World Energy 2001

Million tonnes	1972	1980	1985	1990	1995	2000
Gasolines	564.0	628.4	654.3	754.6	859.5	968.3
Middle distillates	601.3	710.4	787.3	902.5	1085.1	1240.5
Fuel oil	678.9	656.2	465.8	503.2	540.4	519.5
Others*	335.0	361.5	394.5	461.8	533.7	602
Total	2179.2	2356.5	2301.9	2622.1	3018.7	3330.3

* *Others: refinery gas, LPGs, solvents, petroleum coke, lubricants, bitumen, wax, refinery fuel and loss.*

Table/Figure 6: World oil, natural gas and total primary energy consumption 1973–2000
Source: BP Amoco Statistical Review of World Energy 2001

Million tonnes o.e.	1973	1980	1985	1990	1995	2000
Oil	2798.0	3024.1	2833.7	3134.5	3234.7	3503.6
Natural gas	1066.1	1286.3	1459.1	1770.5	1911.7	2164.0
Total primary energy	5913.4	6729.5	7193.5	7855.9	8169.5	8752.4

Table/Figure 7: Annual changes in oil and total energy demand 1974–2000
Source: BP Amoco Statistical Review of World Energy 2001

	Oil	Total primary energy
1974	-1.35 %	0.63 %
1980	-3.74 %	-1.17 %
1985	-0.42 %	2.44 %
1990	1.18 %	-1.96 %
1995	1.28 %	2.10 %
2000	1.19 %	2.56 %

Table/Figure 8: Oil demand by products and regions 1973–2000
Source: BPAmoco Statistical Review of World Energy 2001

USA *Million tonnes*	1973	1980	1985	1990	1995	2000
Gasolines	312.7	305.7	305.4	329.5	345.5	380.5
Middle distillates	200.7	207.9	204.8	230.5	248.6	284.1
Fuel oil	148.3	133.0	67.3	67.2	45.8	49.1
Others*	156.3	147.5	144.2	154.6	167.8	183.7

Western Europe** *Million tonnes*	1973	1980	1985	1990	1995	2000
Gasolines	132.6	142.4	135.6	181.2	180.4	181.4
Middle distillates	248.7	234.0	223.9	272.7	292.4	325.3
Fuel oil	269.9	211.7	117.9	138.5	124.4	108.3
Others*	97.7	92.0	87.2	117.7	126.2	137.8

Japan *Million tonnes*	1973	1980	1985	1990	1995	2000
Gasolines	42.8	42.1	41.5	51.0	64.5	71.7
Middle distillates	50.9	59.9	63.6	83.1	95.3	94.5
Fuel oil	142.6	103.5	62.4	71.0	61.2	43.5
Others*	32.8	32.2	38.8	42.6	47.5	43.7

Rest of the world *Million tonnes*	1973	1980	1985	1990	1995	2000
Gasolines	105.1	138.2	152.6	214.8	269.1	334.7
Middle distillates	145.2	208.3	258.4	342.4	448.8	536.6
Fuel oil	172.5	208.0	172.9	266.8	309.0	318.6
Others*	71.3	89.8	103.7	151.9	192.2	236.8

* *Others: Refinery gas, LPGs, solvents, petroleum coke, lubricants, bitumen, wax, refinery fuel and loss.*
***From 1990, including Eastern Europe.*

Table/Figure 9ab: US economic repercussions 1972–2000
Source: Energy Information Administration (ELA) 2001

Per cent	1973	1980	1985	1990	1995	2000
Price increase (nominal)*	48.95	16.51	-4.01	30.82	7.51	34.62
Price increase (real)*	41.11	2.77	-7.68	24.24	4.54	30.39
Inflation rate	6.20	13.50	3.60	5.40	2.80	3.20
Nominal bank prime rate	8.03	15.26	9.93	10.01	8.83	9.21
Real bank prime rate	1.83	1.76	6.33	4.61	6.03	6.01
GDP growth	5.20	-0.50	3.20	0.80	2.00	5.20
Unemployment rate	4.90	7.10	7.20	5.60	5.60	4.00

North Sea oil.

Table/Figure 10: US oil imports and Saudi oil production 1973–2000
Source: Energy Information Administration (ELA) 2001

Million bbl/d	US oil imports	Saudi oil production
1973	6.26	7.44
1980	6.91	9.99
1985	5.07	3.74
1990	8.02	7.11
1995	8.83	8.89
2000	11.09	9.15

Table/Figure 11: OPEC Middle East military expenditures 1970–1999
Source: The International Institute for Strategic Studies (IISS)

Million US$ 2001	1970	1975	1980	1985	1990	1995	1999
Iran	3,184	31,249	8,657	21,970	4,171	4,741	6,092
Iraq	1,733	3,576	5,566	20,060	11,292	1,419	1,600
Kuwait	n/a	719	2,267	2,554	17,181	3,959	3,493
Saudi Arabia	1,582	19,050	42,669	27,586	41,786	19,517	23,334
UAE	n/a	n/a	2,474	3,185	3,397	2,213	3,399

Table/Figure 12a: OPEC population 1980–2000
Sources: The World Bank 2001; CIA The World Factbook 2001

Million	1980	1990	2000
Algeria	18.7	25.0	31.8
Indonesia	148.3	178.2	228.4
Iran	39.1	54.4	65.6
Iraq	13.0	18.1	22.7
Kuwait	1.4	2.1	2.0
Libya	3.0	4.4	5.2
Nigeria	71.1	96.2	126.6
Qatar	0.2	0.5	0.7
Saudi Arabia	9.4	15.8	22.0
United Arab Emirates	1.0	1.8	2.4
Venezuela	15.1	19.5	23.9
OPEC total	320.4	416.1	531.4

Table/Figure 12b: OPEC oil reserves 1980–2000
Source: Energy Information Administration (EIA) 2001

Billion barrels o.e.	1980	1990	2000
Algeria	8.2	9.2	9.2
Indonesia	9.5	11.0	5.0
Iran	57.5	92.9	89.7
Iraq	30.0	100.0	112.5
Kuwait	67.9	97.0	96.5
Libya	23.0	22.8	29.5
Nigeria	16.7	17.1	22.5
Qatar	3.6	4.5	13.2
Saudi Arabia	168.0	260.0	261.7
United Arab Emirates	30.4	98.1	97.8
Venezuela	18.0	59.0	76.9
OPEC total	432.8	771.6	814.5

Table/Figure 12c: OPEC oil production 1980–2000
Source: BPAmoco Statistical Review of World Energy 2000

Thousand bbl/d	1980	1990	2000
Algeria	1,120	1,345	1,580
Indonesia	1,575	1,540	1,430
Iran	1,480	3,255	3,770
Iraq	2,645	2,155	2,625
Kuwait	1,430	965	2,150
Libya	1,830	1,425	1,475
Nigeria	2,055	1,810	2,105
Qatar	460	435	795
Saudi Arabia	9,990	7,105	9,145
United Arab Emirates	1,831	2,285	2,515
Venezuela	2,425	2,245	3,235
OPEC total	26,841	24,565	30,825

Table/Figure 13a: OPEC oil export revenues 1980–2000

Sources: Energy Information Administration (ELA) 2001; BPAmoco Statistical Review of World Energy 2001

Billion US$ 2001	1980	1990	2000
Algeria	26.09	12.36	10.43
Indonesia	34.14	13.46	5.79
Iran	39.73	27.89	22.63
Iraq	60.10	18.42	21.08
Kuwait	33.89	10.73	16.74
Libya	48.53	13.92	12.09
Nigeria	48.48	19.04	19.11
Qatar	9.66	3.71	6.82
Saudi Arabia	202.61	58.53	61.58
United Arab Emirates	34.98	19.33	19.73
Venezuela	22.80	26.47	22.52
OPEC total	561.00	223.86	218.51

Table/Figure 13b: OPEC oil export revenues per capita 1980–2000

Sources: Energy Information Administration (ELA) 2001; BPAmoco Statistical Review of World Energy 2001; The World Bank 2001; CIA The World Factbook 2001

Thousand US$ 2001	1980	1990	2000
Algeria	1.40	0.49	0.33
Indonesia	0.23	0.08	0.03
Iran	1.02	0.51	0.34
Iraq	4.62	1.02	0.93
Kuwait	24.65	5.05	8.48
Libya	15.95	3.15	2.31
Nigeria	0.68	0.20	0.15
Qatar	42.18	7.63	9.16
Saudi Arabia	21.62	3.70	2.80
United Arab Emirates	33.53	10.48	8.33
Venezuela	1.51	1.36	0.94
OPEC total	147.39	33.67	33.79

Table/Figure 14: World, OPEC and Gulf oil supplies 1960–2000
Source: Energy Information Administration/Annual Energy Review 2001

Million bbl/d	Persian Gulf*	OPEC	World
1960	5.27	8.70	20.99
1965	8.37	14.35	30.33
1970	13.39	23.30	45.89
1975	18.93	26.77	52.83
1980	17.96	26.61	59.60
1985	9.63	16.18	53.98
1990	15.28	23.20	60.57
1995	17.21	26.00	62.33
2000	19.94	29.11	67.98

* Persian Gulf nations are Bahrain, Iran, Iraq, Kuwait, Qatar, Saudi Arabia and United Arab Emirates.

Table/Figure 15: Non-OPEC* oil supplies 1970–2000
Source: Energy Information Administration/Annual Energy Review 2001

Million bbl/d	USA	Russia**	UK	Norway	Mexico	China	Canada	Rest
1960	7.04	2.91	(s)	0.00	0.27	0.10	0.52	1.45
1965	7.80	4.79	(s)	0.00	0.32	0.23	0.81	2.03
1970	9.64	6.99	(s)	0.00	0.49	0.60	1.26	3.61
1975	8.37	9.52	0.01	0.19	0.71	1.49	1.43	4.34
1980	8.60	11.71	1.62	0.53	1.94	2.11	1.44	5.04
1985	8.97	11.59	2.53	0.79	2.75	2.51	1.47	7.19
1990	7.36	10.98	1.82	1.70	2.55	2.77	1.55	8.64
1995	6.56	6.00	2.49	2.77	2.62	2.99	1.81	11.09
2000	5.83	6.48	2.47	3.20	3.01	3.25	1.98	12.65

* Ecuador (withdrew from OPEC in 1992) and Gabon (withdrew in 1994) are included for all the years.
**1960–1991: Former USSR; 1992–2000: Russia.
(s)=Less than 0.005 million barrels per day.

BIBLIOGRAPHY

Abdallah, Kathleen L., 'The changing structure of the international oil industry', *Energy Policy* 23/20 (1995), pp 871–7

Aburish, Saïd K., *A Brutal Friendship* (London: Indigo, 1997)

Adelman, Maurice A., *The World Petroleum Market* (Baltimore: The Johns Hopkins University Press, 1972)

—— 'Mineral depletion, with special reference to petroleum', *Review of Economics and Statistics*, February 1990, pp 1–10

—— *The Economics of Petroleum Supply* (Cambridge, MA: The MIT Press, 1993)

—— 'Modeling world oil supply', *The Energy Journal* 14/1 (1993), pp 1–33

—— *The Genie out of the Bottle* (Cambridge, MA: The MIT Press, 1996)

Agha, Hussein J. and Khalidi, Ahmad S., *Syria and Iran* (London: The Royal Institute of International Affairs, 1995)

Al-Chalabi, Fadhil and Al-Janabi, Adnan, 'Optimum production and pricing policies', *Journal of Energy and Development*, Spring 1979, pp 229–58

Alhajji, A.F. and Huettner, David, 'OPEC and other commodity cartels: a comparison', *Energy Policy* 28 (2000), pp 1151–64

—— 'OPEC and world crude oil markets from 1973 to 1994: cartel, oligopoly or competitive?', *The Energy Journal* 21/3 (2000), pp 31–60

—— 'The target revenue model and the world oil market: empirical evidence from 1971 to 1994', *The Energy Journal* 21/2 (2000), pp 121–44

Aliyev, Kenan, 'US envoy cautions that window could close on a Karabakh settlement', *EurasiaNet*, 14 January 2002, www.eurasianet.org

Allison, Roy and Jonson, Lena, *Central Asian Security* (Washington, DC: Brookings Institution, 2001)

Alterman, Jon B., 'The Gulf States and the American umbrella', *Middle East Review of International Affairs (MERIA)* 4/4 (December 2000)

Amuzegar, Jahangir, *Iran's Economy under the Islamic Republic* (London: I.B. Tauris, 1993)

—— *Managing the Oil Wealth* (London: I.B. Tauris, 1999)

Anderson, J.W., *The Surge in Oil Prices: Anatomy of a Non-Crisis*, Discussion Paper (Washington, DC: Resources for the Future, 2001)

Annual Energy Outlook 1996 (Washington, DC: Energy Information Administration, 1996)

Axelrod, Robert, *The Evolution of Co-operation* (New York: Basic Books, 1984)

—— *The Complexity of Co-operation* (Princeton, NJ: Princeton University Press, 1997)

Ayoub, Antoine, *Le Pétrole – économie et politique* (Paris: Éditions Économica, 1996)

Background Report on Petroleum Production Taxation (Canberra: Australian Government Publishing Service, 1990)

Baran, Amatzia and Rubin, Barry, *Iraq's Road to War* (New York: St Martin's Press, 1993)

Barham, John, 'East–west pipeline: oil and gas to be transported through Turkey', *Financial Times*, 3 March 1998

Bartsch, Ulrich and Müller, Benito, *Fossil Fuels in a Changing Climate* (Oxford: Oxford University Press, 2000)

Beaudreau, Bernard C., *Energy and Organisation* (London: Greenwood Press, 1998)
—— *Energy and the Rise and Fall of Political Economy* (London: Greenwood Press, 1999)
Becker, Gary S., *The Economic Approach to Human Behaviour* (Chicago: The University of Chicago Press, 1978)
Berg, Elin, Kverndokk, Snorre and Rosendahl, Knut Einar, 'Gains from cartelisation in the oil market', *Energy Policy* 25/13 (1997), pp 1075–81
Bezanis. Lowell, 'Joining forces with Iran and Russia', *Transition*, 11 September 1995
Bishara, Marwan, *Palestine/Israël: la paix ou l'apartheid* (Paris: Éditions La Découverte, 2001)
Blair, John M., *The Control of Oil* (New York: Pantheon Books, 1976)
BP Amoco, 'This is how we compete with OPEC', *Petrostrategies*, 19 July 1999
Bradley, Robert L., Jr, *Oil, Gas, and Government* (London: Rowmand and Littlefield, 1996)
Bromley, Simon, *American Hegemony and World Oil* (University Park: The Pennsylvania State University Press, 1991)
—— *Rethinking Middle East Politics* (Cambridge: Polity Press, 1994)
Buchan, David, 'OPEC's dilemma', *Financial Times*, 24 September 2001
Campbell, C.J., *The Golden Century of Oil* (Dordrecht: Kluwer Academic Publishers, 1991)
Campbell, Colin C., *The Coming Oil Crisis* (Brentwood, England: Multi-Science Publishing and Petro-Consultants, 1997)
Cappelen, Ådne and Choudhury, Robert, *The Future of the Saudi Arabian Economy* (Oslo: Central Bureau of Statistics, 2000)
Castells, Manuel, *The Rise of the Network Society* (London: Blackwell, 1996)
Carlson, Richard C., Harman, Willis W., Schwartz, Peter and associates, *Energy Futures, Human Values and Lifestyles* (Boulder, CO: Westview Press, 1982)
Cause, F. Gregory III, *Oil Monarchies* (New York: Council on Foreign Relations Press, 1994)
—— 'Saudi Arabia over a barrel', *Foreign Affairs* 79/3 (May/June 2000), pp 80–94
Chartouni-Dubrarry, Mary, 'Proche-Orient: le compte à rebours', in de Montbrial, Thierry and Jacquet, Pierre (eds), *Ramses 2002* (Paris: Dunod, 2001), pp 141–58
Claes, Dag Harald, *The Politics of Oil-Producer Cooperation* (Boulder, CO: Westview Press, 2001)
Cohen, Ariel, 'Odessa–Brody pipeline creates new option for export of Caspian Basin resources', *EurasiaNet*, 11 December 2001, www.eurasianet.org
Cooter, Robert and Ulen, Thomas, *Law and Economics* (New York: Addison Wesley, 2000)
Cordesman, Anthony H., *Saudi Arabia* (Boulder, CO: Westview Press, 1997)
Cordesman, Anthony H. and Hashim, Ahmed S., *Iraq* (Boulder, CO: Westview Press, 1997)
Corm, Georges, *Le Proche-Orient éclaté* (Paris: Éditions Gallimard, 1991)
Couvaras, George, 'Gas to liquids: a paradigm shift for the oil industry?', *Oil and Gas Journal* 97/50 (13 December 1999), pp 124–6
Cowhey, Peter F., *The Problems of Plenty: Energy Policy and International Politics* (Berkeley: University of California Press, 1985)
Criqui, Patrick, 'Un nouveau partage de la rente', *Le Monde*, 25 September 1990
Crystal, Jill, *Oil and Politics in the Gulf* (Cambridge: Cambridge University Press, 1990)
Cuthberson, Ian, 'Notre destin est en train de se jouer en Asie centrale', *Le Temps Stratégique*, September 1995, pp 30–45
Dam, Kenneth W., *Oil Resources* (Chicago: The University of Chicago Press, 1976)
Dasgupta, P.S. and Heal, G.M., *Economic Theory and Exhaustible Resources* (Cambridge: Cambridge University Press, 1979)
Davis, Jerome D., *Blue Gold: The Political Economy of Natural Gas* (London: George Allen and Unwin, 1984)
Dawisha, Karen and Parrott, Bruce, *Conflict, Cleavage and Change in Central Asia and the Caucasus* (Cambridge: Cambridge University Press, 1997)
Debeir, Jean-Claude, Deléage, Jean-Paul and Hémery, Daniel, *In the Servitude of Power* (London: Zed Books, 1991)
Deegan, Heather, *The Middle East and Problems of Democracy* (Boulder, CO: Lynne Rienner, 1994)

Deffeyes, Kenneth S., *Hubbert's Peak* (Princeton, NJ: Princeton University Press, 2001)

Dinmore, Guy, 'Iran's unsteady ship', *Financial Times*, 12 December 2000

Doblin, Clare P.; 'Declining energy intensity in the U.S. manufacturing sector', *The Energy Journal* 9/2 (1988), pp 109–35

Dolatyar, Mostafa and Gray, Tim S., *Water Politics in the Middle East* (London: Macmillan, 2000)

Donaldson, Robert H., *The Soviet Union in the Third World: Successes and Failures* (London: Croom Helm, 1981)

Durgin, Hullar, 'US administration faces crisis over energy policy', *Financial Times*, 6 December 2000

Ebinger, Charles K. (ed), *The Critical Link: Energy and National Security in the 1990s* (Cambridge, MA: Ballinger, 1982)

Ekelund, Robert B., Jr and Tollison, Robert D., *Politicized Economies* (College Station: Texas A & M College Press, 1997)

Energy Security: Evaluating U.S. Vulnerability to Oil Supply Disruptions (Washington, DC: US Department of Energy, 1999)

Evensen, Jens, *Oversikt over oljepolitiske spørsmål* (Oslo: Ministry of Industry, 1971)

Exploding the myth (London: HSBC, 2001)

Fabriès-Verfaille, Marise, *L'Afrique du Nord et le Moyen-Orient dans le nouvel espace mondial* (Paris: Presses Universitaires de France, 1998)

Fagan, Marie N., 'Resource depletion and technical change: effects on U.S. crude oil finding costs from 1977 to 1994', *The Energy Journal* 18/4 (1977), pp 91–108

Feizlmayr, Adolf H. and McKinnon, Colin, 'Lower costs, environmental protection drive future pipeline technologies', *Oil and Gas Journal* 97/50 (13 December 1999), pp 83–9

Ford, Tim, 'Fuel cell-vehicles offer clean and sustainable mobility for the future', *Oil and Gas Journal* 97/50 (13 December 1999), pp 130–7

Fossum, John Erik, *Oil, the State and Federalism* (Toronto: Toronto University Press, 1992)

Frankel, Paul H., *Essentials of Petroleum*, 2nd edn (London: Frank Cass, 1969)

Fromkin, David, *A Peace to End All Peace* (New York: Avon Books, 1989)

Fundy, Mamoun, *Saudi Arabia and the Politics of Dissent* (London: Palgrave, 1999)

Gaudrey, Jean, *Nouvelle Économie, nouveau mythe?* (Paris: Flammarion, 2000)

Gillespie, Kate and Henry, Clement M., *Oil in the New World Order* (Gainsville: University Press of Florida, 1995)

Gilpin, Robert, *The Challenge of Global Capitalism* (Princeton, NJ: Princeton University Press, 2000)

Graham, Robert, *Iran: The Illusion of Power* (London: Croom Helm, 1978)

Grare, Frédéric, 'La nouvelle donne énergétique autour de la mer Caspienne: une perspective géopolitique', in *La Caspienne: une nouvelle frontière*, Cahiers d'études sur la Méditerranée orientale et le monde turco-iranien 23 (Paris, 1997)

Gresh, Alain, 'Fin de règne en Arabie saoudite', *Le Monde Diplomatique*, August 1995, pp 1 and 8–9

Gülen, S. Gürcan, 'Efficiency in the crude oil futures market', *Journal of Energy Finance and Development* 3/1 (1998), pp 13–22

Hanneson, Rögnvaldur, *Petroleum Economics* (London: Quorum Books, 1998)

Hart, Parker T., *Saudi Arabia and the United States* (Bloomington: Indiana University Press, 1998)

Hawary, Yasser, 'Vers un désordre mondial permanent?', *Arabies* 189 (January 2002), p 14

Hawatmeh, Yasser, 'Tout empire périra', *Arabies*, June 1997, p 5

Heiss, Mary Ann, *Empire and Nationhood* (New York: Columbia University Press, 1997)

Hersh, Seymour M., 'The Iraq hawks: can their war plan work?', *The New Yorker*, 24 December 2001

Hirshleifer, Jack, *Price Theory and Applications* (Englewood Cliffs, NJ: W.W. Norton & Company, 1988)

Hogan, William W. and Manne, Alan S., *Energy-Economy Interactions: The Fable of the Elephant and the Rabbit* (Palo Alto, CA: Energy Modeling Forum, Stanford University, 1977)

Hoopes, Stephanie M., *Oil Privatization, Public Choice and International Forces* (London: Macmillan, 1997)

Hopkins, Nicholas S. and Ibrahim, Saad Eddin, *Arab Society* (Cairo: The American University in Cairo Press, 1997)

Hudson, Michael C. (ed), *Middle East Dilemma* (New York: Columbia University Press, 1999)

Humphreys, R. Stephen, *Between Memory and Desire* (Berkeley: University of California Press, 1999)

Huntington, Hillard G., 'Crude oil prices and U.S. economic performance: where does the asymmetry reside?', *The Energy Journal* 19/4 (1998), pp 107–32

Ibrahim, Anwar, 'Growth of democracy is the answer to terrorism', *International Herald Tribune*, 11 October 2001

Ismael, Jacqueline S., *Kuwait: Dependency and Class in a Rentier State* (Gainesville: University Press of Florida, 1993)

Johnston, Daniel, *International Petroleum Fiscal Systems and Production Sharing Contracts* (Tulsa, OK: PennWell Books, 1994)

Jones, Matthew and Buchan, David, 'Tapping rich stores of offshore co-operation', *Financial Times*, 22 December 2000

Jorgensen, Dale W., 'The great transition: energy and economic change', *The Energy Journal* 7/5 (1986), pp 1–13

Julius, DeAnne and Mashayeki, Afsaneh, *The Economics of Natural Gas* (Oxford: Oxford Institute for Energy Studies, 1990)

Kalicki, Jan H., 'Caspian energy at the crossroads', *Foreign Affairs* 80/5 (September–October 2001), pp 120–34

Karl, Terry Lynn, *The Paradox of Plenty* (London: University of California Press, 1997)

Katzman, Kenneth, *Searching for Stable Peace in the Persian Gulf* (Carlisle, PA: US Army War College, 1998)

Kechichian, Joseph A., *Succession in Saudi Arabia* (London: Palgrave, 2001)

Kéfi, Ridha, 'Après Bachar, Qossai?', *Jeune Afrique – l'Intelligent*, 28 August 2001, pp 34–7

Kemp, Geoffrey and Harkavy, Robert E., *Strategic Geography and the Changing Middle East* (Washington, DC: Brookings Institution Press, 1997)

Kemp, Geoffrey and Pressman, Jeremy, *Point of No Return* (Washington, DC: Brookings Institution Press, 1997)

Khachatrian, Haroutiun, 'Armenian leaders restrained on Karabakh peace prospects', *EurasiaNet*, 12 December 2001, www.eurasianet.org

Khalaf, Roula, 'Why they hate us', *Financial Times*, 5 October 2001

—— 'Saudi suspicions', *Financial Times*, 16 November 2001

Klare, Michael T., *Resource Wars* (New York: Henry Holt and Company, 2001)

Krapels, Edward N., *Oil Crisis Management* (London: The Johns Hopkins University Press, 1980)

Kuzio, Taras, 'Nato reevaluates strategic considerations in Caucasus, Central Asia', *EurasiaNet*, 17 December 2001, www.eurasianet.org

Laffont, Jean-Jacques, *Incentives and Political Economy* (Oxford: Oxford University Press, 2000)

Lane, David, *The Political Economy of Russian Oil* (London: Rowman and Littlefield, 2000)

Lelyveld, Michael, 'Caspian: Moscow attempts to set sea borders', *EurasiaNet*, 12 January 2002, www.eurasianet.org

Lindblom, Charles E., *Politics and Markets* (New York: Basic Books, 1977)

Lynch, Michael C., *Crying Wolf: Warnings About Oil Supplies* (New York: Council on Foreign Relations, 1998)

McBeth, Brian, *British Oil Policy 1919–1939* (London: Frank Cass, 1985)

MacCracken, Christopher N. et al., 'The economics of the Kyoto Protocol', *The Energy Journal*, Special Issue 1999: 'The costs the Kyoto Protocol: a multi-model evaluation', pp 25–71

McKibbin, Warwick J. et al., 'Emissions trading, capital flows and the Kyoto Protocol', *The Energy Journal*, Special Issue 1999: 'The costs the Kyoto Protocol: a multi-model evaluation', pp 287–333

Manne, Alan S. and Richels, Richard G., 'The Kyoto Protocol: a cost-effective strategy for meeting environmental objectives?', *The Energy Journal*, Special Issue 1999: 'The costs the Kyoto Protocol: a multi-model evaluation', pp 1–23

Manning, Richard A., *The Asian Energy Factor* (New York: Palgrave, 2000)

Marr, Phebe, *The Modern History of Iraq* (Boulder, CO: Westview Press, 1985)

Marshall, Alfred, *Principles of Economics*, 8th edn (London: Macmillan, 1994)

Martin, Jean-Marie, 'Le changement des technologies de l'énergie: genèse, modalités et hypothèses explicatives', in Bourgeois, Bernard, Finon, Dominique and Martin, Jean-Marie (eds), *Énergie et changement technologique* (Paris: Éditions Économica, 2000), pp 17–61

Middle East Oil and Gas (Paris: International Energy Agency, OECD, 1995)

Mitchell, John with Morita, Koji, Selley, Norman and Stern, Jonathan, *The New Economy of Oil* (London: The Royal Institute of International Affairs, 2001)

Modis, Theodore, *Predictions* (New York: Simon and Schuster, 1992)

Moïsi, Dominique, 'Tragedy that exposed a groundswell of hatred', *Financial Times*, 24 September 2001

Mork, Knut Anton, *Energy Prices, Inflation and Economic Activity* (Cambridge, MA: Ballinger, 1981)

National Energy Policy (Washington, DC: The White House, 2001)

National Energy Strategy (Washington, DC: Government Printing Office, 1991)

Nicolat, Françoise and Jacquet, Pierre, 'L'actualité économique internationale', in de Montbrial, Thierry and Jacquet, Pierre (eds), *Ramses 99* (Paris: IFR/Dunod, 1998), pp 135–64

Nordhaus, William D., 'Optimal greenhouse gas reductions and tax change in the "DICE" model', *American Economic Review, Papers and Proceedings* 2 (1993), pp 27–50

Nordhaus, William and Boyer, Joseph G., 'Requiem for Kyoto: an economic analysis', *The Energy Journal*, Special Issue 1999: 'The costs the Kyoto Protocol: a multi-model evaluation', pp 93–130

Nore, Petter, *The Norwegian State's Relationship with the International Oil Companies over North Sea Oil, 1965–1975*, unpublished PhD thesis (London: School of Social Sciences, Division of Economics, Thames Polytechnic, 1979)

Noreng, Øystein, 'The world natural gas market and its implications for the world oil market', in *The Future of Natural Gas in the World Energy Market* (Abu Dhabi: The Emirates Center for Strategic Studies and Research, 2001), pp 85–109

Nowell, Gregory P., *Mercantile States and the World Oil Cartel 1900–1939* (London: Cornell University Press, 1994)

Olcott, Martha Brill, 'Pipelines and pipe dreams: energy development and Caspian society', *Journal of International Affairs* 53/1 (Fall 1999), pp 305–25

Owen, Roger and Pamuk, Sevket, *A History of Middle East Economies in the Twentieth Century* (London: I.B. Tauris, 1998)

Parry, Ian W.H., *Are Gasoline Taxes in Britain Too High?* (Washington, DC: Resources for the Future, 2001)

Pauwels, Jean-Pierre, *Géopolitique de l'approvisionnement énergétique de l'Union Européenne au XXIe siècle* (Brussels: Bruylant, 1997)

Pawerlka, Peter, Pfaff, Isabella and Wehling, Hans-Georg (eds), *Die Golfregion in der Weltpolitik* (Stuttgart: Verlag W. Kohlhammer, 1991)

Péan, Pierre and Séréni, Jean-Pierre, *Les Émirs de la République* (Paris: Éditions du Seuil, 1982)

Pearce, David W. and Turner, E. Kerry, *Economics of Natural Resources and the Environment* (Baltimore: The Johns Hopkins University Press, 1990)

Peel, Quentin, 'Washington's balancing act', *Financial Times*, 1 October 2001

Penrose, Edith, *The Growth of Firms, Middle East Oil and Other Essays* (London: Frank Cass, 1971)

Penrose, Edith and Penrose, E.F., *Iraq, International Relations and National Development* (London: Ernest Benn, 1978)

Phelps, Edmund S., *Political Economy* (New York: W.W. Norton & Company, 1985)

Philip, George, *Oil and Politics in Latin America* (Cambridge: Cambridge University Press, 1982)

Piening, Christopher, *Global Europe* (London: Lynne Rienner, 1997)

Pireddu, Giancarlo and Dufournaud, Jean-Christian, *Eco-Taxes in the Italian Age Model: Double Dividend Effects and the Distribution of Tax Burden* (Milan: Scuola Superiore Enrico Mattei, 1995)

Pott, Marcel, *Allahs falsche Propheten* (Cologne: Bastei Lübbe, 2001)

Quandt, William B., 'The Middle East in 1990', *Foreign Affairs, America and the World* 70/1 (1990/91), pp 49–69

Rashid, Ahmed, *Taliban* (London: I.B. Tauris, 2000)

Razavi, Hossein and Fesharaki, Fereidun, *Fundamentals of Petroleum Trading* (London: Praeger, 1991)

Reynolds, Douglas B., 'Modeling OPEC behavior: theories of risk aversion for oil producer decisions', *Energy Policy* 27 (1999), pp 901–12

Richard, Yann, 'La constitution de la république islamique d'Iran et l'état-nation', in *État moderne, nationalismes et islamismes* (Paris: Édisud, 1994)

Richards, Alan and Waterbury, John, *A Political Economy of the Middle East* (Boulder, CO: Westview Press, 1990)

Roberson, B.A., *The Middle East and Europe* (London: Routledge, 1998)

Roberts, John, *Visions and Mirages* (Edinburgh: Mainstream Publishing, 1995)

Roncaglia, Alessandro, *The International Oil Market* (London: Macmillan, 1985)

Rosecrance, Richard, *The Rise of the Virtual State* (New York: Basic Books, 1999)

Rosenberg, Nathan, *Exploring the Black Box* (Cambridge: Cambridge University Press, 1994)

Roy, Olivier, *La nouvelle Asie centrale* (Paris: Éditions du Seuil, 1997)

Sæter, Martin, 'Oljen og de politiske samarbeidsformer, *Internasjonal Politikk* 2B (1975), pp 397–421

Salamé, Ghassan (ed), *Democracy without Democrats* (London: I.B. Tauris, 1994)

Saleh-Isfahani, Djavad, 'Models of the oil market revisited', *The Journal of Energy Literature*, Summer 1995, pp 3–21

Sampson, Anthony, *The Seven Sisters* (London: Hodder and Stoughton, 1975)

Samuelson, Paul A., *Economics* (New York: McGraw-Hill, 1970)

Schelling, Thomas C., *The Strategy of Conflict* (Cambridge, MA: Harvard University Press, 1980)

Scherer, F.M., *Industry, Structure, Strategy, and Public Policy* (New York: HarperCollins, 1996)

Schipper, Lee and Myers, Stephen, *Energy Efficiency and Human Activity* (Cambridge: Cambridge University Press, 1992)

Schipper, Lee et al., 'Linking life-styles and energy use: a matter of time?', *Annual Review of Energy* 14 (1989), pp 273–320

Schurr, Sam, 'Energy efficiency and productive efficiency: some thoughts based on the American experience', *The Energy Journal* 3/3 (1982), p 8

Sèbe, Charles and Le Bras, William, *Indomptable Iraq* (Paris: Le Sémaphore, 1999)

Seymour, Ian, *OPEC: Instrument of Change* (London: Macmillan, 1980)

Shaffer, Ed, *The United States and the Control of World Oil* (London: Croom Helm, 1983)

Shepherd, William G., *The Economics of Industrial Organisation* (Englewood Cliffs, NJ: Prentice Hall, 1979)

Sick, Gary and Potter, Lawrence G. (eds), *The Persian Gulf at the Millennium* (New York: St Martin's Press, 1997)

Sieminski, Adam and Traynor, J.J., 'Mergers, size and value', *Oxford Energy Forum* 1 (May 2000), pp 12–15

Simon, Steven and Benjamin, Daniel, 'Myths of American misdeeds', *Financial Times*, 2 October 2001

Siu, Jaun A. and Weston, John Fred, 'Restructuring the U.S. oil industry', *Journal of Energy Finance and Development* 1/2 (1996), pp 113–32

Skagen, Ottar, *Caspian Gas* (London: The Royal Institute of International Affairs, 1997)

Sluglett, Peter and Farouk-Sluglett, Marion, 'Iraq', in *The Middle East, The Arab World and Its Neighbours* (London: Times Books, 1991)

Smil, Vaclav, *Energy in World History* (Boulder, CO: Westview Press, 1994)

Sohbetqizi, Nailia, 'Pragmatism guides Russian-Azerbaijani deal making', *EurasiaNet*, 11 January 2002, www.eurasianet.org

Spero, Joan Edelman, *The Politics of International Economic Relations* (London: Routledge, 1992)

Spiro, David E., *The Hidden Hand of American Hegemony* (London: Cornell University Press, 1999)

Starr, Chauncey, *Energy Planning – A Nation at Risk* (Palo Alto, CA: Electric Power Research Institute, 1977)

Stevens, Paul, 'Oil prices', *Energy Policy* 24/5 (1996), pp 391–402

—— *Strategic Positioning in the Oil Industry* (Abu Dhabi: The Emirates Center for Strategic Studies and Research, 1998)

Strange, Susan, *States and Markets* (London: Pinter Publishers, 1988)

Terzian, Pierre, *Le Gaz naturel* (Paris: Éditions Économica, 1998)

Tippee, Bob, *Where's the Shortage?* (Tulsa, OK: PennWell Books, 1993)

Tugendhat, Christopher and Hamilton, Adrian, *Oil – The Biggest Business* (London: Eyre Methuen, 1975)

Værnøe, Grethe, 'OPEC-Kartell eller fagforening?', *Samtiden* 2 (1975), pp 65–78

Vaner, Semih, 'Turquie: la démocratie ou la mort', *Politique Étrangère* 4 (1998), pp 763–78

Venn, Fiona, *Oil Diplomacy in the Twentieth Century* (London: Macmillan, 1986)

Verleger, Philip L., Jr, *Adjusting to Volatile Energy Prices* (Washington, DC: Institute for International Economics, 1993)

Victor, David G., *The Collapse of the Kyoto Protocol* (Princeton, NJ: Princeton University Press, 2001)

Wilson, Carroll L. (ed), *Energy: Global Prospects 1985–2000*, Report of the Workshop on Alternative Energy Strategies (New York: McGraw-Hill, 1977)

Wirl, Franz, *The Economics of Conservation Programs* (London: Kluwer Academic Press, 1997)

Wirth, John D. (ed), *Latin American Oil Companies and the Politics of Energy* (London: University of Nebraska Press, 1985)

Wood-Collins, John, 'Mergers, size and value', *Oxford Energy Forum* 1 (May 2000), pp 11–12

World Energy Outlook 2000 (Paris: OECD/IEA, 2000)

Yamani, Hani Z., *To Be a Saudi* (London: Janus Publishing Company, 1997)

Yergin, Daniel, *The Prize* (New York: Simon and Schuster, 1991)

Zorgbibe, Charles, *La Méditerranée sans les Grands?* (Paris: Quadrige/Presses Universitaires de France, 1997)

INDEX